Masters of Networking

Building Relationships
for Your Pocketbook and Soul

Masters of Networking

Building Relationships
for Your Pocketbook and Soul

Ivan R. Misner, Ph.D.
Don Morgan, M.A.

Atlanta•Austin

Masters of Networking
Building Relationships for Your Pocketbook and Soul
Ivan R. Misner, Ph.D., and Don Morgan, M.A.

Copyright © 2000 by Ivan R. Misner, Ph.D., and Don Morgan, M.A.

Bard Press
An imprint of Longstreet Press
2140 Newmarket Parkway, Suite 122
Marietta, Georgia 30067
770-980-1488 phone, 770-859-9894 fax
www.bardpress.com

A Paradigm Productions Book

To order the book, contact your local bookstore or call 800-688-9394.

ISBN 1-885167-48-2 trade paperback

Library of Congress Cataloging-in-Publication Data

Misner, Ivan R., 1956-
      Masters of networking : building relationships for your pocketbook and soul / Ivan R. Misner, Don Morgan.
          p.   cm.
      Includes bibliographical references and index.
      ISBN 1-885167-48-2 (pbk.)
      1. Business networks. I. Morgan, Don, 1946- II. Title.
      HD69.S8 M57 2000
      650.1'3--dc21   00-058641
                                                CIP

The authors may be contacted at the following addresses:

BNI — Business Network Int'l.
199 S. Monte Vista, Suite 6
San Dimas, CA 91773-3080
800-825-8286 (outside So. Cal.), 909-305-1818 (in So. Cal.), fax 909-305-1811
    Dr. Ivan R. Misner: misner@bni.com
    Don Morgan: morgan@bnicanada.ca

Visit the Masters of Networking website at www.MastersofNetworking.com.

CREDITS
Developmental Editing: *Jeff Morris*
Copyediting: *Deborah Costenbader*
Proofreading: *Deborah Costenbader, Luke Torn*
Text Design / Production: *Jeff Morris*
Jacket Design: *Hespenheide Design*
Index: *Alana Cash*

First printing: August 2000
Second printing: October 2000
Third printing: January 2001

To Mike Ryan and Lee Shimmin, two members of the Founding Chapter of BNI who are still members today after seventeen consecutive years. If networking is about building long-term relationships, loyalty, and commitment, then they are truly Masters of Networking.

Ivan R. Misner

To Betty Morgan, a self-described normal person but also published author and wonderful human being, who inspired me to write this book; to my sister Marki, a published author; to my brother Bill, the natural networker; and to Dr. Holland, who at ninety published his second book and at ninety-seven advised, "Reading makes for a full mind, but writing makes for an exact mind."

Don Morgan

Contents

6. Getting into Print

7. Not for Business Only

8. The Power of Word of Mouth

9. Connecting

10. Making a Good Impression

11. Listening to Learn

12. Establishing & Managing Contacts

13. Cultivating Contacts

14. It's Not What You Know . . .

15. Myths, Mistakes, & Misconceptions

16. The Instinct to Help Others

17. The Law of Mutual Benefit

18. What a Little Networking Can Do

19. NETWORKING TO THE MAX

20. THE SKILLS OF A MASTER

21. THE TRAITS OF A MASTER

22. HOW GOOD A NETWORKER ARE YOU?

23. THE ROAD TO MASTERY

About This Book

Our collection of stories, observations, and ideas comes from well-known authors and from many other fine people you've never heard of. It comes from highly successful people, some of whom you may have admired for a long time, and from ordinary people you've never heard of and who are just beginning to achieve success. Through all the contributions runs a common thread: the oddly altruistic yet self-interested collaborative ideal of networking.

Every author in these pages is a networker. Networkers like to network. They live and breathe networking. All of them are people you'd like to know. And therein lies the wonderful, not-so-hidden secret of this book — it is not just a book about networking, it's a sourcebook on masterful networking as well.

When you read a contribution by someone you identify with and would like to learn more from, try an experiment. Turn to the back of the book and read about the author in the Contributions section. There you will also find information on how to contact that person. (You can find the most current biographical information by accessing our website: www.MastersofNetworking.com.) See if he or she might become a part of your own network. As a master networker, this person might very well derive satisfaction from networking with you, and you both could find ways to create and enjoy mutual benefits. (This is, after all, one of the many techniques taught in the book.)

We thank all of our contributors for sharing their tales of personal success and offering their insight and advice on achieving the unlikely, the difficult, and the impossible. This book is written so that we all might be further inspired to persevere in our pursuit of life's greatest challenges.

Dream your dreams, for your goals are merely your dreams, propelled by your determination and guided by your network.

A Way of Life

Did you ever wonder why some people are more successful than you? Why they always seem to get better deals, more sales, bigger promotions, or just live a better life? This is especially frustrating if you feel you are better qualified, have more skills, or offer a better product. Often you may be tempted to explain away their success as simple luck or the result of being in the right place at the right time.

Scratch the surface and you will discover that most of these highly accomplished people are just ordinary folks — people like you and me — who happen to possess highly refined networking skills. These ordinary people achieve extraordinary results as they team up with other ordinary people and engage in the very human activity of networking.

Successful people do not achieve their success on their own; instead, they surround themselves with a well-developed, sophisticated support network. In a world that grows more complex and more competitive every day, networking is necessary not only for survival but also for high achievement.

The central principle of networking is a spiritual ideal common to all the world's great moral systems: the concept of gaining through giving. This ideal is expressed in one form or another by every contributor to this book, from small business owner to corporate executive, from local politician to global operator, from North America through South Africa, the United Kingdom, and Singapore, to Australia. The power of this book comes from its diversity of viewpoints, all reflecting different facets of the same ennobling ideal.

We all network, but some of us — the most successful of us — are networking masters. What is different about masters? How are their lives different? How do they become masters? What actions lead them to greater success than the rest of us? These are the questions this book sets out to answer. And the answers come from the masters themselves. In these pages, the masters share their stories and insights about how they learned to network and how they networked their way to success. Their stories reveal fascinating details about how people skills, communication skills, and an eagerness to help others come together in a symbiotic relationship that benefits everyone.

Master networkers don't turn on their networking prowess Monday morning and switch it off when they go home in the evening; they believe it, they breathe it, they live it every day, all day. They believe in cooperating with others and in helping others achieve success. They have discovered how being supportive in a human relationship will help them achieve professional success and live a satisfying personal life. They have high ideals. They believe that the good they do for others is an integral part of what makes this a good world to live in, as well as a world in which they will experience personal success.

The masters you will meet in these pages discuss a broad range of techniques and strategies for becoming a master networker. As you read stories about Bill Gates, Fran Tarkenton, and Colin Powell and hear the advice of Tom Peters, Harvey Mackay, Deepak Chopra, Susan RoAne, John Naisbitt, Paul and Sarah Edwards, Jay Conrad Levinson, and Mark Victor Hansen, learn from them. Let their minds talk to yours. Rest assured that the skills they use are skills you can learn. When you read the accounts in these pages, you will begin to form ideas that will work for you. All you need to become a successful master are your innate networking skills and a persistent desire to learn how to get networking working for your goals in new, more powerful ways.

> Extraordinary people visualize not what is possible or probable, but rather what is impossible. And by visualizing the impossible, they begin to see it as possible.
>
> — Cherie Carter Scott

1

Why We Network

HUMANKIND SPENDS MORE OF ITS TIME AND ENERGY ON COMMUNICATION THAN ANY other species. And our communication is vastly more complex and sophisticated than that of any other species. We communicate about the past, the present, and the future, how they are connected, how they affect us, how we feel about it, and what we plan to do about it. We communicate in order to dream about things that do not exist, then we communicate to bring them to reality. We communicate to keep in touch with what our neighbors, our peers, our leaders are thinking and doing and how it affects us. We communicate to help and support each other.

In the following four essays, John Naisbitt tells how and why networks form; Deepak Chopra gives us a glimpse into an underlying principle of human networking; Carol Thompson shows why new technology doesn't trump old truths; and Robert French describes how network groups shape and define our social values.

What Is a Network?

John Naisbitt

Simply stated, networks are people talking to each other, sharing ideas, information, and resources. The point is often made that networking is a verb, not a noun. The important part is not the network, the finished product, but the process of getting there — the communication that creates the linkages between people and clusters of people.

Networking, notes Marilyn Ferguson, who has written extensively about the subject in *The Aquarian Conspiracy*, is done by "conferences, phone calls, air travel, books, phantom organizations, papers, pamphleteering, photocopying, lectures, workshops, parties, grapevines, mutual friends, summit meetings, coalitions, tapes, newsletters."

Networks exist to foster self-help, to exchange information, to change society, to improve productivity and work life, and to share resources. They are structured to transmit information in a way that is quicker, more high-tech, and more energy-efficient than any other process we know.

"Networks are appropriate sociology — the human equivalent of appropriate technology — providing a form of communication and interaction which is suitable for the energy-scarce, information-rich future," write Jessica Lipnack and Jeffrey Stamps in *New Age*.

Knowledge Networking

One of networking's great attractions is that it is an easy way to get information. Much easier, for example, than going to a library or university or, God forbid, the government. Washington Researchers, a Washington, D.C., firm specializing in obtaining government information for corporate clients, estimates that it takes seven phone calls to get the information you want from a government agency. Experienced networkers claim they can reach anyone in the world with only six interactions. It has been my experience, however, that I can reach anyone in the United States with only two — three at the very most — exchanges.

Although sharing information and contacts is their main purpose, networks can go beyond the mere transfer of data to the creation and exchange of knowledge. As each person in a network takes in new information, he or she synthesizes it and comes up with other, new ideas. Networks share these newly forged thoughts and ideas.

Describing this process in the magazine *Future Life*, Willard Van de Bogart writes: "Each new thought is being integrated into the next thought, producing a new cumulative awareness of human nature and the universe we live in. These new mental models are being shared within the newly developed networks throughout the world."

Recently I experienced a striking personal example of knowledge networking. Some close friends in my own network are the Foresight

Group, three Swedish business consultants who have sponsored my speeches in Sweden. In late 1981, the Naisbitt Group, the Foresight Group, and our spouses met to discuss future projects. The Foresight Group gave the rest of us a presentation on their latest project, the School for Intrapreneurs (*intrapreneurs* are entrepreneurs working within organizations).

They used a chart that I frequently use in speeches, but their new interpretation brought an additional layer of knowledge to material I thought I knew quite well.

Specifically, the chart graphs the progress of the United States from an agricultural to an industrial to an information society by indicating how many people work in agricultural, industrial, or information occupations.

What my friends pointed out is that the transition times between societies are the times when entrepreneurship blooms. The late agricultural and early industrial era was the time of the great captains of industry (or robber barons, depending on how you look at it). Now, at the beginning of the information era, new businesses are being created at a rate six times faster than in 1950.

For me sitting in the audience, the effect was feeling my own ideas come back at me after being improved and refined by the people in my own network. That is the kind of knowledge networking Willard Van de Bogart is talking about, and it is happening within networks all over the country.

> Networking empowers the individual, and people in networks tend to nurture one another.

There is even a network on networking, notes Van de Bogart: the Consciousness Synthesis Clearing House in Redondo Beach, California, which is "evolving a general understanding of the networking process and the development of an over-arching perspective from which to view this vital phenomenon."

Life within the Network Model

The vertical to horizontal power shift that networks bring about will be enormously liberating for individuals. Hierarchies promote moving up and getting ahead, producing stress, tension, and anxiety.

Networking empowers the individual, and people in networks tend to nurture one another.

In the network environment, rewards come by empowering others, not by climbing over them.

If you work in a hierarchy, you may not want to climb to its top. At a time when decentralist and networking values are becoming more accepted and when businesses must do the hard work of reconceptualizing what business they are really in while facing unprecedented foreign competition, it is not the ideal time to be a traditional-type leader, either political or corporate.

Even in a hierarchy, there is an informal network within the formal structure. Find it. For some people, it is worth the effort to locate and work only in a network-style environment. Outside of work, this is the time to start your own network or join one and get connected with like-minded people.

Today we live in a world of overlapping networks, not just a constellation of networks but a galaxy of networking constellations.

The above excerpt from Megatrends *is used with permission.*

The Law of Giving

Deepak Chopra

The second spiritual law of success is the *Law of Giving*. This law could also be called the *Law of Giving and Receiving*, because the universe operates through dynamic exchange. Nothing is static. Your body is in dynamic and constant exchange with the body of the universe; your mind is dynamically interacting with the mind of the cosmos; your energy is an expression of cosmic energy.

The flow of life is nothing other than the harmonious interaction of all the elements and forces that structure the field of existence. This harmonious interaction of elements and forces in your life operates as the *Law of Giving*. Because your body and your mind and the universe are in constant and dynamic exchange, stopping the circulation of energy is like stopping the flow of blood. Whenever blood stops flowing, it begins to clot, to coagulate, to stagnate. That is why you must give and receive in order to keep wealth and affluence — or anything you want in life — circulating in your life.

The word affluence comes from the root word "affluere," which means "to flow to." The word affluence means "to flow in abundance." Money is really a symbol of the life energy we exchange and the life energy we use as a result of the service we provide to the universe. Another word for money is "currency," which also reflects the flowing nature of energy. The word currency comes from the Latin word "currere" which mean "to run" or to flow. . . .

Every relationship is one of give and take. Giving engenders receiving, and receiving engenders giving. What goes up must come down; what goes out must come back. In reality, receiving is the same thing as giving, because giving and receiving are different aspects of the flow of energy in the universe. And if you stop the flow of either, you interfere with nature's intelligence.

In every seed is the promise of thousands of forests. But the seed must not be hoarded; it must give its intelligence to the fertile ground. Through its giving, its unseen energy flows into material manifestation.

The more you give, the more you will receive, because you will keep the abundance of the universe circulating in your life. In fact, anything that is of value in life only multiplies when it is given. That which doesn't multiply through giving is neither worth giving nor worth receiving. If, through the act of giving, you feel you have lost something, then the gift is not truly given and will not cause increase. If you give grudgingly, there is no energy behind that giving.

> Anything that is of value in life only multiplies when it is given.

It is the intention behind your giving and receiving that is the most important thing. The intention should always be to create happiness for the giver and receiver, because happiness is life-supporting and life-sustaining and therefore generates increase. The return is directly proportional to the giving when it is unconditional and from the heart. That is why the act of giving has to be joyful — the frame of mind has to be one in which you feel joy in the very *act* of giving. Then the energy behind the giving increases many times over.

Practicing the *Law of Giving* is actually very simple: if you want joy, give joy to others; if you want love, learn to give love; if you want attention and appreciation, learn to give attention and appreciation; if you want material affluence, help others to become materially affluent. In fact, the easiest way to get what you want is to help others get what they want. This principle works equally well for individuals, corporations, societies, and nations. If you want to be blessed with all the good things in life, learn to silently bless everyone with all the good things in life.

Even the thought of giving, the thought of blessing, or a *simple prayer* has the power to affect others. This is because our body, reduced to its essential state, is a localized bundle of energy and information in a universe of energy and information. We are localized bundles of consciousness in a conscious universe. The word "consciousness" implies more than just energy and information — it implies energy and information which is alive as thought. Therefore we are bundles of thought in a thinking universe. And thought has the power to transform.

Life is the eternal dance of consciousness that expresses itself as the dynamic exchange of impulses of intelligence between microcosm and macrocosm, between the human body and the universal body, between the human mind and the cosmic mind.

When you learn to give that which you seek, you activate and choreograph the dance with an exquisite, energetic, and vital movement that constitutes the eternal throb of life. . . .

The best way to put the *Law of Giving* into operation — to start the whole process of circulation — is to make a decision that any time you come into contact with anyone, you will give them something. It doesn't have to be in the form of material things; it could be a flower, a compliment, or a prayer. In fact, the most powerful forms of giving are nonmaterial. The gifts of caring, attention, affection, appreciation, and love are some of the most precious gifts you can give, and they don't cost you anything.

When you meet someone, you can silently send them a blessing, wishing them happiness, joy, and laughter. This kind of silent giving is very powerful.

One of the things I was taught as a child, and which I taught my children also, is never to go to anyone's house without bringing something — never visit anyone without bringing them a gift. You may say, "How can I give to others when at the moment I don't have enough myself?" You can bring a flower. One flower. You can bring a note or a card which says something about your feelings for the person you're visiting. You can bring a compliment. You can bring a prayer.

Make a decision to give wherever you go, to whomever you see. As long as you're giving, you will be receiving. The more you give, the more confidence you will gain in the miraculous effects of this law. And as you receive more, your ability to give more will also increase.

Our true nature is one of affluence and abundance; we are naturally affluent because nature supports every need and desire. We lack nothing, because our essential nature is one of pure potentiality and infinite possibilities. Therefore, you must know that you are already inherently affluent, no matter how much or how little money you have, because the source of all wealth is the field of pure potentiality — it is the consciousness that knows how to fulfill every need, including joy, love, laughter, peace, harmony, and knowledge. If you seek these things first — not only for yourself, but for others — all else will come to you spontaneously.

The above excerpt from The Seven Spiritual Laws of Success *is used with permission.*

Relationships Count More Than Ever

Carol Thompson

It might appear to some that networking is a thing of the past — hot in the '70s and '80s, but old hat in the twenty-first-century, high-tech world. If you believe this, you'd better go fetch that hat, because your sales numbers and future success are about to get rained out. Building strong relationships, which is what networking is all about, is even more important now in this new, fast-paced, global business environment.

New technology and ever-increasing bandwidth make communication by telephone and e-mail possible twenty-four hours a day, seven days a week, around the world. So, with all these connection opportunities, why are relationships more important than ever? Here are four reasons:

1. Constant Change. The rate and scope of change in all of our workplaces, not just the high-tech companies, has required all of us to become more innovative in developing new products and services, as well as in the way we work with our customers and clients. With a more flexible virtual corporation becoming the business model, we now have ever-evolving partnerships and alliances. And buyouts or bailouts are often part of our financial agenda. Bottom line: high-trust relationships have a high value in today's business environment. Information comes at a premium — and the most effective way to acquire information is often through relationships.

2. The Tech Mentality. Many people who find themselves in the high-tech workplace by virtue of their education, training, or personality don't fully realize the value of the "people" side of business. To them, technology is the answer. They don't understand that it's *people* who make the decisions to purchase and implement the technology they create. Computers don't decide to hire you, people do. Even the basics of networking, such as returning telephone calls, are important. It seems at times there is an attitude that "unless you left five messages, you must not really want to talk to me." Not the way to build relationships or success.

If you want to increase your bottom line, the human connection is always the place to begin.

3. Broader Roles. In workplaces of the past, roles were narrower and more clearly defined. People could say they were engineers, accountants, architects, or computer analysts and know that people skills were not a part of their job requirements. In today's workplace, almost everyone is selling. Whether it's a product, service, or company you're representing, how well you relate to the people you connect with to perform your job is a big part of your success, and ultimately that of your company. This goes beyond clients and prospects to vendors, employees, partners, the media, and the community at large.

4. More Stress. A more demanding workplace includes more stringent deadlines, tougher competition, and ever-increasing change, and that means stress. Many studies now demonstrate the value of a personal network for one's health. People who network live longer. A strong personal network can serve as a buffer, a support system, and even as an energizer, for all the challenges of this exciting workplace.

On the upside, all this technology allows us to develop relationships more easily and in greater number, not just in our immediate community or industry, but anywhere across the world. If you want to increase your bottom line, or if you want your staff to do that for you, remember that the human connection is always the place to begin. When you go on line, remember that there's at least one other human at the other end of the information highway.

The Global Neighborhood

Robert French

In Elham, a village near Canterbury, I recently met a very unusual couple. Betty and Jack, both in their sixties, had never left Elham. They were quite content to stay home.

I, on the other hand, was visiting my fourth country of the year. Who was living the more unusual lifestyle? I suspect it was Betty and Jack.

But things have changed, of course. Two hundred years ago, most Elhamites, except for the young men who served as soldiers, had never visited even nearby towns. They depended almost entirely on one another for daily necessities, social life, and moral guidance. Their fellow villagers were their reference group. And the reference group's standards of behavior and belief — set by the village elders — were tough and uncompromising, their enforcement swift and harsh. Though they restricted individual liberty, the rules worked to the benefit of all by keeping citizens civic-minded and the village unified and functional.

Betty and Jack are now rare birds, an endangered species. Today we move about freely, settling thousands of miles from our early reference group, the family. We are affluent and mobile; we communicate via long-distance phone calls, faxes, and e-mail; we get our information from nationwide and worldwide television networks and the Internet. At the same time, we are unaccountable, even strangers, to our next-door neighbors.

Living without a reference group is a troubling phenomenon of modern times. Isolated individuals and families easily lose interest in the well-being of their neighbors and fellow citizens. Low moral standards and lax enforcement lead to drug abuse, child abuse, divorce, dishonest business practices, and worse. Many of us find ourselves caught between people we consider fanatical, old-fashioned moralists and amoral hoodlums, unable to associate or communicate with either group for mutual benefit. Ultimately, this dissociation erodes our choices, our liberty. We can't sit on our front porch and chat with the neighbors; we can't walk certain streets after dark.

> For most of us, if we have any reference group at all it is likely to be geographically scattered, diffuse, and ineffectual.

Sometimes new reference groups arise spontaneously, based on the worst instincts of their members. Communities of drug abusers embrace robbery and theft as necessary to their way of life. Fanatical hate groups base their community on a pathological hatred of all who differ in race or religion.

For most of us, if we have any reference group at all it is likely to be geographically scattered, diffuse, and ineffectual. Living in such an unstructured world can be lonely and hazardous. Our natural tendency is to try to regain a sense of community with others, wherever we can find them — to join new reference groups. We may seek safety in the number of groups. We go to the gym and assemble with our fellow fitness seekers once or twice a week. We join a golf club, where we find people who live lives much like ours. Businesspeople join business networking groups and form lifelong friendships based on mutual financial interest. We really can't help it — it's part of our human nature.

Gaining admission to any strong social reference group can restore our sense of accountability. Most modern groups, like their historical counterparts, have a clearly defined organization and structure, along with social and ethical standards, responsibilities, and membership accountability. In the best cases, these global villages are analogous to the geographic villages of old — only with more individual freedom of choice. We can form our associations wherever we wish, independent of where we live.

Helping less advantaged people can become an enlightening, life-altering experience. It is gratifying to see how previously tough-minded businesspeople adept at cutthroat competition suddenly, after joining a business networking group, begin to find deep satisfaction in helping their networking partners.

All groups need standards. Forming communities based on common interests usually invigorates individual moral and ethical

> Forming communities based on common interests usually invigorates individual moral and ethical standards.

standards. Some find this process painful, but without high standards there is little incentive for high performance and results. A group with the courage to set high standards of structure, discipline, and goals will become stronger and help its members. A strong reference group gives members an essential part of their identity — as members in a community, in cooperation with others to accomplish goals the individual cannot achieve on his own.

2

Networking Comes Naturally

NETWORKING IS SUCH AN INTEGRAL PART OF EVERYDAY LIFE THAT MANY OF US DON'T realize we're networking until someone introduces us to the word. Networking is part of family life, and networking is the way we keep our personal lives running smoothly. Below, Karyanne Newton shows us how a parent's lesson for a child translates into the central guiding principle behind networking; Sandy Donovan remembers how, as a child, she learned three lessons in behavior that every good networker should know; and Hazel Walker gives us her take on networking from the perspective of a parent and social volunteer.

Networking for Kids

Karyanne Newton

As parents, we teach our children what to believe and how to behave by our own actions. Sometimes these actions include what we say — or don't say. At certain ages, children left to their own devices can be thoughtless, rude, or cruel. If we ignore this behavior — just sibling rivalry, you say, or they're just tired — we are teaching them lifelong habits that will make life difficult for them and everyone around them.

If, on the other hand, we teach them to treat others the way they would like to be treated, we are teaching them networking.

My oldest daughter, Eve, who is twelve, decided to form a club. Her first new member was a neighborhood boy her own age. They held their first club meeting in our garage, and soon I heard the signs of the first conflict. Eve had banned her younger sister, seven-year-old Shelby, from the club.

The conflict quickly grew shrill and tearful, and I intervened. In our family, I told Eve, we treat others they way we would like to be treated. I explained that it is important to be generous to those who are unable to attain what they cannot attain without others' assistance. We should never exclude people — especially those closest to us, our own family members. You never know, I said, when you might need another friend.

The neighbor boy was moved. "She has a point," he told Eve. He wished his own brother were more friendly toward him, he said, and he also wished that his parents could hear me. He would love to have their help in getting his brother to accept him.

I was both stunned and proud to learn that I was teaching not just my children but a neighbor's child the real meaning of being a giver. Of course, I was only reacting to Shelby's pain at being excluded, but I quickly realized that the impromptu lesson in human relations was something that would help them get along in the adult world.

My career is teaching business networking. I know, and my children are learning, that you are generous to others because that's the way you wish to be treated by them. In networking, we state the Golden Rule succinctly: "Givers gain." Those who network generously and thoughtfully experience great success in all aspects of their lives. They surround themselves, or let themselves be surrounded, by a supportive network of people who admire and care for them.

> This is perhaps the greatest gift I can give my children (as I network with them to pass along my adult wisdom): the lesson that kindness given will eventually come around to them.

This is perhaps the greatest gift I can give my children (as I network with them to pass along my adult wisdom): the lesson that kindness given will eventually come around to them. The more my kids give of themselves to others, the more they will gain in their life, and the more successful I will be as a mom.

How do you gauge success? Is it how much money you earn, how big a house you can afford, how many toys you can accumulate? I find my biggest rewards in learning and in giving. Each time I help someone by offering ideas, information, contacts, or instruction, I invest in a relationship that may some day help me in return.

Ask yourself the same question I was once asked: What will your tombstone read? Mine will say proudly, "She gave and she got back!"

Building Blocks

Sandy Donovan

None of the great networkers I know learned their networking skills in high-level college business courses or in secret executive meetings. Like me, they were taught by their parents. Of course, we didn't know this at the time. We were just learning the art of getting along with our brothers and sisters and playmates. We didn't learn networking in classrooms or boardrooms; we grew up with the essentials of good networking — the keys to success — in our blood.

I resisted, of course. Learning life's hard lessons is not hard-wired into the child. Parents need to possess and use great patience and perseverance. It was not until much later that I learned the wisdom of their lessons: that making the effort now brings a payoff later, and that the rewards are worth waiting for.

Here's what my mother and father told me, as often as necessary, until the lessons took:

"YOU HAVE TO LEARN TO SHARE."

This was not a lesson I was fond of learning. What was mine was mine! Not my cousin's or my sister's or my playmate's — mine! But share I learned, and share I did — my toys, my clothes, even my room when we had guests. But gradually I became aware of a funny thing about human nature: when you share with others, others want to share with you, too.

In business, we are all focused on getting ahead, achieving our own goals, advancing our individual careers. But if we've learned to share, we realize that we reach our greatest heights when we pool our strengths and see how high we can soar together. By focusing on helping others achieve their goals, we get back tenfold, and reaching our own goals somehow becomes easier.

As Stephen Covey says, moving from independence to interdependence helps take us to the highest level of leadership. Learning to share in the business community through ideas or referrals builds trust, loyalty, and camaraderie between individuals. What better way to establish your reputation than as an individual who is always looking to help others?

"DON'T FORGET TO SAY THANK YOU."

Soon after I learned the basics of reading and writing, I discovered the downside: I had to write thank-you notes for birthday gifts. I was not particularly fond of this ritual, but was aware that it was important, even if I wasn't sure why. In any event, it became a habit, and I have since found it to be quite an effective tool in establishing strong business relationships.

I look for reasons to send people notes — and not just thank-you notes, but any kind of note that gives me regular communication with a business associate, client, friend, contact, or colleague. I clip and send my contacts articles showing them at a charity function, promotions that might interest them, news that might affect their business. Why? Because I know most people don't do it, and it helps give others a positive impression of me. It shows them I'm thinking of them. You never know whose path you'll cross who could someday influence your career, and I'd rather have that person on my side if I can help it.

"YOU MADE A PROMISE; NOW KEEP YOUR WORD."

We've all battled our parents on this one, haven't we? "I know I said that, but I didn't mean it!" "I told them I'd go, but they'll never notice

I'm not there!" Of course, our parents were right. Part of growing up is learning to keep a commitment — and a good definition of commitment is doing the thing you said you'd do long after the mood you said it in has left you. Doing things we don't want to do, but promised to do, gradually brings to light the better angels of our nature. And these angels are the ones most likely to bring us success. How can we be great networkers without cultivating great relationships? How can we build positive relationships without trust? And who will trust us if we don't do what we say we'll do?

Thanks to technology, we can work more efficiently and achieve our goals faster than ever before. But our modem-to-modem instant communication ability can't replace the person-to-person virtues and values that make us a vital part of the business community. What sets us apart from our competition is how well we have learned and adopted the lessons our parents taught us.

Mothers Are Natural-Born Networkers

Hazel Walker

Networking is as old as the human race. Bob Burg describes networking as the cultivation of mutually beneficial, give-and-take, win-win relationships. The term "networking" brings to mind the "old-boys' network," with big men in smoky rooms swapping favors and business (exclusively) with one another. The reality is that we each network in one way or another, and we all know people who seem to be very good at meeting people and making connections; we just don't recognize it as networking. I believe that effective networking is an acquired skill that takes patience and practice.

As a mother and avid PTA volunteer, I often have the opportunity to observe the natural networking of women at different events — seemingly informal conversations among women who are not aware they are networking. I often hear tips about babysitters, play groups, housekeeping services, garage sales, and other information important to their jobs as mothers and home caretakers. They pass information freely to those in their contact spheres. What is commonly referred to as the "hen party" is, in reality, old-fashioned networking.

Through my involvement in structured business networking groups, I have become aware of the dynamics of word-of-mouth advertising and find it very interesting to note how formal hen-party networking really is. There are definite protocols followed in these groups.

While doing volunteer work at a food pantry, I had the opportunity to hear how networking really works. Moms exchanged information about

- whom to speak with at the trustees' office for help with the rent,

- who is the best counselor at the utility agencies,

- how to get financial aid for the bills,

- which church pantry can help with babysitters, and

- what agency in town can provide birth control and day care.

When one mother needed help with a sick child, several mothers volunteered names and phone numbers of the clinics that would be willing to help.

As I listened, I realized that what they were doing was exactly what I teach businesspeople to do to build their businesses by networking. I asked a few of the ladies if they would mind speaking with me about their networking. I asked them how they found out about the various agencies, special contacts, and services. Was there a book or list of places to go for all the help they were getting? They explained that much of the information and help available to the poor comes from word of mouth. There are many people willing to help those in need who are not a part of the formal system. The only way to access this help is through verbal referrals and common associations.

Most of these women see the same people at different places. They build their relationships while they stand in one line after another. It becomes natural to share experiences and information. When asked, some had a vague idea about what was meant by networking, but they certainly did not realize that they were doing formal networking every day. To many, what they are doing is simply surviving for both their children and themselves.

They were very clear that they did not share this information with just anyone. Referrals are passed only to those they have become familiar with over time. This is similar to the way we teach people in our business networking organizations. They must first build relationships and earn trust before they do business with each other.

Passing leads and information and giving testimonials are just basic survival skills for this group. They are never without pencil and paper. When Debbie needed help with dental problems, Susan told her about a dentist who would do the work at a very low cost and allow bill payment in affordable installments. Susan wrote the name and telephone numbers of the dentist on a piece of paper and passed the lead on to Debbie. An outstanding testimonial was given for an attorney who works hard for very little, and a compassionate gentleman at the electric company was given high marks. On the other hand, these women are very outspoken when they have been given bad service or treated with disrespect.

> Knowing where to get help to raise their families was just as important to these women as new business referrals are to the businessperson.

I shared with these mothers how businesspeople network with each other to exchange business referrals. One mother responded that this was indeed (also) their business. Knowing where to get help to raise their families was just as important to these women as new business referrals are to the businessperson. With no formal training in networking, they have learned to ask for specific referrals. They have goals, they build relationships with each other, they always follow up, and they practice the "Givers gain" philosophy. Their very survival depends on their ability to network.

I realized that these women could teach many of the businesspeople I work with how to build relationships and develop word-of-mouth business. I also learned how important this type of communication is to everyone, whether personal or business. The pantry ladies taught me that many people have the natural ability to network but success depends on refining this ability. By setting their goals, working their contacts, and being always ready to give referrals, these women have proved that the very essence of networking is people caring about other people. Donna Fisher says, in her book *Power Networking*, "Even if you learn all the skills, say all the right things, and go through all the right motions, networking is only truly powerful when genuine human caring exists."

3

Starting Up

NORTH AMERICANS ARE HEIRS TO A RICH AND RECENT PIONEERING TRADITION, AND nothing excites us more than coming into virgin territory and staking a claim. The entrepreneurial spirit lies behind the following four articles — two of which, it must be noted, concern activities by citizens of other nations. Mary Anne Marriott demonstrates how a little networking can lead to big dreams and accomplishments; Linda Macedonio relates her story of building her accounting practice by networking; Stacia Robinson tells us how her marketing business took off as a result of networking; and Todd Evans, Mike Levin, Sim Chow Boon, and Mervin Yeo chronicle the spread of networking organizations across borders and beyond oceans.

Exploring Wonderland

Mary Anne Marriott

"**W**ould you tell me, please, which way I ought to go from here?" asked Alice.

"That depends a good deal on where you want to get to," said the Cat.

"I don't much care where — " said Alice.

"Then it doesn't matter which way you go," said the Cat.

This wonderful quote from *Alice's Adventures in Wonderland* crossed my desk a few years ago. It meant little to me at first, but over the years it began to mean a great deal. You see, I didn't know where I was going until someone pointed me in the right direction.

For eight years I had worked in an office environment and expected to be there for the rest of my life. I had no real dreams of doing anything else. I had an office and decent pay and was treated well. My responsibilities included dealing with salespeople. I developed an aversion to sales. I never wanted to sell people things, and I didn't like being pressured to buy.

One day, however, I met an interesting young saleswoman, Melodie Stewart, who was selling ad space in a local women's magazine. Over coffee she told me the wonderful things she could do for the company I worked for if we advertised in her magazine. I was impressed by her ability to put me at ease and gain my confidence. I decided that I wanted to do business with her and believed it would help my company.

Melodie and I spent a lot of time putting together copy for the ads. We became friends, and it was her persistence that got me to attend my first networking event, a Christmas social for the Women's Network. I walked into the room, shy and nervous — a little like Alice must have felt. When I spotted Melodie, I attached myself to her until I felt more comfortable talking to new people. Although I am not terribly shy by nature, this was a new environment, and I was a bit intimidated by all the professionals.

Shortly after this event, Melodie called me and said she had a great opportunity for me. There was a new and exciting business networking group called BNI being established in Halifax, and she was sure I would want to be a part of it. Later that week I attended my first business networking referral group. I was impressed and decided to get involved, even though it meant meeting at 7 AM. I still did not know where my career was heading, but something in me made me want to find out.

This decision changed the course of my life. I quickly fell into a new role as a business networker. Through my association with the

Marriott's Wonderland Travel Tips

- Be aware of the value of important chance encounters.
- Seek out new experiences and make new contacts.
- Learn from those around you.
- Surround yourself with the best people possible.

members of the group, I became more comfortable with salespeople and ultimately learned to be a salesperson myself. Soon I decided that a part-time business operated from my home might be a good idea. After all, it would reduce my income tax bill, and my "real" job was helping people with their credit issues.

The entrepreneurial bug bit me. I became involved with a part-time, home-based, direct-sales program, and six months later I won a sales contest and qualified to attend a conference with the BNI referral program in Toronto, Canada. Not long afterwards, I accepted a position as a part-time assistant director with BNI in Halifax.

Since my first exposure to business networking, I have been president of the Women's Network, a board member of the Young Atlantic Entrepreneurs Association, and a member of the Halifax Chamber of Commerce and Pro-Net Business Connections.

More recently I left my ten-year office job to work my home businesses, BNI and direct sales. I'm doing the things I love. I've met wonderful people and formed great friendships. I'm surrounded by positive people who are available to me at a moment's notice. My personal network now includes people who can fix my car, paint my portrait, and help me establish and achieve personal goals.

Now I know where I want to go, and networking is the tool to help me get there. Networking has truly changed my direction and my life.

Becoming a Networking Bookkeeper

Linda Macedonio

When I started my home-based bookkeeping business, I knew I would have to find a way to sell my business — and myself. The only way I could think of was to mail letters to local CPAs introducing myself and follow up each letter with a call.

The thought of cold-calling terrified me. Before I could pick up the phone I had to take five deep breaths and press the knot forming in my stomach. I hated every minute of it, but I thought I had to do it if my business was to be successful. After twenty-five letters and countless follow-up calls, I had found only two CPAs who would meet with me.

When I was first introduced to networking, I had no idea how to do it. What interested me was the idea of forming relationships with other businesspeople and getting business through referrals. The good news: No more cold calls!

The bad news: Being basically a shy person, I didn't realize that I had to learn how to initiate contact with strangers. I thought that by simply showing up at networking events, I was networking. The problem was that I was talking to the same people each month.

GOING PUBLIC

I didn't realize how little I knew until I joined a strong contact networking organization with regular weekly meetings. Part of the weekly format was an opportunity for each member to give a sixty-second commercial about his or her business. This forced me to do two things I had never done before. First, it made me evaluate my business. The idea of the commercial is to tell members what is a good referral for your business. Preparing for it made me ask myself, "What is a good referral for me?" I never had thought of my clients as a "target market." This made me focus on the type of clients I wanted and those I did not want. Little did I know then that this is a basic exercise for marketers.

> The opportunity to give a sixty-second commercial at weekly meetings forced me to do two things I had never done before: evaluate my business, and talk about it in front of others.

The second step was to prepare my own sixty-second commercial, and talk about my business in front of others. Since the commercial had to be different every week, the night before my meeting I would prepare a flyer presenting a different angle to my business. I would address issues such as reconciling your bank account or not mixing business and personal expenses. Sharing these bookkeeping tips with my fellow members helped me to build trust and to show that I did have the technical background necessary for my clients.

Each week I got nervous waiting to do my commercial, so nervous that the butterflies wouldn't let me eat until after my turn. Part of the structure of the meeting was that one member each week would do a ten-minute presentation. *Ten minutes!* How would I survive?

When the week came for my ten-minute presentation, I was a nervous wreck. But I prepared carefully, and on the appointed day, I felt I was ready. The presentation was about an hour into the meeting. After about twenty-five minutes, the woman next to me asked if I was okay. I asked what she meant, and she told me that I kept coughing and choking. I was so nervous about speaking that I hadn't even realized I was doing it.

I got through my presentation fairly well, and I don't think most people realized how nervous I was. As time went on, my confidence and my speaking skills improved with the weekly one-minute commercials. I can actually improvise a little now. The next time I did a ten-minute presentation, it came a lot easier — and I managed not to have a coughing fit!

HARVESTING BENEFITS

Two years later, I have realized two great benefits from networking, one that I expected and one I did not. As I anticipated it might, my business has grown from ten clients and no employees to thirty-five clients and an assistant, and I'm even subcontracting work to other independent bookkeepers. The surprise is that, despite my shyness, I am now comfortable meeting strangers and speaking before groups. Not only am I doing one-minute commercials each week, but I also conduct workshops, training sessions, and other presentations for local chambers of commerce and other organizations. If I had been told two years ago that I would be doing this, I wouldn't have believed it.

I truly believe networking is priceless. Not only does it help you grow your business, it can provide benefits that you never expect until they happen.

Serving Networking ICE

Stacia Robinson

A new delicacy being served in Montgomery, Alabama, is Networking ICE — not the cold stuff you may be visualizing, but a delicious combination of ingredients that, when served with relationships, brings added satisfaction and success to your business.

My story goes back to when I was a captain in the U.S. Air Force. As a communications computer officer, my duties included planning, implementing, and coordinating computer information systems, such as the Defense Data Network. In 1986, when I transferred to Montgomery, I was responsible for developing the interface between the government's and vendors' computers. This led to a computer technology conference that is now one of the biggest conferences in the city.

I left the Air Force in 1991 and started my own marketing business, armed with little more than my own confidence and the knowledge that success breeds success. Through my research into small businesses, I discovered networking as a business tool. A book by Paul and Sarah Edwards, *Working from Home,* introduced me to a business referral organization called BNI. A few phone calls later, I started the first BNI referral chapter in Montgomery and began discovering my recipe for Networking ICE: investment, cultivation, and enrichment.

INVESTMENT

I was committed to learning and developing effective networking skills. I have a genuine love for people, and networking seemed to hold answers for my new business. I soon discovered that learning to network and to develop and cultivate relationships requires a substantial investment of time and resources.

My first business networking goal was to get clients for my marketing company. I devoured information about networking from books such as Harvey Mackay's *Swim With the Sharks Without Being Eaten Alive* and *Dig Your Well Before You're Thirsty*. Ivan Misner's *The World's Best Known Marketing Secret* encouraged me to practice my emerging networking skills at every opportunity. I had to broaden my networking focus and goals.

A big return on my research investment came in 1992, when Sonya Buckner, vice president of small business at the chamber of commerce, took me under her wing. Together we conducted the award-winning, three-year "Buy Montgomery" campaign, which brought a 30 percent increase in the city's sales tax revenues.

CULTIVATION

To cultivate my networking skills, I decided to brush up my people skills. The basics, such as the arts of etiquette and conversation, are not as simple in practice as they sound. I also had to learn that making a contact is only the beginning of networking, and that trying to sell a contact when you first meet him is a great way to ruin a potential networking relationship before it begins.

> Trying to sell a contact when you first meet him is a great way to ruin a potential networking relationship before it begins.

One of my biggest mistakes was trying to meet all of Montgomery right away, leaving myself no time to follow up on contacts. I soon learned that when I allowed time for follow-ups, people actually remembered me from one meeting to the next, and relationships did not have to be reestablished.

One of my mentors, James Belton, the sales manager of our local NBC affiliate, guided me through the world of advertising and encouraged me to become involved in the Montgomery Advertising Federation. I asked him once when I would see the payoff; first give, then get, he quietly reminded me. For me, the payoff came when, through my efforts as president of the Montgomery Advertising Federation, we won the National Award for Diversity Advertising.

ENRICHMENT

After I told my sister Dana Fisher (the Little Rock, Arkansas, network queen) how much I admired George Fraser's book *Success Runs in Our Race* for its discussion of networking in the African-American community, she arranged for us to meet at the Black Expo in Atlanta. I followed up on this contact, and soon he was under contract for keynote speeches for my friend Sonya Buckner at the Small Business Banquet in Montgomery and at my chamber of commerce workshop, "How to Advertise on Network Station WOMM: Word-of-Mouth Marketing." Shortly thereafter, George and I teamed up for a workshop based on his book. Our opportunities multiply with every contact.

Since 1991 I have volunteered for many business, civic, and professional organizations, which has helped me anchor my business as "the" hub firm in Montgomery. I've become the first African-American female board member of the chamber of commerce. Meeting advertising leaders at regional and national conventions lets me network to my heart's content.

> When done well, networking brings meaningful, lifelong relationships, material and spiritual enrichment, professional success, and personal satisfaction.

Networking has given me a whole new perspective on future career possibilities. I've learned that, when done well, networking brings meaningful, lifelong relationships, material and spiritual enrichment, professional success, and personal satisfaction. The people in my network have honored me by sharing their success secrets, encouraging me to take risks, and becoming valuable business contacts and friends.

This is how learning the not-so-secret recipe for Networking ICE transformed a former air force captain into a successful businesswoman. My wish for you is that you are enriched by a serving of Network ICE, a dish best served warm.

In Another Country

In the last decade of the twentieth century, the growth of referral networking has been astronomical — especially that of BNI, founded by Dr. Ivan Misner in 1985. Expansion throughout the United States has been followed by startups in several other countries. Three BNI directors describe how the philosophy and rationale behind networking operate in different cultures.

CANADA, BY TODD EVANS

Networking was something I enjoyed as far back as high school. But it wasn't called networking; it was simply organizing and getting involved in as many activities as possible, keeping in touch with everyone, and helping others. Later, while attending college and becoming active in my fraternity, I stayed in touch with friends and associates and used a card file to keep track of them. These contacts proved valuable when I began paying for my college education by exporting Canadian cars to the United States.

After graduating, getting married, and starting a family and a career, I joined a local networking group and later became a member of the Ottawa Board of Trade. I shared business referrals with my growing network of friends and contacts. Among these was Marc Bonneville, with whom my toddler Katie and I often had breakfast.

My father, a Toronto businessman and a believer in face-to-face contact, had taught me by example the value of networking. In 1995 he suggested that I check out a fast-growing structured network referral organization — BNI — that was looking into expanding into Canada.

I learned about BNI's program at a lunch meeting with its founder. A light went on. I agreed to set up a chapter in Ottawa. The first person I called? Marc Bonneville. The two of us became the founding members of the Ottawa chapter. I went on to become a manager and soon thereafter purchased the marketing rights. Many of the early members came from my extensive informal network of contacts.

BNI's Ottawa region now boasts hundreds of members. From my own perspective of nearly forty years, what began as my group of school chums has grown into a substantial and productive system of business contacts — the largest such referral network in Canada.

South Africa, by Mike Levin

In 1994, from the ashes of apartheid, a new South Africa was born. As international trade sanctions were lifted, the powerhouse economy of sub-Saharan Africa reentered the world.

Despite the promise and optimism of the new government, however, the legacy of apartheid's inequities weighed heavily on South Africa. Housing and school programs fell short of their goals because of poor management and underfunding. A recession saw unemployment shoot up to 34 percent. Funds for development were severely curtailed. Crime became an attractive option for many, a problem that now threatens the entire country.

The government now considers small business the key to economic renewal. It is in this scenario that I find myself.

A happily married man with a secure but unstimulating business, I often caught myself thinking fondly of my early days in the retail business — the excitement and challenge experienced by the small businessperson, starting something new. I desperately needed a change.

It wasn't until 1998, on a business trip to London, that I found what I was looking for. A friend invited me to a BNI meeting. I sat through the proceedings thinking how well the program would work in South Africa. The concept was simple: a structured business referral program, businesspeople supporting and helping each other increase their business through word-of-mouth referrals; as relationships and support grew, so would results.

I was excited. What better place for a business networking organization than a country with thousands of new small businesses?

Word of mouth was the ideal marketing technique. The moral for myself, I thought, was to be ready to network wherever I go and keep my mind and eyes open for new opportunities.

Back home in Cape Town, I contacted BNI's international head office. Not long thereafter, I signed a business agreement to introduce the program to South Africa.

Singapore, by Sim Chow Boon, with Mervin Yeo

Networking can mean different things to different people, independent of their profession or training. To many, networking is meeting as many people as possible, primarily as prospects for future business. To others, the prospect list becomes a source of referrals.

It has always been a wonder how networking comes naturally for some but is uncomfortable for others. Oftentimes we waste the contacts we already have by not turning them into salespeople for our business.

What's networking to me? Having been in sales for more than ten years, I was already in the habit of referring others. But this was not good enough. I had always wanted to be a "trade directory": to know at least one salesperson or businessperson, preferably two or three, from each of thirty or more trades or professions. However, I realized that such a list would not be easy to build, and to keep it up to date I would have to stay in touch with everyone.

Networking in Singapore often takes the form of recreation, such as golf, or happens in social or community service organizations. Whatever the venue, social restraint must be observed. Although everybody knows that one's objective is to cut business deals with others, it is considered impolite to let this become too obvious too soon. Your prospect knows you're there to talk business, but both of you are ill at ease waiting for the right time. It's a slow, inefficient process.

Organizations like Toastmasters, Lions Club, and Rotary Club are by nature ad hoc networks — that is, they do promote contact but are inefficient ways to generate referrals. Their primary function is, and should remain, to serve the community.

There are also ad hoc networking groups, in which one or two enthusiastic individuals invite perhaps twenty businesspeople to have dinner, socialize, and exchange business cards. Since there is no organization or calendar, they may not meet again until six months or even a year later. Often they fail to keep in touch with their contacts, and the business cards become obsolete. These ad hoc meetings lack several factors essential to productive networking: structure, program, coordinators, frequency, even identity.

Networking is most efficient if it is clear from the start that the primary motive for getting together is to generate referrals for one another. That is why it is obvious to me that Singapore is ripe for a structured referral networking organization. Starting from zero, BNI is sure to be a success within a few years.

4

Starting Over

PEOPLE WHO HAVE NETWORKED KNOW WHAT A POWERFUL TOOL NETWORKING CAN BE. So, naturally, when they are faced with beginning again in a new place or a new situation, their thoughts turn immediately to making valuable connections as a way to jump-start their next successful venture. In this section, Dr. Misner relates how football star Fran Tarkenton networked his way into new ventures before his professional gridiron career was over; Nancy Giacomuzzi tells what it was like to be uprooted from an established business community and expected to start over in a new community; and Phil Campbell describes a similar experience, with the added hurdle of starting in a new profession.

Tarkenton after Football

Ivan R. Misner

"**M**any people have told me I'm lucky," says Fran Tarkenton. "They say everybody talks to me because I'm a well-known sports figure, and that's why I've been so successful. My question is this: if that's true, why aren't most football players successful in business after their playing careers end?"

Tarkenton's words to me on the phone reminded me that the professional life of sports figures is short. Once it's over, many are left with no idea of what to do next. After years as highly paid celebrities, largely through the efforts of others, they feel that people will always take care of them. They try to live on past glories, and it's hard to make a career out of that. Some, like Don Meredith and Frank Gifford, have the personality and talent to stay close to their sport by becoming announcers or coaches. Others, such as Jim Brown and Alex Karras, stay in the public eye by becoming actors or performers.

On the whole, though, former sports celebrities are often reluctant to do ordinary work. There are exceptions, of course. Roger Staubach has made a big splash in real estate. He did this by leveraging his celebrity and — most significantly — through skillful networking.

Practicing for Action

Like all professional football players, Fran Tarkenton spent hours learning and practicing his skills every day during the regular season. He had the help of coaches, trainers, and other players. Early on, though, he realized that his football career wouldn't last forever and that he needed to plan a future career. He knew that to be a success in business he would have to learn and practice business skills the same way he learned and practiced his skills in football — by networking.

Learning from others has always come easy for Tarkenton. "Having a curiosity about what people are about and what they are doing, that's what networking is all about to me. Throughout my years in sports and in business, I've found that by listening to people's ideas, concerns, and challenges, I could discover a million opportunities."

Tarkenton resolved to apply the same strategy, the same work ethic, in his business interests that had worked for him in football. "The problem was that I had spent most of my life studying to be the best football player I could be." He had little choice but to start with those skills, and with the opportunities they had given him to meet other people, and apply them to the next phase of his life.

Out of every year Tarkenton had seven months during which football did not fill his life. He asked himself, "Are you going to waste that time, or are you going to use it to prepare for the day you leave football?" He decided he would learn all he could about business — any business.

He went to work for the Wilson Trucking System in Sioux Falls, South Dakota, for $600 a month. His job was to persuade shipping clerks to ship via WTS. This is how he learned about selling. Most important, he learned something valuable about sales that helped him achieve eventual success in his own business: "It wasn't about cost, it was about service and relationships."

It wasn't glamorous work. Some professional athletes would never take such a job. But it taught Tarkenton some of the fundamentals of business, the same way the unglamorous work of training, conditioning, and scrimmaging taught him the essential skills of football.

Lessons from the Field

For seven months of the year, he left the celebrity role behind. He went out and knocked on doors. "I met and talked with as many people in as many places as I could. I didn't know I was networking; I just knew I had to be in business and the way to do that was to talk to people."

Tarkenton learned that business was about who you know. Many people look for shortcuts in business; they want to build a business without taking the time to learn about their customers, their employees, their colleagues and competitors. This is like building a house without a blueprint.

He learned that business was about relationships. People who concentrate entirely on the material and financial aspects of business fail to realize that in the end all business is conducted through personal relationships. Your customers must have confidence in your ability to meet their needs.

> People who concentrate entirely on the material and financial aspects of business fail to realize that in the end all business is conducted through personal relationships.

He learned that business was about knowledge. People who were serious about doing business didn't want to talk to him about just football. They wanted to talk about things that concerned them — products, services, money. "People want to 'wow' you with how much they know. . . . I wanted people to tell me about what they knew. I knew that I would learn by being curious about what people knew."

To broaden his base of knowledge and experience, Tarkenton went out on the speaking circuit while he was still a player. But he didn't do sports groups; he spoke to business groups, talking about motivation and leadership. Sometimes these audiences included coaches and players, but before and after his talks he tried to meet and talk with people in other fields. "As a speaker, I could meet many business professionals. . . . I spoke with management, salespeople, production personnel, and administrators. I asked questions and listened to their issues. This was like getting an on-the-job masters degree in business. It opened up a whole new realm of contacts that took me away from sports and into the world of business."

New Teammates

Tarkenton built a friendship and contact base that encompassed a wide range of people, from CEOs to shipping clerks. Jimmy Robinson, chairperson of American Express, has said that Fran Tarkenton was personally acquainted with more chief executives than anyone else he knew. And he learns from all of them. Many people want to hang out with just the CEOs, he says. By doing so, they limit their opportunities to learn. He feels that listening to people at all levels gives him access to information he wouldn't otherwise get. The CEO can help you in important ways — especially when it comes to big ideas and big-time support. But the shipping clerk can teach you things the CEO doesn't know about his own business.

> The CEO can help you in important ways, but the shipping clerk can teach you things the CEO doesn't know about his own business.

While giving a talk at Kodak, he met Bill Close, chairperson of the Spring Mills textile company, and told him he would like to come see his plants. Next thing Tarkenton knew, they were on a whirlwind tour of Close's plants by helicopter, meeting the people who ran the plants. "I was learning. I didn't know where it was going to lead, but I had a real interest in the business and saw an opportunity." He learned that the textile industry suffered from low margins, largely because of massive worker turnover. And he saw the reason for that turnover: poor working conditions and poor worker motivation.

"I started a consulting company called Behavioral Systems Inc. Brought experts from Harvard and worked on Skinner-type positive reinforcement systems." With its first customer, Cannon Mills, Tarkenton's company went straight to the workers to find out what motivated them. "What if we coached them to help implement feed-back plans?" he asked. "We trained them and kept a consultant on board to assist." Using this strategy, Behavioral Systems cut turnover by two-thirds at Cannon Mills and in all the textile companies they later worked in.

By getting acquainted with industry leaders, Tarkenton learned about business and business opportunities — in particular, how to start a company that would address some industry needs. But what he and his company learned about motivating people, they learned from the people, not from management. If they had spent all their time up in the executive suite, they would not have learned how to fix the problem.

"I made twenty speeches in one year to IBM. By doing this I got exposed to people in many fields — sales, production, marketing. I de-veloped relationships with some of the top management of IBM at the time, people like board chairperson John Akers, U.S. General Man-ager Terry Lautehchech, and Chief Technical Officer Earl Wheeler. With that experience, I started a high-tech company of my own. When I had some problems, I was able to contact these people for ideas and support. As a result, IBM became a 10 percent partner in my computer company. This helped increase our sales from $6 million to $129 million a year.

"Now I speak for pay about fifty times a year. It's the greatest laboratory in the world. I touch fifty industries a year — food, produc-tion, sales, manufacturing, marketing."

Tarkenton says that the people he meets share enough informa-tion, experience, and expertise to give him an MBA in their business. He's accumulated such a broad base of knowledge that he can speak on many topics. These knowledge and people connections have brought him far more money than he could ever have earned from speaking alone. "Knowledge really is power," he says.

"It's important to put yourself in play. You must be out there where it's happening. I can't put myself in play by watching the NFL every Sunday afternoon." On the other hand, he notes, you don't have to get invited to the Governor's Inaugural Ball either, which most guests attend merely to feed their ego. The way to succeed is simply to meet people who can teach you about business.

The Game Plan

Tarkenton's strategy can be summed up in three simple rules:

- Be curious; ask questions and listen to the answers. People love a good listener who is interested in what they do.

- Learn from everybody. Talk with people at all levels, because everyone can teach you something.

- Cultivate contacts with people in power who can bring you ideas and support and opportunities, people who enjoy making money and whose hearts and interests are like your own.

And here's one more: Enjoy the trip.

The Success Connection

Nancy Giacomuzzi

It may sound absurd, but I went from Utah to Minnesota via the Caribbean! I had been a longtime resident of Salt Lake City, an active community volunteer, committee member, and golf enthusiast, and had a thriving real estate business. As I packed for a vacation-week cruise, little did I know I was setting a course that would take me down the matrimonial aisle, out of Utah, and into the Land of 10,000 Lakes. I met Al Giacomuzzi on that cruise. Two years later I found myself shopping for a winter parka and getting new business cards printed.

Starting over in real estate in a new part of the country, far from my Utah social and business contacts, would be difficult. But I knew the first thing I needed to do was connect. I had to find other business owners, professionals, and entrepreneurs who depended on referrals and word-of-mouth marketing. We needed to band together — to network. Besides, there was no way I was going to go knocking on doors in the snowy season. No sir, no cold cold calls for me.

So, as Old Man Winter howled outside the house, I got busy employing the proven techniques of networking. I gathered names of people Al and I had met or done business with, and I made a list of businesses essential for the support of a busy realtor. Soon I had formed a small networking group that met once a week solely to give and receive referrals.

Before long, our small group became bigger, and we began looking forward to each week's meeting with our new circle of friends, where we could talk, learn more about one another, and help one another succeed. It's a great feeling to pass a referral to a friend, as well as to receive one. By the time the snow melted and the lilacs began to bloom, I was back in business.

Networking continues to be the backbone of my business. I still look forward to our weekly meetings and passing referrals to the members. It's easy to see why I recommend networking — it works!

The philosophy of networking is simple: help others to succeed and you will be successful. Networking is not a method for only a select few, but rather a formula for success for anyone who is willing to help others succeed. Make the success connection.

Bootstrap Networking

Phil Campbell

When my wife took a position as a controller in a rural community, I figured I would have no trouble finding a job. I had been a successful loan officer for a commercial loan broker and thought my skills would be valued anywhere. So we packed our bags and set off for the relaxed pace of small-town living.

Although I had a pretty strong résumé, I was surprised to discover that I could not find sales work. I realized that the best way to go was to start my own business. I tried to figure out what industry would be successful in that community. After studying the community I decided to open a catering company. Now that I had given myself a job, I needed to generate business.

I thought about advertising in the yellow pages but learned that I had missed the deadline. I also considered direct mail, but I didn't think it would be successful for this venture, because I needed to get customers quickly. Instead, I decided to create a business referral network.

FROM THE GROUND UP

From one local bank that specialized in small businesses, I got the names of some up-and-coming professionals: an attorney, a CPA, and others. I invited six of these entrepreneurs to dinner at a local restaurant and suggested that if we pooled our resources, we could generate more business. We agreed to meet weekly and to do business with one another when possible. Even though we allowed only one member from each industry, the group's membership quickly grew to eighty-seven people. At every meeting, each member could pass out business cards and give a one-minute commercial.

The first benefit I realized by starting the networking group was that I developed immediate credibility. I had been in business only a couple of months, but already I had prospects, simply by virtue of going to the meetings and making myself available to other members. Although there were other catering companies in town, I got all the referrals generated by my networking partners. When I was in competitive selling situations, I could refer to prominent community members with whom I had a good relationship. This was often the critical factor in closing deals. For all the people in my network who did not have a friendly caterer, I became that friend.

LEARNING ON THE JOB

Never having been in the catering business before, I had a lot to learn. I got to know some of the other catering companies in town and offered to handle their overflow. On busy weekends I got some business through them. All of this was accomplished without doing any radio, TV, newspaper, or direct mail advertising.

As a member in a local "knowledge network" (Kiwanis), I found employees for my business. I learned — from a fellow member who happened to be the county health officer — about health requirements for the catering industry. I also learned to approach nonprofit agencies (e.g., Cancer Society, Lung Association, Red Cross) for cooperative ventures that would raise money for them while creating jobs for me. I did all the work, they got money, and I got paid.

I didn't know anyone in town when I first moved in, but I quickly became a strong competitor bidding for local catering business. Looking back, the only thing I feel would have made my success more rapid would have been to join an existing network instead of starting my own. My advice to you is to find a business referral networking group (such as BNI) in your area, because this is an active source of new business.

When you join a referral group, take time to get to know the other members. Don't join just to get business for yourself. Learn about the other members' businesses; keep your eyes and ears open for business you can steer their way. In your everyday business and personal affairs, you will run across people who need something that members

TIPS FOR SUCCESSFUL NETWORKING

- Attend every network meeting.
- Be on time for every meeting.
- Quickly get to know the people at each meeting.
- Let the members know that you are reliable and can be trusted, that your word is credible, and that you are punctual.
- If you have a business referral for a member, don't wait for the next meeting — call immediately and give that member the lead.
- Provide good service to any lead that comes through your networking experience and to your fellow members.
- Return phone calls promptly.

of your network offer. The more you keep your fellow members in mind, the more they will keep you in mind.

You never know where business might come from. I once generated $55,000 for my company directly through a referral. There was no way I would have gotten it without the help of the network.

After building my business for one and a half years, I was forced to sell when my wife was again transferred. Even so, networking once more came to my aid. I sold the company for a healthy profit to one of my fellow network members, and of course the membership was a factor in the sales price.

I now run a successful marketing company that specializes in promoting businesses through networking. Our slogan is "We Put More Eyes and Ears to Work for You."

THREE WAYS TO GENERATE BUSINESS

There are only three ways to generate business in any industry:
- Cold-call advertising (newspaper, direct mail, knocking on doors)
- Renewals (calling old customers for repeat business — difficult when you have a new business)
- Referrals — by far the best use of your scarce time, especially if you are a small business owner, a sales representative, or a consultant who wears a lot of hats.

5

Making the Big Time

WE SOMETIMES ENTERTAIN THE ILLUSION THAT PEOPLE KNOWN WIDELY FOR THEIR accomplishments have made it entirely by virtue of their own talents and efforts. If you look behind the scenes, though, you can see that the best of the best had the support and encouragement of a wide network of friends and associates. Candace Bailly's and Connie Hinton's account of Colin Powell's impressive career demonstrates this fact vividly, as does Connie Hinton's saga of the richest man in the world, Bill Gates, and Arlette S. Poland's and Ron Stark's interview with Ed Asner.

The Colin Powell Story

Candace Bailly and Connie Hinton

Networking skills are human relations skills. Few people exemplify this connection better than General Colin Powell, a man for all seasons whose military career spanned the presidencies of Republicans Eisenhower, Nixon, Ford, Reagan, and Bush, and Democrats Kennedy, Johnson, Carter, and Clinton.

According to the man himself: "It's the story of a black kid of no early promise from an immigrant family of limited means, who was raised in the South Bronx and somehow rose to become the national security advisor to the president of the United States and then chairman of the Joint Chiefs of Staff."

Powell learned or inherited much of his networking talent from his father, Luther, an immigrant from Jamaica. Like millions of others who came to America before and after him, Luther Powell lived a meager existence with his family in a small apartment while pursuing a better life. "Our family was a matriarchy," said Powell. "I loved my uncles; they were the sauce, the fun, and they provided the occasional rascal. But most were weaker personalities than their wives. The women set the standards, whipped the kids into shape, and pushed them ahead. The exception was my father. Luther Powell, maybe small, maybe unimposing in appearance, maybe somewhat comical, was nevertheless the ringmaster of this family circus."

His father was an instinctive networker. Surrounded by people of various personalities, talents, and dreams, Luther Powell got them all to work for the common good of the family. Overcoming the inevitable problems was surely not substantially different from pulling together a good fighting unit, the kind of challenge that Colin Powell would face again and again throughout his military career.

DESTINED FOR LEADERSHIP

Colin Powell's talents, intelligence, and human relations skills during two tours of Vietnam marked him early as a natural leader. His networking skills — making and cultivating contacts, regardless of political persuasion, and showing people his ability to get the job done — made his rise through the ranks swift and sure. Consider the following career highlights:

Nixon administration: Promotion to major; White House fellowship in Office of Management and Budget under director Casper Weinberger and deputy director Frank Carlucci.

Carter adminstration: Promotion to brigadier general; assistant to deputy secretary of defense; assistant to secretary of energy; promotion to major general.

Reagan administration: Assistant to Frank Carlucci during Defense Department transition; senior military assistant to Secretary of Defense Casper Weinberger during the invasion of Grenada and the raid on Libya; commanding general, Fifth Corps, Germany; assistant to National Security Advisor Frank Carlucci; promotion to lieutenant general; assistant to the president for national security affairs; coordination of technical and policy advisors for the president's summit with Soviet leader Gorbachev; national security advisor.

Bush administration: Promotion to four-star general; head of U.S. Forces Command; chairman of the Joint Chiefs of Staff; commander of forces in Operations Desert Shield and Desert Storm.

It is obvious that Powell was a military man of many skills, which he developed through service both in the field and in the centers of power. His mentors, among them Weinberger and Carlucci, recognized his ability to handle a wide range of duties and responsibilities, and his rapid rise to the top was due in large part to networking with friends and contacts of long standing. By 1989 he had accumulated the skills and experience, and was in the right place at the right time, to become the youngest-ever JCS chairman. When he commanded the highly successful Desert Shield and Desert Storm operations in 1990 and 1991, his skill as a communicator with his subordinates, his superiors, the media, and the public made him a national hero overnight.

After continued service as JCS chairman during the early months of the Clinton administration, he retired from the military. But his service to the nation continued. Powell joined former President Carter and Senator Sam Nunn in 1994 on a diplomatic mission to Haiti, which resulted in the end of military rule and the peaceful return to power of the elected government of that country. Because of his popularity, many people encouraged the retired general to run for president in 1996; however, he did not see himself as a partisan, and he wanted privacy with his family, so he took himself out of consideration for any elected office. At that

> It was Powell's skill at communicating with all factions that helped lay the groundwork for his path in military and civilian service to the nation.

time his approval rating was above 70 percent, and at least one poll showed him to be "the most trusted living American."

A CITIZEN OF DISTINCTION

In Powell's public but private life he lectures worldwide, consults with Congress, sits on several boards, and devotes much of his time to helping America's youth. In less than a year, he took a good idea for getting American corporations involved in public service for children and turned it into a national movement: America's Promise. This fast-growing organization now has over 300 commitments from corporations, government, religious communities, and nonprofit organizations.

Powell is a man who radiates confidence, honor, and charm, and so it's not unexpected that one of his most important issues is personal responsibility. Despite being in the public eye, he discreetly coordinates clothing drives and delivers bedding to a homeless shelter.

In his years in public service, General Powell never disclosed his political sympathies; he was registered to vote as an independent. He served in both Republican and Democratic administrations and his aim was to serve whatever president was in office. It was his skill at communicating with all factions that helped lay the groundwork for his path in military and civilian service to the nation.

The motto that best describes Powell comes from his own list of "13 Rules" that he kept under the glass of his Pentagon desk: "Perpetual optimism is a force multiplier."

The Bill Gates Story

Connie Hinton

One common business networking activity is to attend events where business professionals gather to meet one another and exchange business cards. The whole purpose of making contacts is to transform the initial contacts into long-term relationships that offer value to each member. In today's competitive and increasingly complex world, building relationships with an eye to strategic alliances is a key to success for many companies.

The story of Bill Gates and Microsoft exemplifies how powerful strategic alliances have proven very successful. Bill Gates is considered a software visionary and an extravagantly successful businessperson. His success came out of a series of strategic alliances with important and timely network contacts. However, his business empire was not built through networking in the current sense of attending business-card exchanges.

All the Right People

Mr. Gates built his strategic alliances from the outset. He learned to surround himself with people of diverse talents who supported his vision. As a high school student, Bill Gates learned about computers and software with his friends Paul Allen and Steve Ballmer, relation-ships that continued through his Harvard University days and into the present. These men became the core group designers for BASIC, a programming language created specifically for the first micro-computer. The Bill Gates story shows that it's never too early to start building strategic alliances.

The phenomenon of Microsoft was built on the same kind of drive and passion that typifies Bill Gates's own personal style. Gates attracted people to him who lived and breathed computers and who loved to work. The alliances that Gates created during the early Microsoft days formed the foundation for Microsoft's skyrocketing growth.

> Bill Gates learned to surround himself with people of diverse talents who supported his vision.

As a business professional, it is very important to diligently seek out and align yourself with people who are able to help promote your business, while at the same time not alienating past business relationships. Microsoft's critical alliances included John Roach of Tandy Computers; Kuzuhiko Nishi, who was instrumental in opening the Japanese markets to Microsoft products; and IBM executives, who facilitated Microsoft's quantum leap into the com-puter software industry.

A Family Connection

Bill Gates may have learned valuable networking lessons about the power of association from his mother. Mary Gates may also have played a large role in an early, critical Microsoft alliance. She was involved in many community service and civic organizations, including the

National Board of the United Way. The relationship between Mary Gates and a fellow member of this board — John Opel, CEO of IBM — probably eased the way for a deal between Microsoft and IBM. Networking often helps close a deal through such a "trilogy of trust" — the trust that one person has in another, which is then passed along to a third referred member.

Even though Bill Gates may not resemble a typical networker, he nevertheless mastered networking skills by establishing long-term relationships with talented people — individuals who shared a common vision and goal and offered their unique talents to the larger-than-life team effort of Microsoft. "For me," he says, "a big part of the fun has always been to hire and work with smart people. I enjoy learning from them."

Bill Gates and Microsoft exemplify the power and success that we can all achieve by building upon strategic alliances. The next time you attend a networking function, keep Bill Gates's success in mind. While collecting business cards, consider the people you meet as potential strategic partners, not just commercial prospects. Build a working team and create the successes you've only experienced in your dreams.

The Ed Asner Story

Arlette S. Poland and Ron Stark

Today his name has household recognition. But there was a time in Ed Asner's life when that wasn't true. To become the successful actor that he is, Ed used five key elements of networking to open doors, and his abundant talent to keep those doors open.

"When I started in Chicago," he told us one afternoon, "I did lots of drama on stage. I used to ask anyone and everyone to call or write another person for me. Then it was up to me to prove that I was a capable performer." One production he liked was *Threepenny Opera*; naturally, he was cast as J. J. Peachum, the "heavy."

LOADING UP WITH CONTACTS

Before long, Ed decided he would have to move to New York to further his goals. To get ready for the move, Ed asked everyone he knew for names and phone numbers of contacts in New York.

A photographer friend of Ed's had a friend in Chicago who made custom neckties. Ed wanted to make a good impression in New York and thought these ties would help, so he looked up the tie maker and bought several. Out of habit, he asked the man if he knew anybody in the Big Apple. The tie maker knew only one person there; he gave Ed a name and a number.

In New York, Ed called every number he had been given. The contact from the tie maker turned out to be a radio show producer, from whom Ed got a series of parts.

DEMONSTRATING INTEGRITY

Aiming to resume his stage career, Ed gathered up all his chutzpah and went to the New York producer of *Threepenny Opera* to ask for the J. J. Peachum part. He offered to take over the role, which was already cast, whenever it next came open. The producer had never heard of Ed, but he was so impressed with the actor's direct approach that he offered him a small role in the show on the spot.

ED ASNER'S TOP NETWORKING TIPS

- Ask everyone for contacts.
- Follow up on all contacts given.
- Believe in yourself and your work.
- Make a good, positive first impression.
- Build and maintain a good reputation.

The offer was tempting, but Ed reluctantly declined. He was still doing the radio show, he explained, and even though the radio part was small and he performed only one night a week, he could not walk away from it.

The producer admired Ed's integrity and promised to keep him in mind. Sure enough, when Ed's commitment ended, the producer again offered him a small part.

Ask and You Shall Receive

"Part of the role I was offered was to understudy the part of Tiger Brown. It was common to understudy a larger part while playing a smaller one. Later, the guy playing Tiger Brown wanted to give notice that he would leave the show soon. I was afraid I would get stuck with that small part, when I really wanted to do the part of J. J. Peachum, like I did in Chicago."

Ed knew that if you don't ask for what you want, you probably won't get it. "See, I knew the guy playing Peachum was leaving the show even earlier than the one playing Tiger Brown. So I told the guy playing Tiger Brown how I wanted to play Peachum. He was sympathetic and agreed to time his departure so I would have a chance to try for the part of Peachum — and I got it." Ed played J. J. Peachum for about two and a half years and loved it.

"Back in those early days in New York I stayed away from comedy. My agent and I focused on dramatic roles. The worst year of my professional life pushed me to break that mind-set. There was a director who used me in two different movies. One was a two-hour movie pilot that was a *Perry Mason* takeoff, produced by the same people who did the *Perry Mason* show.

Becoming Lou Grant

"The other show wasn't a comedy, but the writing for my character cried out for comedy, so I started doing the part using 'shtick.' The producers were a bit worried but amused nonetheless. One of them saw the dailies [a film of the day's shooting]. It was Grant Tinker.

"Grant Tinker was just then creating the *Mary Tyler Moore Show.* They were looking for someone for the part of Lou Grant. They weren't sure I could do the comedy for the part until they saw those dailies."

Ed jumped at the opportunity to stretch his acting skills. With his typical *carpe diem* attitude, he asked for an audition.

"The first time I read for the part, I read it conventionally. They said, 'We'll bring you back to read with Mary, and do it more broadly then for comedy.' I told them, 'No, let me reread it now. If I can't do the comedy now, then you don't have to bring me back.'

"I wanted to know right then and not wait around for a couple of weeks to find out that I didn't get the part anyway. The second time I read it I had no idea what I was doing. I just did it like a real whacko. They laughed! So they asked me to read it with Mary. Years later I found out that Mary looked at them after we read together at the callback and asked, 'Are you sure you want him?'"

A Commitment to Public Service

Ed Asner is deeply dedicated to the betterment of humanity and has the courage to stand up against all odds for his beliefs. This was strongly displayed when he ran for and won the presidency of the Screen Actors Guild in 1981 and held it for four years. "I always wanted to give something back. I had great success, and I believe that the guild helped me. It was an obligation of sorts."

In the early 1970s, the guild had a reputation for being an "old-boys' network." Ed had experienced it that way and wanted to break the pattern. He used his well-honed reputation and ability and began extending his network relationships within the guild.

"Friends contacted friends on my behalf. I had the success of the *Mary Tyler Moore Show* working for me, so I made a good front man. I went to the streets and started talking about how I felt. Apparently people got ignited.

"The secret of good networking is to parlay one name into three. My biggest difficulty is that I have trouble remembering names," Ed laughed. "Clark Gable was good at that, he could remember everyone.

"Once, on the *Mary Tyler Moore Show*, Ted [Knight] had a friend's daughter visiting the set. I was introduced to her but couldn't remember her name, so I circled behind her and motioned to Ted 'What is her name?' He said out loud as a joke, 'What is her name!' I was embarrassed, but everyone laughed. If you fess up to it, people can be very forgiving."

Ask everyone you see for names and numbers to call on. Follow through with all your contacts. Believe in yourself and your work. Make a good first impression. Build and maintain a good reputation. If you apply these five basic keys to networking to your own life, you may end up being a household name, too.

6

Getting into Print

GETTING YOUR NAME BELOW THE TITLE OF A BOOK IS ANOTHER WAY OF BECOMING a public figure. Though writing is a solitary occupation, the publicizing and selling of a book is a major networking activity. Joe Tye turned a chance meeting into a valuable connection for selling his book — an experience on a small scale that can be a model for larger-scale networking, as Ed Craine proves to us with the story of Mark Victor Hansen's blockbuster series of bestsellers.

A Lucky Coin

Joe Tye

Last winter, I took my family to Florida for a vacation. We spent one day in Key West, where my son and I rented a motor scooter and putted around the island while my wife and daughter took the credit cards for a stroll.

Midway down Duval Street, the island's main drag, the word "Courage" caught my eye. It appeared to be the title of a short poem in a shop window. As the author of a book called *Never Fear, Never Quit*, I was naturally curious.

We circled around the block and stopped in front of a little shop called Last Flight Out. The store was filled with T-shirts, baseball caps, and other products, some sporting the poem "Courage." The store was quite busy, so I simply took a business card from the counter and left.

After I returned to Iowa, I contacted Clay Greager, the owner of the store. I sent him a copy of the book, and he sent me a "Courage" T-shirt.

What happened next confirmed my belief in the networking dictum: Always follow up. It turned out that Last Flight Out was not just one store, but a franchise with many locations. It also turned out that we had many interests and values in common. Later I spent several days visiting Clay and his partner, Elise Franzetta, who wrote the poem, discussing ways we could help each other.

They were both intrigued with *Never Fear, Never Quit,* and it is now the only book being carried by Last Flight Out stores. They actually sell more copies every day than all but the busiest retail stores. Every week or so, I get called by an old friend or acquaintance who is standing at the counter of the Last Flight Out store in Key West looking at a picture of me with the owners.

One of the chapters in *Never Fear, Never Quit* is entitled "A Lucky Coin Is What You Make of It." I've learned to be on the lookout for opportunities to transform what appears to be mere coincidence into genuine serendipity. After all, isn't that what networking is all about?

> I've learned to be on the lookout for opportunities to transform what appears to be mere coincidence into genuine serendipity. After all, isn't that what networking is all about?

In *Never Fear, Never Quit,* Rafe says, "Whatever you most need in life, the best way for you to get it is to help someone else get it who needs it even more than you do." The people at Last Flight Out are helping me get the word out about my book, which has now grown from a single book into an organization with members across the United States and Canada.

I am now writing a sequel, which will include a chapter set in Key West. One of the scenes takes place in Last Flight Out and includes (with permission) reproduction of Elise's magnificent "Courage."

When that book hits the bestseller charts, business will take off at Last Flight Out as readers stop in to see why the place grabbed my imagination the way it did. Givers gain!

Coincidence? No, serendipity — an opportunity not missed.

Mark Victor Hansen's Networking Victory

Ed Craine

Mark Victor Hansen and Jack Canfield, coauthors of the *Chicken Soup for the Soul* series, are best-selling proof that networking works. After thirty-three publishers rejected their manuscript, their agent said it would never sell. Undaunted, Mark and Jack took their manuscript to the American Booksellers Expo in Anaheim. Walking from booth to booth and talking to hundreds of publishers, they eventually found the one who would read and eventually publish *Chicken Soup for the Soul*. The book sold 1.3 million copies during the first year and a half.

Mark Victor Hansen believes that the two most important skills for business in the next century are networking and innovation. The benefits of networking are easy to recognize: "It's a proven fact that we grow from the people and projects we associate with. Innovation gives networking direction." According to Mark, "Networking without a goal is an exercise in going nowhere fast." He says the best innovations take shape when we interact with others, allowing ideas and concepts to become something concrete.

POWER OF TWO IN ALIGNMENT

Mark believes that with "the power of two in alignment" one can create a team that has potential to accomplish almost anything. "If you can sell one other person enough on what you are doing to get them to align with you, then you can do anything. From this union, you will build a team that others will want to join."

Mark used this theory when he partnered with Jack to write *Chicken Soup for the Soul*. Mark and Jack have been friends and colleagues, as trainers and motivational speakers, for over twenty-five years. One day, over one of their regular breakfasts, they started talking about writing a book: a compilation of some of the best stories they used in their motivational speaking careers. The idea for *Chicken Soup for the Soul* was born.

ON INNOVATION AND GOALS

Once an idea is hatched and turned into a goal, and you have enlisted the power of two, the next step is to network. Through networking, an idea or goal becomes refined, enhanced, and expanded. We all experience this when we brainstorm for a better way to do something. We come up with an idea, then improve and perfect it by bouncing it off others. When Mark and Jack first created the concept for the book, they contacted 101 best-selling authors and asked them what they would have to do to sell their book. The information they gathered helped them shape the content of the book and the way it would be marketed.

The key to innovation, according to Mark, is to dream big and tell your goals to as many people as possible. With the *Chicken Soup for the Soul* series already a huge success, Mark is planning seventy-four more books, aiming at eventual sales of 100 million copies. His more immediate goal is to sell a million books in a single day. This may seem farfetched, but Mark has built a team of people, including his coauthor, who will most certainly help him achieve his goal.

GIVERS GAIN

Networking can take a lot of time and effort to get the desired result. But, as in *Chicken Soup for the Soul,* the result can be far more than you imagined. Now that Mark and Jack have proved the importance of the power of two in alignment, they are practicing the principle that the more you give, the more you gain. For each book sold, Mark donates one dollar to charities benefiting children. He has already surpassed a million books — a million dollars to charity.

As Mark Victor Hansen's career illustrates, networking is much more than giving out your business card. Setting goals, the power of two in alignment, persistence in the face of rejection, interacting with many people, and being open to innovation all play a role.

What are you waiting for? It's your life. You have the power to create your team. What are you willing to do? Go find that partner, think big, build your team, and create your miracle.

7

Not for Business Only

BUSINESSPEOPLE USUALLY THINK OF NETWORKING AS A BUSINESS ACTIVITY, BUT experienced networkers know that networking is a versatile tool that can be used to get practically anything done. The four authors below illustrate this powerfully. Gillian Lawson describes an intriguing round-robin of networked bartering that features businesses, charities, the performance arts, and royalty; Craig W. Campana tells of his family's experience using networking to bring a new child into their life; Kathleen Mathy reminds us of the rise of a twentieth-century phenomenon, the self-help group; and Nancy Holland tells us how she networked her way to success in an Olympic sport and in business.

Charity Networking with a Princess

Gillian Lawson

"**I**ntelligent networking can yield almost any result you wish to achieve, particularly if you start by thinking how to help others before your own cause."

This thought-provoking statement was spoken by my husband, Martin, in a discussion about how to raise money for one of the charities of the late Princess of Wales. I am involved with her musical charities, and the charity development committee had invited my husband to inject a commercial orientation into our fundraising activities. Martin got us onto a path that resulted in a highly successful program.

I was at the time somewhat embarrassed by Martin's statement, and others were skeptical. But as the explanation unfolded, we all started to realize the potential of that provocative idea.

Our starting point was to realize that between us we knew a very large number of people across a wide range of industries and organizations. The second step surprised most of us: Martin asked us to think of another charity that needed help as much as or more than we did, and to be prepared to give them half of everything we raised. What was not yet clear was that we would succeed as well as we did.

"Intelligent networking can yield almost any result you wish to achieve, particularly if you start by thinking how to help others before your own cause."

Then it was time for all of us to delve into our contact networks to identify businesses or organizations we knew like insiders — organizations where we had assiduously cultivated our contacts or where we had a good contact who could offer us insights about the company. We were looking for organizations that needed certain things or had surpluses of certain commodities or resources and were prepared to trade.

A Chain of Needs and Benefits

What we were being taught to do was to match the diverse resources and needs of a large group of organizations. We were looking for players in the chain who had a need and were prepared to work with other organizations in a partnership. It is usually difficult to match two organizations' needs in this way; although the first might need a commodity and have something to trade, the second, which could potentially supply the first organization's need, might not need what the first has to offer. As we faced this dilemma, we also enlarged the circle to include a third and fourth player and created a program that served all organizations.

Our networking research yielded information about one of the largest insurance companies in the world, which sought access to new and underdeveloped markets in the United Kingdom. This company had recently acquired a competitive health insurance company, which wanted to increase its market share without appearing to be profiting from the ill health of customers.

Our research also turned up information about a large book and record club business that felt its future prosperity would be enhanced if it could offer its subscribers unique privileges. Its belief was that creating membership privileges would be an incentive for customers to maintain their subscriptions longer. We discovered that this company had never allowed its client list to be used by any other company, but it might consider sharing its list if a uniquely prestigious musical event were to be organized exclusively for its membership and attended by Princess Diana.

It's Who You Know

Our hook was that we had access to Her Royal Highness the Princess of Wales, who was the royal patron for our charity, the London Symphony Chorus. We used our contacts at the palace to find out what other organizations were blessed with the patronage of the princess. Our decision was to focus on medical charities that might be able to help the insurance company, which in turn would be interested in an opportunity to promote its product by mail to the book and record club members. These members would have an exclusive opportunity made available only through their membership in the book and record club.

We found such a charity, the British Lung Foundation. One of our contacts, in a senior position, explained that although 30 percent of all deaths were related to lung disorders, less than 5 percent of medical research funding was focused on lung disease. The opportunity to help the British Lung Foundation, one

> Our hook was that we had access to the Princess of Wales.

of HRH's favorite charities, would provide enormous favorable publicity for the insurance company and help it acquire new customers.

It then became an organizational issue of persuading Princess Diana to attend a performance at London's magnificent and historic Royal Albert Hall exclusively for customers of the book and record club. The members heard one of HRH's favorite works, Walton's *Belshazzar's Feast*, performed by the London Symphony Chorus, and the benefits went to the British Lung Foundation. The insurance company made a generous donation to the charities as a sponsoring organization, and had the privilege of using the book and record club mailing list for its marketing.

This fundraising strategy, coordinating the diverse needs of organizations into a fundraising network, was very effective. Since then, what started as a labor of love has turned into a sideline business for Martin and me. We now have to our credit a whole series of successful fundraising events. One of these was a birthday concert for the Princess of Wales, featuring world famous tenor Jose Carreras, in the largest venue in Britain. We have raised more than one million pounds for charities through the strategy of "thinking how to help others before your own cause."

Parenthood by Networking

Craig W. Campana

It was Friday night, and I was out ordering up a traditional Lent dinner of fried fish to take home to my family. The waitress, whose face seemed familiar, asked for my last name. "Campana," I said.

She looked up. "Craig?"

Then I remembered — she had worked for a production company I had used as a video producer. "How are you, Karen?" I asked.

We talked for a few minutes. Then Karen asked a question that made time stand still and brought back warm memories: "How's your baby doing?"

I answered that our "baby" was now an active six-year-old.

Karen told me that she never forgot the day my wife and I brought our baby home. She had taken the message that told me, at work, that we were finally to be parents — through networking!

Eight years earlier, my wife and I had discovered that we were not biologically able to conceive. After draining our financial and emotional resources on medical attempts to achieve our family, we joined an infertility support group.

Like many other group members, we soon decided to try adoption. We learned all we could about adoption by attending support group meetings and classes and by talking with adoptees, adoptive parents, and birth parents. Gradually we gained the confidence and knowledge to pursue "marketing our needs to the contacts we knew." We decided to create a strong message and send it out to as wide an audience as possible. Although we didn't recognize it at the time, we were networking.

We created a business card with a simple message: "We desire to adopt." The card had a caricature of a duck and the phone number of an adoption hotline we had installed in our home. We had our photographs taken. We even produced a video showing my wife and me in family and home surroundings (this seemed to be a novel idea in adoption circles). We added our adoption cards to an extended Christmas card list of 250 diverse contacts, including relatives, friends, high school and college contacts, church friends, co-workers, former co-workers, medical professionals, and members of the clergy. We gave cards to anyone and everyone we met and asked each one to pass them along to anyone considering putting up an unborn baby for adoption. We also asked them to present, along with our cards, an endorsement for us as a couple. We believed that someone out there might know someone who could contact the right person.

Finally, after a lot of patience, planning, and perseverance, we began to realize our desired goal.

In creating our mailing list, we had wrestled with the idea of sending our card to one individual, a pastor in Montana, who we thought probably would not remember us. In fact, it was this card that made the difference. Exactly one month after Christmas, the pastor called me at work to let me know that he had a woman in his congregation who wanted to place her baby for adoption. This man knew us from a previous relationship, and told the mother he thought we would make good parents. She called that evening and the relationship was formed that would result in our becoming parents by adoption four and a half months later.

Our son Corey was born in June 1991 — coincidentally, in the same state I was born in. As we flew to Montana to receive him from the hospital, we were amazed at how a contact made through a simple (but unique) business card would lead to the result for which we had hoped and prayed for so long.

Our newly expanded family was the cover story in a national magazine affiliated with our church. After we began to get phone calls from other couples across the country who also wanted to adopt, we spearheaded the development of the Independent Adoption Network. This support group has, over the past six years, helped many couples locate children for adoption. It has also taught them the power that networking can have in transforming their lives.

Networking for Your Health

Kathleen Mathy

In this age of fast, easy communication, we routinely use networking as a tool to achieve business success. We get positive feedback from satisfied customers and refer friends and family to networking partners. We meet trusted associates and exchange valuable technical insights. But how important is networking in our personal lives?

Pretty important, if we consider the growth of self-help groups in Western societies. These small groups, formed for special purposes and mutual aid, are basically analogous to business networks. Their core functions include socialization, affirmation, information sharing, advocacy, and support. They help participants acquire coping and planning skills and deal with powerful emotions.

Many studies have documented the importance of basic social support to our health and well-being. We have support groups for everything from cancer, substance abuse, AIDS, and bereavement to Elvis sightings. Whether their purpose is to share information or experiences or to teach new coping skills, they offer an alternative to formal psychological or health intervention. Joining one also gives participants a better chance of success than going it alone.

Although we often think of support groups as a modern phenomenon, small social groups have been an important part of personal development and spiritual healing throughout history. The medicine man of legend conjured healing therapies for groups of sufferers that included family, friends, and the religious community. Later communities supported similar practices. It is only in modern times, with its isolated, alienated suburban families, that group therapy seems novel.

> Although we often think of support groups as a modern phenomenon, small social groups have been an important part of personal development and healing throughout history.

A little over a year ago, I became a keen observer and believer in the power of personal support and networking. Over a period of fourteen months, a client of mine became gravely ill and needed several surgeries, followed by extensive therapy and rehabilitation. I visited her at first, but hesitated to stay involved, rationalizing that it would be too intrusive. Besides, I didn't know her well outside our business relationship.

Fortunately, her many friends and colleagues were health and social workers who understood that she would need active support, even if she didn't ask for it. They visited her constantly, shared her burden, and kept her from becoming depressed. As a group, they focused on getting her well; they studied her disease, became experts on research into treatments and cures, sought the best medical care available, and kept her medical team well informed. They contributed excess sick leave, comp time, and vacation days to her; although she missed nearly five months of work, she was never without a paycheck. Her personal support network would not let her worry about anything except getting well.

When I visited her recently, she looked great! She said she was feeling well and that the doctors were very optimistic. "We're going to make it!" she said. And I believe "we" will.

Networking to the Olympics and Beyond

Nancy Holland

It's never too late to learn — and I've been learning for a long time, through two successful careers. In the first, I was an Olympic and World Cup alpine skier, racing downhill at breakneck speed, alone against my competitors. In the second, I am a successful businesswoman, constantly working with my friends and associates to give and receive business referrals — a skill I had to learn in order to succeed professionally.

But that sounds like I became a champion skier on my own, doesn't it? Well, the truth is that it took every bit as much networking to succeed in that solitary sport as it did in business — only I didn't know it at the time. From my earliest attempts to develop my talents, I had my own support network, although I didn't think of it in those terms. In fact, it was my closest associates — my coaches, sponsors, chaperones, and parents — who opened doors for me by networking their own contacts.

As a child, I studied with the Canadian National Ballet. Later, as a teen, I was encouraged to apply my athletic talent to alpine skiing. As a member of the national team, I participated in two Winter Olympics and a World Championship and was ranked in the top ten in the world. My only job was to go downhill fast, get back up, and go downhill again. In those early days I intuitively knew that I was able to compete not only because of my personal attributes, but also because I had a networking team supporting my effort.

It was not until 1989 that I was first introduced formally to networking. Now I own a growing national franchise employing more than thirty people. I've also become a networking specialist. I see clearly that having a support network was as crucial to my success as an Olympian as to my current business, and that networking is crucial to the success of everyone's career, whatever it is.

I've also come to realize that the same individual strengths that are the mark of an athletic champion also apply to being a master networker. Here are some that have been important for me.

CONTROL YOUR FEARS

In my early days as a young competitive skier, I had to compete in all types of events. I liked the slalom and giant slalom best. I didn't much like going flat out straight downhill. I was afraid of falling, something that is inevitable in downhill racing. I had to psych myself up just to get into the starting gate — tell myself that I really loved the speed! I knew that when the mind doubts, the body hesitates.

This insight made it easier for me to overcome fears in the world of business and business networking. My biggest fear is public speaking, which is an essential part of what I do. When I feel those starting-gate jitters, I tell myself that there's nothing in the world I enjoy more than standing up in front of a large group and spouting off. I also steel myself by planning thoroughly and practicing what I'm going to say. When I do give a good speech, I feel as though I just won a race. The best antidote for fear is to prepare well — then blast out of the starting gate, focused on your goal! Later, when I've finished and settled down, I turn to my network for feedback on how to improve. My network becomes my coaching staff.

KNOW YOUR STRENGTHS

Everyone grows stronger by facing and overcoming trouble. Living and working in bad weather, falling down and picking myself up time after time on the slopes taught me that I could live with pain, recover from injuries, and regain my determination, my competitive edge. These strengths sustain me when I encounter setbacks in business. They spur me to do things I know I need to do, especially when I really don't want to do them. Being active in my network enhances my strengths and keeps me going. I find the help I need, when I need it — and I am given the opportunity to help others overcome setbacks.

BUILD A SUCCESS TEAM

In today's complex and competitive world, success cannot be achieved by working alone. Olympic athletes rely on mentors, coaches, sponsors, therapists, teammates, technicians, friends, and family. Businesspeople rely on a similar network of helpers. This network may be structured more loosely, with many people sharing similar interests and goals and support flowing in all directions, not just toward a star athlete.

In skiing, I was the star and champion, but when I started my own business, I had to shift gears and assemble a support network in which I was more of a coequal participant. It was a struggle at first. I disliked having to ask my old friends and associates for help in my new career. But it got easier once I discovered that I was able to help them in return, and now that I've been networking for ten years, it seems quite natural. I am once again becoming a star and a champion.

In either case, the secret of networking mastery is to develop contacts who can help you accomplish your goals and who can quickly help you correct any mistakes you make. When developing your networking success team, pick your coaches and players carefully. Sometimes all it takes is a single phone call to put you in touch with someone who will pull you along in the right direction. Don't allow yourself to be around people who pull you in the wrong direction.

The world tends to put top athletes on a pedestal, but athletes are just people doing what they are passionate about, some of whom achieve great success. In other words, they are like the rest of us, striving for excellence in manufacturing, sales, service, or anything else. We all need help to reach our goals — and networking is the key to finding and providing that help.

8

The Power of Word of Mouth

THE SECRET OF WHY NETWORKING WORKS IS IN ITS SMALLEST-SCALE FEATURE: THE person-to-person connection. People trust other people, not large, anonymous organizations; one person's word to another can influence more actions, get more things done, make more sales than whole trainloads of mass advertising. This is why businesspeople value the good word of a single customer, and why networking is so effective: the person-to-person connection, multiplied by a network of friends and associates, is disproportionately influential.

In the five articles that follow, Tom Peters discusses a systematic approach to word-of-mouth marketing; Jay Conrad Levinson gives tips on how to make it work for your business; Jerry Wilson tells why a single disgruntled customer can hurt you as much as eleven happy customers can help you; Richard Poe describes an entire category of enterprise — multilevel marketing — based on the science of word of mouth; and Pam Sheldon spins a vivid political tale of how a good word from an individual can sway an entire community.

Systematic Word-of-Mouth Marketing

Tom Peters

Buying a new personal computer? Trying to figure your way through the jungle of new personal financial services? Where are you likely to go for counsel? Certainly you don't sit in front of the TV waiting for an ad to appear. And you're not likely to "let your fingers do the walking." You probably ask a re-spected friend, neighbor, or colleague who's been down the same route recently.

Now switch sides. If you were the would-be seller of a new service or product, how could you tie into that network of friends and experts who advise potential buyers? Most sales of services, complex prod-ucts, and especially new products and services, come via word of mouth. As a seller, you need not passively sit by. *You can be just as organized, thoughtful, and systematic about "word-of-mouth advertising" as about media buys.*

However, marketers tend to over-rely on mass-media advertising and under-rely on the careful development of reputational campaigns, according to Regis McKenna. He goes on:

> Word-of-mouth communication can take on many different forms. Industry participants form "old-boy networks" to keep each other informed about new developments. One recent market-research report showed that such a network plays a key role in the telecom-munications industry. Gaining access to the network is critical to success. . . .

> Word of mouth is so obvious a communications medium that most people do not take time to analyze or understand its structure. To many people, it is like the weather. Sure, it is important. But you can't do much about it. You never see a "word-of-mouth communi-cations" section in marketing plans. . . .

> Of course, much of the word-of-mouth communication about a com-pany and its products is beyond the company's control. But a company can take steps to put word of mouth to its advantage. It can even organize a "word-of-mouth campaign."

> . . . [T]he company must decide who should receive the message — and who from within the company should deliver it. By the nature of word-of-mouth communications, it is not possible to spread the message too widely. Luckily, there is no need to. Word of mouth is governed by the 90-10 rule: "90 percent of the world is influenced by the other 10 percent." . . . A word-of-mouth campaign should be based on targeted communication. Word of mouth is not an efficient means for distributing information widely. . . .

The targets for a word-of-mouth campaign fall into several categories:

The financial community. Who backs a company is often more important than how much money is behind it. . . . A company's initial backers can use word of mouth to spread the company's message.

Industry-watchers. Rapid-growth industries are filled with consultants, interpreters, futurists, and soothsayers who sort out and publish information through word of mouth. . . .

Customers. Companies can use word of mouth to reach customers at trade shows, technical conferences, training programs, and customer organizations. [New-product test] sites and early customers become especially important.

The press. More than 90 percent of the major news stories in the business and technical press come from direct conversations. All journalists have networks of sources they use for background, opinions, and verifications. It is valuable to become part of this word-of-mouth network.

The selling chain. The selling network includes sales representatives, distributors, and retailers. . . . Word of mouth is needed to generate enthusiasm and commitment toward the product.

The community. Every person who is interviewed, or delivers a package, or visits a company walks away with an impression. If company employees communicate properly, every person who comes in contact with the company becomes a salesperson for the company, a carrier of good will about the company.

Ev Rogers of the University of Southern California is the leading expert on "diffusion of innovation." He has examined how new ideas and new products spread. His dozens of studies have analyzed new commercial products, the adoption of birth control techniques, and agricultural technology to determine the reasons behind the typical thirty-year and forty-year delays in the widespread dissemination of innovations — delays which mark even products and services which demonstrate crystal-clear, decisive advantages from the start.

Rogers, like McKenna, emphasizes the overriding power of networks: "Most individuals do not evaluate an innovation on the basis of scientific study or its consequences. Most depend mainly upon a subjective evaluation of an innovation that is conveyed to them from other individuals like themselves who have previously adopted the innovation. This dependence on the communicated experience of near-peers suggests that the heart of the diffusion process is the imitation by potential adopters of their network partners who have adopted previously." Study after study that Rogers reviews reveals that (1) an innovation takes off only after "interpersonal networks have become activated in spreading subjective evaluations" and that (2) "success is related to the extent that the change agent or marketer worked through opinion leaders."

I write, I must admit, with the zeal of a true believer. My first book, *In Search of Excellence*, was launched by an unsystematic (but, in retrospect, thorough) word-of-mouth campaign. A 125-page presentation of what became the book's principal findings was first bound in 1980, fully two years before the book was published, and circulated surreptitiously among business executives. My coauthor, Bob Waterman, and I eventually printed 15,000 presentation copies to meet the underground demand, much to the misguided consternation of our publisher, who was certain we were giving away most of our future sales. We also assiduously courted opinion leaders in the media over a period of several years. Thus, within days of the book's launching, supportive reviews appeared, and the network of 15,000 (plus at least an equal number of photocopied knockoffs) hurried to buy the real thing, often in bulk for their subordinates. We could not have more effectively marketed the book if we had planned the process meticulously.

The most critical word-of-mouth activity is targeting early adopters.

GETTING WORD OF MOUTH ORGANIZED

The important point, to which McKenna speaks so passionately, is that the process can be systematized. For instance:

- Careful charting of official and unofficial opinion leaders can be conducted.

- Disproportionate selling time can and should be aimed at highly reputable, would-be early adopters.

- Sales incentives should encourage working with early adopters.

- Events that pair happy new customers with a wider audience can be stated on both a one-shot and an ongoing basis.

- User newsletters can be established, then circulated to targeted nonusers.

- Testimonials can be systematically gathered and circulated.

- All of these programs and others can be put together in a detailed, written, step-by-step "word-of-mouth" campaign plan.

THE SEARCH FOR SMALL, PROGRESSIVE BUYERS

The most critical word-of-mouth activity is, of course, targeting early adopters. *Above all, look for the innovative adopters, not necessarily the big ones.* Sure, you'd like to launch your new workstation by signing up GM. Yes, you'd like the chairperson of the town's biggest firm to be the first to buy your new personal financial planning service. But such giants, though certainly helpful to word-of-mouth diffusion, are usually laggards when it comes to adopting new products and services. Therefore, you'd be wise to look to smaller firms or individuals with a reputation for progressiveness; they're much more likely to become early adopters. Pouring almost all of your energy into getting a couple of these leaders on board is usually a worthwhile strategy.

The above excerpt is from Thriving on Chaos: Handbook for a Management Revolution *by Tom Peters. Copyright © 1987 by Excel, a California Limited Partnership. Reprinted by permission of Alfred A. Knopf, a division of Random House, Inc.*

Elementary Word of Mouth

Jay Conrad Levinson

It is possible to generate word-of-mouth advertising. There are several ways to accomplish this. The first, of course, is to *be so good at what you do,* or to offer products that are so obviously wonderful, that your customers will want to pass on the good word about you. Another way to get the ball rolling is to *give brochures* to your new customers. This reminds them why they patronized you in the first place and spurs word-of-mouth endorsements. A third way to obtain positive recommendations is literally to *ask for them.* Nobody is better equipped to talk up your company than you — or perhaps your best customer. Tell all your customers: "If you're really satisfied with my service or products, I'd sure appreciate it if you'd tell your friends." Finally, *you can bribe your customers.* Tell them, "If I get any customers who mention your name, I'll send you a free gift (or give you a 10 percent discount) next time you're in." Which of these methods should you employ? As a guerrilla, you should use all of them. Testing will tell.

The point to remember is that no large corporation can succeed by means of word-of-mouth advertising alone, and some entrepreneurs can. But do yourself a favor and don't leave everything up to the recommendations of your happy customers. They probably have more important things to talk about. Even for a guerrilla, consistent marketing is crucial to success.

An overall marketing plan for a person engaged in individual enterprise might consist of a listing in the yellow pages, a mailing of circulars and business cards, a posting of signs, and a follow-up telephoning to prospects to whom the promotional material was sent. That four-pronged effort (yellow pages, mailing, sign-posting, and telephoning) might be all it takes to get a business off and running. You can be certain that no big company has a marketing plan so short and simple — and inexpensive.

Imagine a staple gun and a handful of circulars as the only marketing tools necessary to conduct a business. IBM would boot me out of its corporate offices for suggesting such a thing. But many a successful home-typing service uses these devices and none other. A typist I know started out by typing her circulars, thereby lending credibility to her typing ability. Then she posted them with her staple gun on bulletin boards throughout local college campuses. These days, she posts no more circulars, and her staple gun gathers dust. Word of mouth has taken over, and she gets all the business she needs through referrals.

The above excerpt from Guerrilla Marketing *is used with permission.*

What Do Your Customers Say about You?

Jerry R. Wilson

Have you ever stood in a checkout line with twelve other people and wondered, "Are they ever going to open another register?"

I was standing in just such a line in a hardware store once when an assistant manager came by. I asked him if management planned to open another line. He said, "I don't know — I'm going to lunch," and left.

I stayed in line and struck up a conversation with the guy next to me. What did we talk about? Crowbars and screwdrivers? No. We chatted about what a bunch of idiots these people were. We agreed that businesses are not murdered . . . that they commit suicide by their attitudes and behavior toward customers. . . .

Most managers seem oblivious to what their company really looks like to others and many are most emphatically deaf to the talk factor.

They don't even try to ask themselves, "What are people saying about us?" They worry about managing things — numbers and people — but don't understand that managing word of mouth might be the most important management activity of all. Why would they ignore word of mouth, a factor Regis McKenna calls "the most powerful form of communication in the business world"? . . .

TALK CAN BE SCARY

Everybody has a horror story about goods and services. People *love* to tell horror stories. I guess inquiring minds want to know the worst.

In fiction, writers love to talk about ghosts and werewolves and demons and evil spirits. Those things sell because people love to share horror stories. Face it, bad news sells newspapers. How often is the lead story on the front page of your paper a positive one? Not nearly as often as it's negative. What keeps the screaming exposé tabloids selling at the supermarket checkouts? Certainly it's not articles on the good done by Mother Theresa. Nope, it's the infidelity of celebrities, illegitimate births, human deformities, tragedy, and perversity. What's hot on television? Crime reenactments and bizarre confessions. A fascination with horror seems to be part of the human condition.

In business, this predisposition takes a seemingly harmless form. People love to tell about their horrible experiences with rude clerks, apathetic waiters, and shoddy merchandise. If you're in a business involving customers — and who isn't? — you don't want to be the object of such stories. Why not? Because of the rule of 3-33.

> . . . For every 3 people willing to tell a positive story about an experience with your company, there are 33 others who will tell a horror story.

That's right, a satisfied customer might tell 3 people a happy story about you and your business. And yes, an irate customer might tell up to 33 others the horror story. Depending on the business, the ratio of bad to good stories varies. The White House Office of Consumer Affairs finds that a dissatisfied customer reveals the unpleasant experience to 9 others. A California market research firm shows that dissatisfied automobile customers tell their stories to 22 others. A Dallas researcher says that in banking, a dissatisfied depositor will tell 11

others about a bank mistake and that those 11 will tell 5 more people —
an average of 55 horror stories.

I use the rule of 3-33 because it's more descriptive. It isn't enough
to make the arithmetic reduction and say somebody tells 11 horror
stories for every good story. I find that people don't usually find more
than three occasions where they can say something positive. For some
reason, it's far easier to complain to somebody.

The problem is not that dissatisfied customers complain, but that
they don't take their complaint to the owner or manager of the business that made them feel disgruntled. They complain to their families,
friends, and co-workers. You can't
afford that sort of bad advertising.
The horror stories that might be
told over cocktails and at lunch may
easily number into the hundreds.
That's the talk factor at its scariest.

> The problem is not that dissatisfied
> customers complain, but that they
> don't take their complaint to the
> owner or manager of the business
> that made them feel disgruntled.

Most of my personal horror
stories concern airlines and hotels.
I once called to make a hotel reser-
vation in Las Vegas. When we came to the part about paying, the nice
woman said, "Yes, we accept credit cards, but if I put this on your
Visa we'll bill you $5.75 for handling the transaction." I said, "You're
going to bill me for buying from you? I don't want to pay you a service
charge for the right to pay you." She said, "What we would rather
have you do is to send us a money order by Federal Express for the
entire amount and save the charge." I said, "I'm not going to be able
to get a postal money order at 1:00 in the morning, am I?" She said,
"Probably not, sir." Then I asked, "At this point in the conversation
with you, what do most people do?"

She answered, "They hang up."

Me too.

The talk factor.

Of course, there are plenty of positive tales too. I love the story
that circulated about Nordstrom, the Seattle-based retailer legendary
for customer service. This story made the *Wall Street Journal*. According to this story, an irate woman brought in a set of tires. She was
adamant that she wasn't happy with those tires, and she demanded
her money back. So Nordstrom returned her full purchase price.

Big deal, you say? Think about this: Nordstrom does not even *sell* tires. The store took a loss on unsatisfactory merchandise that had been sold to the woman by somebody else — no arguments, no hassle. The woman simply *thought* that she had bought them at Nordstrom, so in her mind, she *had* bought them there, and the store's reaction to her demand for satisfaction would forever be the yardstick by which she measured the store — the story that she told most often would be this one, either negative or positive. The company was more concerned about managing negative talk, and more concerned about keeping a customer happy, than about refusing to take back those tires. The result? A whole lot of positive talk. If you didn't read about it in the *Wall Street Journal*, you're reading about it here, right?

Now, ask yourself these questions: What would have happened to that woman in *your* store or business? Would that woman have left your premises happy? Or would she have left feeling humiliated? Are your employees inclined to argue when customers err? What kind of talk factor would you have generated? All too often, the talk generated would be negative.

Nordstrom and others are so concerned with the word of mouth generated by their service, you could actually say they are obsessed by it. Nordstrom will do anything to satisfy the customer, whereas most businesses will do *almost* anything.

Do you have to be a giant retailer to make such a commitment? Emphatically not. I know the world's best painter. His name is Curley, and he owns a small automobile body shop. He once painted a car, and the owner brought it back nitpicking about things that are out of a spray-painter's control — things like a run out of sight under the rocker panel. Curley listened to the litany of complaints and said, "Hold on a second." He went back into his office and returned with an $800 check, which he handed to the customer. He looked the guy in the eye and said, "Nobody could paint your car any better, but even I can't do a perfect job. Nobody can! Here's your money back, because I can't afford to have you running around town telling people what a lousy job I did." I know this story is true because I witnessed it. I know Curley was absolutely obsessed with service and with controlling what people said about him. I also know that Curley is not stupid, so he would never accept another job from that customer. Finally, although the nitpicker is probably inclined to tell horror stories about businesses, he would have no basis for ever saying anything negative about Curley.

Do you think Curley lost on that $800 deal? Perhaps. But we'll never know how many more customers might never have gone to him if the nitpicker had run around town spreading negative word of mouth. If he does say anything, people probably will consider him a jerk and Curley a hero. Curley is someone who doesn't take chances. Today his shop is fifteen times the size it was then, and he has a waiting list of customers. Enough said.

The above excerpt from Word-of-Mouth Marketing *is used with permission.*

The Word-of-Mouth Factor

Richard Poe

For Paul Zane Pilzer, cocooning is far more than a concept in a book. It is a destructive force of nature that nearly ran his company into the ground. Like so many entrepreneurs and corporate executives today, Paul saved his business only by turning to network marketing. In so doing, he set his company on the road not only to recovery, but to unparalleled growth.

Paul is no ordinary businessman. He is a respected and brilliant economist. At age twenty-three, he became the youngest vice president at Citibank. Paul served as an economic adviser to Presidents Reagan and Bush. He warned Congress of the impending $200 billion savings and loan crisis, years before official Washington was willing to listen. Although a professor of economics, Paul disdained academia and set out to test his theories in the marketplace. He amassed a personal fortune of tens of millions of dollars through real estate development and wrote smash bestsellers on economics such as *Unlimited Wealth, Other People's Money,* and *God Wants You to Be Rich.*

THE NEW BREED

On the surface, at least, Paul seemed a most unlikely convert to MLM [multilevel marketing]. The industry had long been associated, in the popular mind, with blue-collar dreamers, infomercial junkies, and hucksters in leisure suits, out for the quick buck. But such stereotypes were already out of date by the time Paul entered the industry. The new breed of networker was a sophisticated, highly educated professional, searching for a profitable niche on the cyber-frontier. And Paul fit that profile with admirable precision.

Paul's long and winding road to MLM success began in 1989, when he produced his first CD-ROM — an inspirational program based on a videotape in which Paul traded economic ideas with popular motivational speaker Anthony Robbins. The success of his *PowerTalk* CD gave Paul an idea. Why not use this new medium for educating children? Paul felt that the undivided attention children normally reserved for video games could be channeled into their algebra lessons, if only those lessons could be enlivened with exciting, interactive graphics. Paul's vision was well ahead of its time. The potential market was enormous. But Paul's game plan lacked a crucial component that nearly cost him everything.

THE PROBLEM

Paul had not figured out how to penetrate the cocoon. And without such a strategy, his business was doomed. Paul would spend years attempting to sell his educational CD-ROMs through conventional channels, such as direct mail, retail stores, and schools. His Dallas-based firm, Zane Publishing, poured $25 million into marketing. But every distribution channel lost money. In order to make a sale, Paul had to penetrate not one, but three mental barriers. First of all, most parents did not see the need to get personally involved in their children's schoolwork. That was the schools' job, they thought. Secondly, parents did not understand why they should waste their money experimenting with this newfangled medium. And, finally, customers had no way of discerning, in the few seconds it takes to make a retail buying decision, how Paul's CDs were better than competing brands. Deeply cocooned in their established routines, they ignored Paul's flyers and in-store displays. Cocooners viewed such come-ons as nothing more than psychological intrusions, in a world already oversaturated with advertising media.

PERSON-TO-PERSON

A solution to this problem was already available, but Paul knew nothing about it. He did not realize that what he needed was a personal sales approach. Paul needed salesmen who could get right in the customers' faces, hold their attention, gain their trust, and explain, in great detail, the benefits of this technology. In short, he needed word-of-mouth marketing.

The mainstream business world offered no strategy for delivering personal testimonials, face-to-face. Conventional marketers looked upon word-of-mouth promotion as a *result* of good advertising, not a strategy for conveying it. They assumed that a good ad campaign would generate a buzz. But a buzz, by its nature, was thought to be as unpredictable and uncontrollable as the weather.

Network marketers, on the other hand, looked upon word-of-mouth marketing as a science. They knew that, through hard work and the application of certain well-known principles, a word-of-mouth buzz could be generated, time and again, with reliable and often lucrative results. This was, in fact, precisely what network marketers did for a living. It would be some years before Paul even realized that multilevel marketing existed. But once he did, he would quickly become one of the industry's most fervent advocates.

THE DISTRIBUTION FRONTIER

Paul was introduced to the industry by a happy accident. One day in 1991, an Amway distributor named Don Held sat down and listened to an audiotape version of Paul's *PowerTalk*. On the tape, Paul explained to Anthony Robbins that the big money in the 1990s was to be found not in building better mousetraps, but in finding better ways to distribute those mousetraps.

On the tape, Paul offered a memorable example to illustrate his point. He recalled a famous scene from the movie *The Graduate*, in which a well-meaning businessman offers career advice to Ben (the character played by Dustin Hoffman). The advice takes the form of a single word: "Plastics." Back in the 1960s, that was good advice. The best money, in those days, was to be made in figuring out ways to reduce the cost of manufacturing. One way of doing this would be to make objects from plastic rather than metal. By 1991, however, this opportunity had largely disappeared.

Advancing technology, Paul explained, had driven the production cost of an item down to where it typically represented less than 20 percent of the retail price. That left little room for reducing production costs further. Distribution costs, on the other hand, now accounted for a whopping 80 percent of an item's price. There was plenty of room left to push these costs down. For that reason, Paul explained, the big opportunity now lay in finding ways to *distribute* products more cheaply.

THE MLM CONNECTION

Paul did not know it at the time, but one of the best ways to reduce distribution costs is through network marketing. Unlike a conventional sales force, MLM distributors receive no compensation beyond their commission. Their word-of-mouth advertising can penetrate markets more effectively than conventional, multimillion-dollar ad campaigns, while costing the manufacturer next to nothing.

Despite all his credentials as an author, presidential adviser, economics professor, and entrepreneur, Paul did not know these basic facts. Indeed, he had never heard of network marketing. But listening to the *PowerTalk* tape, Don Held grasped the connection right away.

"He was saying that the big money now was in distribution," Don remembers. "When I heard that, I said, 'My God, that's what we're in!'" Don tracked down the famous economist and retained him to speak at an upcoming Amway rally.

THE AMERICAN WAY

Paul Zane Pilzer, of course, had never heard of Amway before. But behind the scenes, this company had been quietly revolutionizing American business since 1959. That year, two boyhood friends from

Grand Rapids, Michigan — Rich DeVos and Jay Van Andel — broke away from Nutrilite Products, Inc. The pair had made a fortune distributing vitamin and mineral supplements for Carl Rehnborg's original MLM company. But DeVos and Van Andel thought they could do better on their own. Using an improved version of Rehnborg's MLM compensation plan, they formed a new entity that they called the Amway Corporation.

Having served in the Army Air Corps during World War II, DeVos and Van Andel were fiercely patriotic. They were also committed Christians, reared in the stern Protestantism which their immigrant forefathers had carried over from Holland. From the beginning, the partners intended that Amway would epitomize America's old-fashioned virtues. Its very name was an abbreviation of the American Way. Amway's revival-style sales rallies, to this day, open and close with sing-alongs of "God Bless America" and "The Star-Spangled Banner," to the accompaniment of Old Glory waving on a giant video screen; its distributor force is composed, in large part, of devout churchgoers. God, country, and multilevel marketing find a happy synthesis in the Amway worldview.

INTO THE UNKNOWN

Amway's formula has proved remarkably successful. What began as a tiny enterprise, selling a biodegradable all-purpose cleaner called Frisk, has now grown to a $5.7 billion transnational corporation, with 3 million independent distributors worldwide, offering more than 6,500 different products and services, and managing one of the largest retail web sites on the Internet. Amway's research and manufacturing facilities alone encompass eighty buildings, totaling 4.2 million square feet. DeVos and Van Andel appear routinely on the annual lists of American's wealthiest individuals, published in *Fortune* and *Forbes* magazines.

Paul knew nothing of these matters when he agreed to speak at his first Amway rally. To him, it was just another convention gig, but Paul had unknowingly taken the first step on a journey that would one day lead him to the cutting edge of twenty-first-century innovation. He was going where no mainstream economist had gone before. Had they known what he was up to, Paul's old professors at Wharton

Business School would undoubtedly have frowned with disapproval. Yet they would also have marveled at the stunning opportunity Paul was about to uncover.

Pigpen Networking

Pam Sheldon

Effective networkers understand that word of mouth is not just an expression — it's a way of life. The best politicians, who are among the most accomplished networkers, have understood for centuries that a positive word-of-mouth campaign can make the difference between victory and defeat at the polls.

When I decided to run for office, I didn't understand the significance of word of mouth. But I learned it by winning.

I was a city girl. Born and raised in Toronto, I was a newcomer to the beautiful rural area that my husband and I had moved into with our two small children. Nothing could have prepared me for the daunting task of winning over the agricultural community in the local municipal election. I knew what the farm issues were. After all, I'd read all about them. Surely it was just a simple matter: tell all the farmers that I knew what to do and they'd vote for me.

What I was unprepared for was the farm community's distrust of outsiders. I had never farmed, never driven a tractor, never mucked out a stall. And I was a woman. There had never been a woman on the municipal council. Women's Lib had not quite appeared over this town's horizon.

The farmers were always polite, but whenever I attended a fair or other agricultural event, I could feel a distinct wall between us. I knew

I was in trouble. I heard gossip: the farmers called me "that woman from the city."

Every politician knows that to get elected, you have to go out and knock on doors — the political equivalent of cold-calling. You meet your constituents, hand out your brochures, and ask for their vote. A few of the farmers would mention that pothole in the road or ask what I proposed to do about saving farmland. I learned quickly that when this happened it was far more effective to listen to what they were saying than to tell them what needed to be done.

One day I drove up a long lane to a farmhouse and, finding no one at home, put on a pair of rubber boots I always carried and strolled over to the barn, where I heard an engine running. A pungent odor wafted out and assaulted my nose. I stepped inside. The floor was ankle deep in fresh pig manure. In the middle of this mess, a farmer maneuvered his tractor, busily pushing the wet pig excrement into vast, steaming piles.

When he caught sight of me, he shut down the tractor, sat back, pushed his hat back on his head, and crossed his arms. He didn't say a word; just sat there and looked at me beneath bushy eyebrows. I knew what he was thinking: "That woman from the city!"

> I've never forgotten that farmer mucking out his barn, because I know he had a lot to do with my success. I know, because the story of the woman standing ankle-deep in pig poop came back to me many times over the next few years.

I will never know where I found the courage. Without missing a beat, I took a step forward and marched, slop slop slop, praying I wouldn't slip and fall, right up to the tractor. I said, "How ya doing today? Just thought I'd drop by and introduce myself." He sat there and I stood there, and we talked and chatted for a good fifteen minutes about taxes, rural roads, and those durned city slickers who come here and try to change everything. Not once was pig manure mentioned.

In November I was elected — the first woman on the council. I've never forgotten that farmer mucking out his barn, because I know he had a lot to do with my success. I know, because the story of the woman standing ankle-deep in pig poop came back to me many times over the next few years. When I went to see him, I was networking, but when he told all his farm friends that the woman from the city was not afraid of barn smells or a little pig poop, that became positive word of mouth — the most powerful form of advertising there is, far more powerful than all the posters and flyers I could have printed and handed out or all the radio and television ads I could have spent a fortune on. That one farmer did more for my political fortunes than I could have done by knocking on a hundred doors. He told people, who told people, who told people, and from that day forward, instead of being known as "that woman from the city," they referred to me as "that gutsy lady councilor."

Word of mouth can just happen. It happened for me. But next time, I'll know how to make it happen.

9

Connecting

EXPERIENCED NETWORKERS KNOW THAT THE FASTEST WAY TO EXPAND AND ENHANCE their network is to regularly attend gatherings where networking takes place. Having many people with overlapping interests within arm's reach facilitates the process of making connections based on mutual benefit. Here are seven articles that spell out the strategies and tactics of making the most of these meetings. Cindy Mount and Jeremy Allen outline a six-part foundation for success at networking events; Anna Banks provides a tool that will help you overcome your natural modesty and promote your own interests; Joe McBride illustrates the value of establishing name recognition; Dr. Misner shows you how to grab your audience's attention and stick in their memory with a few well-chosen words; Mel Kaufmann outlines what to do and what not to do while attending a meeting; Anne Baber and Lynne Waymon provide a detailed game plan for attending and getting the most out of conventions; and Susann Linn offers twelve valuable guidelines for being an effective networker when attending meetings.

Attending the Networking Event

Cindy Mount and Jeremy Allen

As every good networker knows, one of the fastest ways to grow your business quickly and successfully is through word-of-mouth marketing. That's the fundamental reason networkers attend networking events. And people who have made a science of systematic networking keep six essentials in mind. Each time they attend an event, they have (1) a purpose, (2) a goal, and (3) a plan, and they make sure to (4) execute the plan, (5) evaluate their efforts, and (6) follow up on all contacts.

Think of each networking event as a journey. You have a purpose for taking the trip, a destination in mind, and a plan for getting there; you start driving; you evaluate your progress and modify your plan as you go; and once you reach your destination, you keep using what you learned on the trip.

Following the same logic, as discussed below, will help you get the most out of your networking time and effort.

1. PURPOSE

What's your reason for attending the event? Do you expect to show up, shake hands, and exchange business cards and phone numbers just to be sociable? No. To build business or increase sales? Maybe. But, really, aren't you there because you see networking as a complete philosophy of doing business and living your life — that helping others is the best route to helping yourself?

> Aren't you there because you see networking as a complete philosophy of doing business and living your life?

If this is true, then it's good to keep in mind at all times. It will motivate you to attend every meeting, meet every new person, and give freely of your time, effort, and expertise to help others. It will help you do the work. If your reason is not strong enough to motivate you, find another purpose or desire.

2. GOAL

What is your destination? What do you need to accomplish at the event? What do you expect the outcome to be? How many contacts do you need, and in what kinds of businesses? Do you need to become a gatekeeper as a step in obtaining your outcome? Ask yourself these questions.

Think of the professions, trades, or business owners that would most likely hear of or see people who need your services or products.

Target these people for your networking efforts. For example, a maid service sees inside many homes and might be able to refer business to finishing carpenters, carpet cleaners, personal organizers, electricians, painters, and decorators.

3. Plan

Once you know your destination, you need a map to show you how to get there. A complete map will show you trouble areas and point out good rest and refueling stops. A good networking plan will include these things:

Research. Who do you have to meet? Where do they have lunch? What do the target company's annual plans say? What are some of the new trends within your target industry?

Competition. Who are your competitors? What is their market share, and how much market share do you expect to capture? What edge does your competition have? What are your strengths and advantages?

Resources. What resources do you need, and where will you get them? Do you need guidance? Are your listening skills good enough to get you your money's worth?

Backup. Do you need to recruit new contacts or associates who can take over some of your duties or help you reach your goals faster?

Schedule. How much time have you given yourself to achieve your goals? Do you have contingency plans in case you encounter problems along the way?

4. Execution

Plans don't work unless they are implemented. To be successful, you must begin executing your plan — so grab your map and start driving. Your time and project management skills will be tested. Use a time management planner and project organizer that can show you a week at a glance. Mark dates when you expect certain results, then work backward to monthly, weekly, and daily completion of specific objectives. If your target for accomplishing your goal is twelve months, decide where you need to be in six months, three months, three weeks, and one day.

5. EVALUATION

As you reach each checkpoint in your plan, stop and evaluate your results. Did you find what you expected along the way, or did detours throw you off course? Do you need a new route? If you find that a particular network group is not meeting your goals, adjust your plans. You may need a new way to work the group, or you may need a new group. If after a suitable interval you're not getting referrals, it's time to evaluate the reasons. You may need a new skill or some help to meet your goals. You may also need rest or relief to reenergize your mind.

6. FOLLOW-UP

Once you've arrived at your goal, take a moment to savor your accomplishment. Then it's time to get back to work. Make complete notes on everybody you met, keep their business cards and brochures handy, and think about the potential of each new contact you've made. Begin making appointments to meet and work with these contacts as soon as practical. Don't let a recent introduction grow cold and be forgotten; if cultivated, it could turn into a rewarding relationship.

A well-organized contact management system is critical for future networking success. Keep it current. Master networkers include among their essentials an electronic contact management system that includes an e-mail program, project planning software, and a database. If you don't already have it, consider buying and using a personal digital assistant to manage information that you might need at any time.

> Don't let a recent introduction grow cold and be forgotten; if cultivated, it could turn into a rewarding relationship.

Once you've established your contact management system, use it to contact each member of your network every six to eight weeks, depending on the nature of the contact and your objectives. This keeps you in your contacts' minds when they consider their own purchases or their friends' needs.

The key word in "networking" is "work." It takes time, effort, and patience. But the payoff of powerful networking will be a personal marketing strategy that accelerates the achievement of your goals.

Learn to Brag

Anna Banks

We know that effective advertising often means the difference between success and mere subsistence. We also know that word of mouth is the oldest and most effective form of advertising. Networking is basically a systematic and purposeful marketing plan that harnesses the power of word-of-mouth advertising.

The effectiveness of your word-of-mouth promotion depends on four actions. You must

- offer a product or service that is valuable and that people desire,

- talk convincingly about the value of your product or service,

- motivate others to speak highly of you and your product or service, and

- deliver the product or service as promised.

For many of us, the most difficult of these actions is the second. Your customers (and the contacts who refer customers to you) must be persuaded to go to you, not your competitor, for what they need. Although most of us can provide plenty of technical information about our product or service, many of us don't like the self-promotion that is required to convince others of its value. In fact, however, the most important item you are selling, in any business, is yourself. And this is especially true in word-of-mouth advertising.

Why do so many of us find self-promotion so difficult? Because our parents and teachers taught us it was not polite to brag. It's still true, in a social setting, but in the world of business we all have to blow our own horns to get attention. Modesty will get you nowhere.

Networking works for you when others begin to spread the word about how good your products are or how well you provide your service. But you have to get the ball rolling yourself. You have to let your networking partners know what you do and how well you do it, and you need to give them your promotional ammunition. To get them to brag about you, you have to do a little bragging of your own.

One way to overcome your shyness about marketing yourself is to join the kind of networking organization (such as BNI) that teaches

GAINS PROFILE

Use this form to record goals, accomplishments, interests, networks, and skills — your own, or those of your network members or others with whom you want to build a relationship. Use one form per individual; attach sheets as necessary. Date each entry so you will know how old the information is. Use extra sheets to record information that doesn't fit one of the categories listed.

Name _____ Date _____

Goals _____

_____

_____

_____

Accomplishments _____

_____

_____

_____

Interests _____

_____

_____

_____

Networks _____

_____

_____

_____

Skills _____

_____

_____

_____

you how to speak appropriately about yourself. The GAINS profile, which originally appeared in *Business by Referral*, by Ivan R. Misner and Robert Davis, is one of the tools you learn to use to tell others about your skills, interests, and so forth. It is a summary of personal and professional information that helps people decide to do business with you or to promote your business to others.

To increase your business referrals through networking, you need to learn not just to stand up and talk about yourself but to use all the other networking techniques that have been devised and refined by experienced networkers. You can learn these on your own, but why spend all your time reinventing the wheel? You can learn it faster and better from the experts, and increase your business at the same time, by joining a formal business referral organization. By the time you learn the art of bragging, you'll be well on your way to becoming a master networker.

Speaking Your Own Name

Joe McBride

Not long ago, at an informal gathering, a businessman mentioned to me that his company was being hurt by inaccurate rumors. I immediately thought of my friend Sarah, who owns a highly regarded advertising and public relations agency. I gave him Sarah's card and recommended he contact her. His reaction surprised me:

"Oh yeah," he said. "I know her. She spoke at my Kiwanis club last year. You're right. I'll give her a call."

Within two weeks, both he and Sarah called to thank me for putting them together.

It occurred to me later that, although I had helped him make the connection, the fact that the businessman recognized her name was the key to the success of this referral. When I mentioned this to Sarah, she told me that achieving name recognition in the local business community was a part of her word-of-mouth strategy.

There are many paths to name recognition. Massive advertising, mailing out press releases, and keeping a high profile in organizations are a few time-honored routes. But none of these comes close to the power of what Sarah does. She speaks to twenty-five to thirty business, civic, and professional groups each year. She feels her other networking activities are at least three times more effective because she has good name recognition.

STANDING UP IN FRONT

On any given day, thousands of civic, business, and service organizations hold meetings. For you, each of these meetings is a target-rich environment — a place to increase your name recognition. And the most effective way to do that is to speak to as many as you can.

Finding the right opportunity is amazingly easy. In most local newspapers you can find information on upcoming community meetings, including when and where and whom to contact. The contact can tell you who is in charge of selecting speakers.

Ask what kinds of speakers and topics the group likes best. If your topic fits their needs, briefly describe your program and offer to send information. Your particular message will not be right for every group, but there are lots of groups, and with some thought you can usually find an angle that will work. A professional photographer I know of offers all the groups in his hometown, from women's church groups to the Campfire Kids, a program he calls "How to Take Great Vacation Photographs," with ten easy-to-remember hints for better snapshots. When people who have heard him need a photographer, they are likely to remember his name, or at least recognize it in the yellow pages.

There are many reasons a group might ask you to speak. You could discuss new regulations or new technologies that affect your business or theirs; you might clarify a current issue that is misunderstood; or you might promote a civic project that has nothing to do with your business. Whatever the topic, if you make it interesting and relevant, your audience will learn more about you, and you will gain name recognition.

THE FRIGHT FACTOR

"Who, me? You've got to be kidding. I can't speak in public!"

Yes, I know. Don't worry about it. Your competitor will be glad to do it.

Now that you've thought about it for a minute, here's a tip: Join Toastmasters International. It's easy to find in the phone book or through your local chamber of commerce, and it will help you get over the jitters.

In seventeen years with Toastmasters, I've never seen anyone who honestly tried the program who did not benefit from it. Toastmasters doesn't promise to keep the butterflies out of your stomach, just to get them flying in formation.

Having a clear strategy in mind helps keep your nervousness under control. Here are three key actions you can take.

Use your introducer effectively. Here's a chance to gain credibility from a third party who is usually well known and trusted by the group. Find out who is introducing you and contact that individual at least a week ahead. Send this person several documents: (1) a short biography — a page of facts about yourself, about two thirds of which should establish your credentials on the topic, the rest lighter facts of a personal nature; (2) copies of three to five letters from satisfied customers praising you or your company; (3) a sample introduction including some of the above information. My experience is that about seven out of ten introducers will simply read the sample introduction; the others will usually introduce you even more glowingly.

> Here's a chance to gain credibility from a third party who is usually well known and trusted by the group. Find out who is introducing you and contact that individual at least a week ahead.

Fit your speech to the group. If you have customers or clients in the group (and it doesn't violate professional ethics), mention them in your speech; compliment them in a way that benefits both you and them. (Asking their permission will usually create strong allies for you after you leave.) Find references the group can relate to; if you're speaking to chiropractors about computers, give examples of how other chiropractors have benefited from computers.

Exchange names. Help your audience keep your name with them after they leave, and get as many names as possible from the audience. The photographer I mentioned prints up his list of ten tips, with his studio's name, address, and phone number at the bottom, and hands them out during his speech; most audience members take them home. As he begins, he passes around a basket and invites everyone to deposit a business card, to be drawn after his speech for a free portrait. The rest of the cards? He takes them home to add to his mailing list, and each audience member gets a quick follow-up letter containing a coupon for a special offer.

How to Make a Memory Hook

Ivan R. Misner

Whether you realize it or not, you already know a lot about memory hooks. You've been using them, consciously or unconsciously, since you were small. What was your best friend's nickname when you were in the third grade? Where were you living when "MacArthur Park" was playing on the radio? Who do you think of whenever you hear someone say, "Ehhh — what's up, Doc?" Mere fragments of phrases, jokes, songs, and rhymes remind us of people, places, and events we have not seen or experienced in years — and they stay with us all our lives.

WHAT MAKES A GOOD MEMORY HOOK?

The key word in "memory hook" is "memory." If it's going to work the way you want it to, to pop into the prospect's mind whenever the need for your product or service arises, it has to be easy to remember. The best way to make it memorable is to make it vivid and short.

See It, Hear It, Feel It

A good memory hook often appeals to the basic senses — sight, hearing, taste, smell, touch. When meeting people in person or presenting your product or service using marketing materials, you should invoke the senses as strongly as possible — in a pleasurable way, of course. Here are some good examples:

"For balloons with a flair, remember the bear in the air." This memory hook, for a retail seller of toy balloons, grabs the visual imagination and paints an image that sticks in the mind. The next time a prospect discovers a need for balloons — for a party, a wedding, a convention — she may well find the image of the "bear in the air" popping into her mind. Or she may be driving down the street and see the balloon shop's big bear sign and think, "Oh, yeah, I need to remember this place next month when I start decorating the gym for the class reunion."

Here's a memory hook, used by a travel agency, that conjures up the memory of a popular song: "Come fly away with me." Most people of a certain age will be reminded of Sinatra's hit of several decades back. With the exception of smells, nothing cranks up a pleasure trip into nostalgia like the fond memory of an old song.

Make 'Em Laugh, Make 'Em Cry

Another "sense" that is often invoked in the best memory hooks may be the most important one of all: the sense of humor. When you want to catch and hold someone's attention, tickling his funny bone is perhaps the surest way of being remembered. In fact, one thing that most memory hooks have in common is that they are funny. Making people laugh is one of the fastest ways of breaking down the barriers between strangers and of winning the prospect's good will.

Puns are a form of humor that everyone groans at but tries to remember to pass along. The power of the pun comes from the element of surprise; your listener (or reader) thinks you're saying one thing but suddenly discovers that you're saying something else because you've either distorted the word or defined it another way. Here are some examples of memory hooks that use puns or word play:

- "We check your shorts," an electrician offers.

- "We're dyeing to save you money," says a company that can change the color of your carpet.

- "Be true to your teeth or they will be false to you," warns an Ohio dentist.

For pure name recognition, some of the most effective puns are made on a company's or person's name:

- Bob Howe, a mortgage lender in Irvine, California, says, "Know Howe to get your next loan!"

- The people at Truecolor Screen Print & Graphics of Vernon, Connecticut, use their company name in their invitation: "Let us help you show your true colors."

Verse — or Worse

Using verse is a sure way to catch someone's interest. Before most people could read, storytellers passed down tribal legends in verse form to make them easier to remember. The tradition lingers. Most people can recite from memory poetry or doggerel or humorous verse, whether sonnets or limericks, and anyone who can read is instinctively attracted to words that rhyme. If you can use your name as part of the rhyme, so much the better. Here are some examples:

- "When things go blurry, don't stop to 'ponda'; stumble to 17th Street and see Dr. Honda" (an optometrist).

- If you find yourself in trouble with the authorities, perhaps the following poem, penned by a lawyer in Portland, Maine, will spring to mind: "When the cops are in the foyer, call Marchese, your friendly lawyer."

Piracy or Parody?

Many memory hooks work by taking a familiar saying and rephrasing it, usually with humor — that is, parodying a song or a phrase the reader or listener will recognize. But you have to be careful; some authors, especially songwriters, are quite militant about copyright infringement.

- "When you're in a commotion, who're you gonna call? Law in motion!" proclaims paralegal Gloria Jones of Long Beach, California. It's a good bet she's seen *Ghostbusters*.

- Thomas Quirk, a banker in White Plains, New York, offers this thought, perhaps borrowed from a farewell speech by a famous WWII general: "Old bankers never die — they just lose interest!"

The Old Double Reverse

One of the most powerful language devices is a statement in which the second part either rephrases or reverses the first. The original meaning may be reinforced, slightly altered, or turned around entirely, leading to intriguing mental juxtapositions. For instance:

- "A business without a sign is a sign of no business" (a sign company in Canyon Springs, California).
- "If your hair is not becoming to you, then you should be coming to me" (a hair stylist in Covina, California).

These approaches should give you an idea of some of the tools and resources you can use to construct your own memory hook. Notice that many memory hooks use a combination of these techniques. Almost anything you do in the line of word play will come out funny — and that's the way it should be, unless you'd rather appeal to the heart. Song lyrics usually rhyme, so if you parody a song, it should rhyme as well. And any of these techniques can be more effective if your memory hook is short and snappy and appeals to the senses.

WHEN AND HOW TO USE A MEMORY HOOK

The best memory hook is one that you can use in many contexts. It should work in a pure word-of-mouth setting, as when you are attending a meeting of a networking group. It should work on your business card, on your letterhead, your calendars, your giveaway pens (another reason to keep it short), even your print ads and — at the top of the expense scale — your broadcast ads. Whether it's mass advertising or face-to-face, you want people to think of you, and you alone, when they see, hear, or remember your memory hook.

The above excerpt from Seven Second Marketing *is used with permission*

How to Pick & Choose

Mel Kaufmann

The $100,000 question . . . "How do you pick and choose the professional you need to meet?" . . . Answer . . . Arrive at each event 30 minutes early . . . Pay your dues . . . Make out your name tag . . . Greet the registrar . . . Greet the host . . . Greet the *speaker* . . . Stand 15 feet from the entrance . . . Face the door at a 45 degree angle . . . Don't look like a hungry vulture . . . Keep your eyes riveted on their name tag . . . Do not judge their dress . . . Their hairstyle . . . Their jewelry . . . Their bodily contours . . . Focus on their name tag . . . Look at the picture not the frame . . . If you become enamored by the frame of another you will miss the financial picture . . .

Kaufmann Corollary #2: Networking and Selling Don't Mix . . .

Networking and *selling* are like oil and water . . . Both are vital for your financial engine . . . But keep them in separate containers . . . Some professionals equate *networking* to selling . . . Not so! . . . I often hear professionals say as they leave a luncheon . . . "Boy! . . . am I a good *networker* . . . I just got 3 deals" . . . That's selling . . . Selling *severs* a relationship . . . *Networking bonds* a relationship . . . Unless you have taken the vow of poverty . . . STOP selling at events . . . If you keep asking for the order . . . The next event you attend . . . the people you want to meet will avoid you as if you had the measles . . . *Gather information . . . not deals!* . . .

Kaufmann Corollary #18: Choose One Committee

Never join a civic organization without becoming involved . . . Involvement is where *bonding* begins and *bonds* are nurtured . . . If you are turning pancakes next to the CEO of Xerox at a homeless shelter . . . You will *bond* . . . I guarantee!! . . . This means you must have an agenda . . . Know which committee members will be at the pancake breakfast . . . Then from the members who are attending . . . Determine by whom you want to flip pancakes . . . You are the CEO of your financial Universe . . . And the Universe is always generous . . .

Kaufmann Corollary #48: The Letterman Lunch

In the 1920s . . . Elmer Letterman was an insurance salesman in New York City . . . He reserved a table for 4 at the Fours Seasons Hotel 5 days a week . . . He would call a client or prospect and ask them who they would like to meet . . . He would arrange a luncheon for no more than 3 guests . . . His plan was to help his clients or prospects develop contacts that would enhance their career . . . He carried *no* brochure . . . He carried *no* rate book . . . He sold *no* insurance . . . If anyone asked him about insurance . . . his comment was . . . "I will have my partner give you a call." . . . Elmer became a *multimillionaire* . . .

Kaufmann Corollary #68: The Watering Hole

Everyone has a professional they need to meet . . . Some executives will not return your phone calls . . . Everyone you need to meet has a favorite *watering hole* . . . Search for the events they frequent . . . Charities they patronize . . . Organizations where they are members . . . After-hours social affairs . . . Their favorite attitude adjustment pub . . . This collapses the time between the *Search* and the *Salient Sale* . . .

The above excerpt from The Link *is used with permission.*

The Convention Connection

Anne Baber and Lynne Waymon

What's so hard about going to a convention? You send in your registration, buy your plane ticket, pack your suitcase, and go. Right?

Wrong. That's the way *most* people go to conventions. What you actually gain from a conference depends on the tactics you use to get the most out of the experience. You could read a book or current professional journal and get virtually the same information you'll receive from attending a convention. The difference, though, is obvious. A conference brings people face-to-face. If you don't make effective contact with the other people at the convention, you'll go home feeling vaguely dissatisfied.

If you think about it, you'll realize that you — and your organization — have expectations about how the experience will benefit you. You probably assume you'll gain valuable knowledge. Your organization assumes they are paying for you to get something out of that week in Miami besides a suntan. . . .

Amazingly, there are shelves and shelves of books in the library devoted to *planning* meetings and conventions. But there are no books on how to be an effective participant. Using the ideas in this book, you can make conventions a valuable business experience, one that's worth your time and effort.

Expand Your Expectations

Bringing people together face-to-face is expensive. In the business community, there's lots of talk about replacing meetings with video teleconferencing. On the other hand, there are strong arguments for convening in person. Your organization isn't going to continue paying the price for you to attend conventions, however, unless you can bring back bottom-line benefits. There are ways to sell your organization on footing the bill. . . .

Take Advantage of the Meetings in the Hallway

If you want to carry back more than souvenirs and stuff from exhibitors, plan ahead to make the most of all the informal and unstructured moments, "the meetings in the hallway." You make them happen when you introduce yourself to someone sitting near you before the keynoter begins to speak, when you strike up a conversation with someone in the hotel lobby or at a luncheon, when you welcome a newcomer, or when you congratulate a new board member at the opening reception.

The hotel can be awful, the weather can be lousy, the speakers can be mediocre, but if you meet just one person who can help you boost your sales, advance your career, land a new job, or solve a problem that's festering back on your desk, you'll call the convention a success. . . .

GET READY, GET SET, BEFORE YOU GO

Take these six steps to get ready.

1. Set your agenda.

Make a written list of your GIVES and GETS. By making an agenda, you customize the conference so that it exactly meets your needs.

On the GIVE side, jot down things to share with the people you meet:

- new resources you've discovered,
- special expertise you've developed,
- problems you've solved, and
- successes you've had.

If you are a newcomer, list some insights you might offer from other arenas. If you are a veteran, make a note about information you can provide to those just coming into the field.

On the GET side, go for the gold and make your list as long as possible. Jot down what you want to find:

- answers to challenges you're facing,
- solutions to problems you're dealing with,
- resources you need to succeed, and
- people you'd like to meet. . . .

2. Take along other people's agendas.

Not everyone will be able to spend the time and money to go to the convention. A great way to get more bang for your buck and build your relationships with colleagues, your boss, your salespeople, or your business partner is to collect their concerns and hunt for answers for them at the meeting. . . .

3. Choose your sessions in advance.

Select your sessions before you get to your hotel room. Advance planning while you're still in the office will allow you to shape your experience to your goals. . . .

4. Design your own sessions.

Recognize that some of the best sessions are not listed in the conference brochure — they're set up by you! Arrange them *before* you leave for the conference.

Here are some ideas:

- Visit a branch office or corporate headquarters to increase your knowledge of the business or to get to know an internal customer.

- Meet with a key prospect or customer in the city where your conference is being held.

- Contact a speaker before the conference begins to suggest getting together for breakfast or lunch.

- Set up a meeting with a board member, a guru, an expert, a counterpart from a similar organization, or a colleague you've lost touch with. . . .

- Plan an out-of-the-ordinary experience to stimulate your creativity. It might have a business payoff. . . .

5. Build in time to relax, unwind, exercise, and see the sights.

Get information about the city before you go. A request to the chamber of commerce will bring you lots of information in the mail. Search the Internet for that city's web home page. Also browse through travel magazines. How can you take advantage of the location of the conference? If you don't find ways to take advantage of the site, you might as well be staying at home. . . .

6. Volunteer for a job at the conference.

Call ahead and offer to help out. Find the name of the chairperson of a committee on which you'd like to serve, and volunteer your talents. It's a rare group that can't use an extra pair of hands. You'll find it easy to make contact with people that way. You'll also gain professional visibility, mingle with the leaders, and build a nationwide network.

Or give *yourself* a job to do at the conference. Before you leave home, arrange to bring back a report on an aspect of the conference to a person in your organization, to your company newspaper, to your city newspaper, or to your local professional group. Having a job to do will strengthen your agenda, and you'll feel as if you have an even better reason to meet people, ask questions, and take notes.

SHOW UP AT THE CONFERENCE

Show up! Set aside thoughts of the work stacking up back on your desk and the messages piling up in your voice mail. Use these ten tips for making great convention connections.

1. Get to the convention early.

The important people — speakers, conference organizers, association leaders — are likely to arrive early for "pre-meeting meetings." Get with the successful people. They are the ones with the knowledge. Find a mentor or a role model.

2. Wear a smile.

Make your body language say, "I'd be easy to talk to." React to visual clues. Comment on jewelry, a necktie, a T-shirt, a name tag listing a state you've traveled in. If you're in line to pick up theater tickets with someone who is wearing the same kind of convention badge you are, go with the obvious. Say, "Hi, I'm Jack, Jack Armstrong. I'm at the NCAC convention, too."

3. Volunteer (again!) to help.

Give out name tags, fill in for a panelist whose plane got fogged in, distribute handouts for the speaker. Participation leads to relationships.

4. Introduce yourself to speakers or panelists.

Welcome them before the program and let them know why you chose their session. Often they are eager for more information on who's in the audience, so if they aren't busy getting ready, talk to them. They may mention you in their presentation — instant visibility! . . .

5. Participate in the sessions.

Ask a question. This does several things. It forces you to think actively rather than just sitting passively and taking it all in. When you ask your question, stand and talk loud enough to be heard. Introduce yourself and tell where you're from or what organization you're with. You'll be remembered because you have been seen. Your visibility makes it easier for people to come up to you after the session and start a conversation. . . .

6. Sit with strangers.

At sessions and meals, don't sit with people you already know. Use that time to meet someone new. Tell yourself that there are no accidental meetings, and try to figure out what you and the other person have in common. Find out what others are looking for and help them connect with resources and contacts.

7. Look for excuses to introduce people to each other.

Listen for commonalities, then be a great connector. "Fred, I've got to introduce you to Sam over there. You both grew up in Chicago." "Mary, I want you to meet Sunita. You are both program chairs for your chapters. I know you'll have lots to talk about!"

8. Consult the list.

You may get a list of attendees in your registration packet. Use it and the conference registration materials to see who's on site. Look for people you'd like to meet. Make it a game. Take every opportunity to start conversations.

Welcome first-timers. Thank an association leader for his or her hard work. Say hello in the elevators. Meet people who have the kind of job you have now. Meet others who have the kind of job you think you'd like to have next. . . .

9. Give feedback.

Offer suggestions to the meeting planner and conference committee about how the convention could be made more network-friendly. Complaining is strictly off-limits. Make positive suggestions. Offer to help so you'll stand out as a creative contributor.

10. Be prepared to job hunt — even if you don't think you're looking for a job.

Update your résumé and take a dozen copies with you. Make sure your business cards are up to date also. Put together a few samples of your work. Throw in a U.S. map. If you are interviewing for a job, you may want to be able to locate Bigville on the map. Find out what you're worth. If there is a placement service, sign up and set up interviews with prospective employers. This lets you practice your interviewing skills. It also gives you an idea of your marketability and the going rate in other parts of the country for the kind of work you do.

If you are in the process of hiring, interview people for your job opening. Even if you don't fill the job with a person you interviewed at the conference, you'll have an idea what kinds of people would be interested in your job opening. You'll have a benchmark against which to measure the people you interview when you get back home. You also may be able to pick up a job description for a job you are creating. Then, you won't have to write the job description yourself from scratch.

FOLLOW UP AFTER YOU GET HOME

Sit down at your computer with your notes, and compile a list of major ideas, resources, and contacts. Turn sketchy notes into action steps. Make a list of people to follow up with. Do it within a week. Did you promise to send your counterpart, a franchisee in Albuquerque, that interesting article on selling to Baby Boomers? Do it! Did you say you'd review someone's résumé and send it back? Do it!

Tell your boss about the conference. Then, follow up with a memo. Pass along all of the exciting ideas you heard. Tell the boss who you

CONNECTING

talked to, what sessions you attended, what you learned, and why it's valuable to you and the organization. . . .

Later on, Get Re-inspired

Finally, six months later, take out your notes and reread them. Choose a rotten, rainy Monday for this exercise. You'll find that all the ideas and enthusiasm and inspiration you felt while you were at the convention come flooding back. That's what a convention is for: to give you ideas and to stimulate you. William James, the psychologist, was talking once about the time it takes for the unconscious to incubate ideas. He said, "We learn to swim in the winter and skate in the summer." You may find that ideas from the conference have now incubated and are ready to be hatched.

Also, at this six-month point, send notes to some of the people you talked with at the last convention. Ask them if they are going to be attending the next one. Keep in touch with your contacts. Put them on your holiday card list. That will make going to the next conference much easier: you'll be looking forward to seeing, not strangers, but your valuable business contacts.

The above excerpt from Smart Networking *is used with permission.*

Widening Your Circle

Susann Linn

What is networking? In its broadest sense, networking is using your contacts to get what you want. Commonly, though, the term refers to group situations in which businesspeople can interact. It's a current buzzword for an age-old principle: "It's not what you know, but who you know."

People network for many reasons: to make friends, get information, gain a support system, find jobs, stay current in their profession, change careers, locate business prospects, learn about new industries, develop leadership skills, gain publicity, and — particularly for those running a small business — market their products or services. In business especially, the bottom line is that people do business with and hire people they know. For job security and future business, it's a good thing to be known by a lot of people.

Here are a dozen good tips for making yourself an effective business networker:

• Carry business cards with you at all times. Your card is your silent salesman, reminding people of you after you've left.

• Try to meet five new people at any gathering. Make a point of talking to at least five people you don't know. It may be safer and a lot easier to remain with friends, but the purpose of networking is to widen your circle of contacts.

• Networking is an active behavior. Being a wallflower is not effective in a business situation. Make an effort to walk up to a stranger and introduce yourself.

• Put yourself in new networking situations regularly. Networking opens doors you never knew were there. Even if you're not prospecting for business, you can make contacts for future career possibilities or pick up useful information.

• Talk to everyone. You never know who the person next to you might be. I once met a new client in front of a merry-go-round while we both waited for the optometrist's office to open.

• Let the other person speak. People would rather talk than listen. Ask questions and try to learn about the person you're conversing with. Find common interests and get a clear idea of his or her line of work.

• Be helpful and other-directed. Maintaining a "What's in it for me?" attitude will severely limit your networking possibilities. Take the focus off yourself and notice that you no longer feel self-conscious or shy. See what you can do to help those you meet. Make suggestions, introduce them to others, or offer to brainstorm with them on problems they may have.

• Volunteer your expertise to the group. The best way to become known in an organization is to be active and visible. Ideally, become a board member or get on a committee. If you don't have much time to give, you can still help sign people in or assist with hospitality at the meeting. Act like a host; if you're shy, this gives you something to do and a reason to talk to people.

• Don't make a beeline for your seat. Wait until the meeting has officially started before you sit down. You'll have plenty of time during the meal to get to know your tablemates. Try to position yourself next to people you haven't met.

• Be memorable. If the group you're attending allows self-introductions, say something funny, witty, or different that helps people remember you. Using a clever prop as a visual aid can get you even more notoriety.

• Be concise. When introducing yourself to individuals or to the group, describe what you do simply and briefly, in plain language. There's no greater turnoff than someone who drones on and on about his business in a torrent of jargon.

• Remember: networking is not sales! It's about developing relationships with people. Out of these relationships can come all the things you want or need, such as a new job or more business. First, though, you have to establish credibility with people. Otherwise, you are still a stranger, and why should they trust or do business with a stranger?

10

Making a Good Impression

To establish the vital person-to-person connection that is basic to networking, you need to be aware of how people perceive you at first glance, before you've even had a chance to speak, and especially in the first few minutes of an acquaintanceship. In the next four essays, Susan RoAne tells you how to overcome common obstacles to forming a mutually rewarding lasting relationship; Catherine Bell focuses on your appearance and on how to make it work in your favor; Morris E. Goodman shows vividly the power of nonverbal communication when it's all you have; and Darrell and Donna Ross discuss what people say when they're not saying a word.

Removing Roadblocks

Susan RoAne

For every roadblock [to networking], there is a remedy. . .

Remedy #1: Redefine the Term "Stranger"

Mom says not to talk to strangers? Okay, let's redefine the term. Obviously, we have to exercise some caution in today's society. Not every street corner in town is a suitable place to mix and mingle. And there will always be some people who, for some inexplicable reason, make you feel very uneasy. Go with your gut reaction.

But if you are attending a meeting of professional colleagues, you're not really with strangers. If you go to a PTA meeting, you may not know anyone in the room, but you all have a common interest in quality education for your children. When you go to a new health club, a new church, a new synagogue, a new charitable or political organization, you have a *common interest* with those people.

When you go to a party, you probably know the host or hostess. At a wedding, you have some connection with the bride or groom. At a baseball game, notice how everyone talks to everyone else who is rooting for the same team.

Look for what you have in common with people at an event. This is the planning that helps you feel more comfortable and more prepared. You share interests with anyone who does the same kind of work you do, who is interested in your work, or whose work interests you. . . .

REMEDY #2: PRACTICE A SELF-INTRODUCTION

Scarlett O'Hara may have needed a "proper introduction," but we live in a different world. We may never meet another living soul if we wait for a Fairy Godperson or Ed McMahon to appear and introduce us around. We'll just stand in the corner, watching the real "room workers" who seem totally comfortable moving around the room, meeting strangers, conversing, and circulating through the crowd.

Every so often, you actually get lucky and attend an event that has a greeting committee. The problem is, not everyone on the committee knows who you are, who you want to meet, or how to introduce people properly — so they may not be able to give you much of an introduction, and they may not give it to the right people. . . .

The truth is that only Johnny [Carson] gets Ed McMahon to introduce him. The rest of us are on our own. Therefore, we need to have a *planned* and *practiced* self-introduction that is clear, interesting, and well-delivered.

What you say about yourself will depend on the nature of the event. At a chamber of commerce reception, for example, you should say your name and what you do — with energy. But at a purely social function, your occupation may not be as important as how you know the host or hostess. Your self-introduction should be tailored for the event. . . .

REMEDY #3: MOVE FROM "GUEST" BEHAVIOR TO "HOST" BEHAVIOR

There is no need to get gray hair waiting for "good things to come to you." Here is a remedy.

Dr. Adele Scheele, author of *Skills for Success,* says that people in a social or networking situation tend to behave either as "hosts" or as "guests."

The "hosts" exhibit gracious manners — meeting people, starting conversations, introducing others and making sure that their needs are met. "Hosts" are concerned with the comfort of others and actively contribute to that comfort.

"Guest" behavior is just the opposite. "Guests" wait for someone to take their coats, offer them a drink, and introduce them around the room. Often, the wait is interminable. If no one performs these services for them, "guests" move to the corners of the room and stand there until someone rescues them. They may be suffering the agonies of shyness, but other people interpret their behavior as "standoffish."

The bottom line is, "hosts" have something to do and "guests" do not. Dr. Scheele suggests that the key to success is moving from "guest" behavior to "host" behavior. We all have it in us to be "hosts." After a presentation I gave for the National Speakers' Association in San Francisco, my colleague Winston Hoose asked me, "Susan, how did you learn to work a room?" After a moment's thought, I shrugged my shoulders and told him the truth: "My mother made me!" Most of us were taught the same. . . .

What exactly do hosts do? Basically, the host's job is to extend himself or herself to the guests and make them feel comfortable. If you are having company or throwing a party, you plan a guest list and a menu. You clean out the hall closet. When the guests arrive, you welcome them at the door, take their coats, and invite them in. You smile and greet them. You offer them food and get them something to drink. You introduce them around, mentioning the things they have in common with other people. You provide conversation starters, perhaps an interesting story or piece of information about the guest. At the end of the evening, you retrieve their coats and thank each guest for coming. . . .

You might try volunteering to be on the greeting committee of your organization. You get to meet everyone who comes in the door; it's your job to meet people and make them feel comfortable. You have something specific to do, and it is just the thing you want to do anyway — meet and connect with people. You have an excuse to be as outgoing as you want to be. . . .

Remedy #4: Respond to Rudeness As You Would to the Flu — And Fly the Coop!

Fear of rejection is sometimes a self-fulfilling prophecy. If we're afraid that people will reject us, they may! Even when it comes at us from out of the blue, it's hard to take. It's no fun to put yourself out, extend a hand and a smile, introduce ourselves, and get a withering stare in return.

The only advice I can offer in response to this kind of rude behavior is to move on. Don't try to escalate the battle. The other person is probably ready and willing to "out-rude" you, and there is no point in stooping to his or her level.

Instead, simply walk away. The other person's behavior probably has nothing to do with you; he or she most likely treats a lot of people that way. Respond to this kind of inappropriate behavior as you would a deadly flu bug — and fly the coop!

Remedy #5: Anticipate the "Intercepted Pass" While It Is Still on Your End of the Field

With so many men and women working together today, we have to watch our P's and Q's — or some behaviors that are not intended as sexual will be misinterpreted as such. However, there are several things you can do to prevent your words, gestures, clothing, and manner from being perceived as suggestive.

The first is to ask yourself if your behavior really is being misinterpreted, or whether you actually do have an interest in this person. If your interest really is romantic, face the truth yourself and proceed in a way that won't jeopardize your professional relationship.

If you aren't interested, and you don't want the issue to surface again with someone else:

- Don't dress for misperception. Avoid see-through blouses and other suggestive clothing in the office.

- Stay away from double entendres and off-color comments.

- Be conscious of body language.

- Be clear about your purpose. Stick to business.

- You might even want to "lose your touch" a bit, at least in situations where it is apt to be misinterpreted.

We can't control others' thoughts and actions, but we can be aware of the signals we send — and of whether or not we want to send them. Continue to be friendly and outgoing . . . just be aware.

The above excerpt from How to Work a Room *is used with permission.*

Is Your Image Working for You?

Catherine Bell

Are you aware that it takes less than ten seconds to make a first impression? In a networking situation, during these few seconds the person you are meeting for the first time forms an opinion as to your economic status, educational background, credibility, and confidence.

In today's competitive marketplace, if you are well groomed and appropriately clothed, and if you display the right attitude, social skills, and personality, you stand a good chance of making a positive first impression. To be a master at networking, you need to ensure that the messages you send to others are congruent with your professionalism, the reputation of your company, and your chosen image. All of this has to be present during the first ten-second encounter with the individuals that you meet.

Your image does play a role in networking. The way you use your image determines how you are received by those who will influence your level of success. Dynamic networking is a process that begins when you come face-to-face with another person. If you make a positive impression, the encounter continues and a relationship based on trust has potential to unfold. The more attention you pay to your image, the less you need to convince people that you can be trusted. Once they are comfortable with your business ethics and abilities, they are ready to recommend you to others.

WARDROBE STRATEGIES

Your wardrobe and appearance should be part of your strategic networking plan. It's important to be familiar with contemporary trends in clothing, hairstyles, accessories, and eyeglasses. If your appearance or attitudes reflect another era, others will question your awareness of current affairs. Update these image factors regularly, but never be a slave to fashion or blindly adopt a style that goes beyond your comfort zone. If you're not comfortable with your appearance, you will not be sincere and self-confident.

With today's general tendency to dress more casually, you should strike a balance between the rigid "dress for success" regimentation of the eighties and the ultra-casual clothing that is best relegated to the weekends. Learn to dress down without bottoming out. In businesses where a navy or dark suit is still essential, replacing the white shirt or blouse with one in an interesting color, texture, or pattern will make you seem more approachable, yet still professional. In a more casual work environment, a sports jacket or blazer will keep you in the business casual zone. Subtly patterned jackets worn with colored shirts, dress pants, and ties are miles ahead of polo shirts and jeans. Keep a blazer handy to throw over more casual clothing if you suddenly meet an important client on a dress-down Friday. As the thermometer rises and polo shirts become an option, team them with dress slacks and dress shoes instead of khakis and docksiders.

Dressing Down by Degrees

The number of pieces of clothing worn at one time, the color combinations, the pattern and texture of the fabric, and the style of the garments are variables that affect the perceived formality of your clothing.

- The greater the number of pieces of clothing worn at one time, the higher the degree of formality. A three-piece suit is the most formal: pants and T-shirt are at the most casual end of the scale.

- Dark colors project an image of power and authority, especially when worn with high-contrast garments. Similarly, switching from dark colors to mid-tones, such as mid-gray or taupe, makes you appear more approachable. Combining a jacket of one color with pants or a skirt of another color will always be less formal than a matched suit.

- The smoother and plainer the fabric, the more formal the garment. Knitted fabrics are less formal than woven fabrics. Worsted wools and silks are considered better quality and therefore more formal than most cotton, linens, and synthetic blends.

- A tailored, collared shirt is more formal than a collarless shirt, blouse, or T-shirt. A fully tailored garment will carry more influence than a softly constructed version. Women should take note that wearing a dress will have less impact than a suit, unless the dress is a structured coatdress, or the dress is worn with a jacket. Dressy or formal garments are not appropriate for business, just as a business suit is out of place at an informal social gathering.

Image Indicators

Once you have deciphered the networking event and have strategically chosen your wardrobe pieces, you must also consider the finishing touches that will influence the quality of your appearance. The garments must suit your physique and fit impeccably, especially in the collar and shoulder area of a jacket. They should be clean and in good repair.

Your shoes will give clues to others about your attention to detail and your economic situation. Shoes that are unpolished or have heels that are run down should be avoided. Remember to polish the back of your heels. This is the last thing people see when you leave.

Strive to buy quality accessories. A leather briefcase, portfolio, purse, or billfold will look better and last longer than vinyl. A worn belt will detract from a new suit or pair of slacks. A good quality pen is very important if you will be writing in view of business associates. A broken umbrella never makes a good impression.

MAKING YOUR ENTRANCE

You've arrived at your destination and are about to begin networking. You pause at the door to straighten your clothing. The garments you're wearing have been chosen with great care to create a professional image. Using the reflection in the window, you discreetly check your hair and take one last look at your shoes. You have prepared what you will say and are ready to enter.

The speed and confidence of your gait should display awareness and self-control. When you enter a room, do not stand meekly inside the door. Walk with deliberation a few steps into the room and stand equally balanced on both feet while you examine the people around you. Approach either a person standing on his own or a group of more than two. Smile and introduce yourself. Offer your hand in greeting; shake the others person's hand firmly two or three times, and release.

THE LOOK OF SUCCESS

People like to associate with those who appear successful. However, image is more than mere polishing of the exterior. It starts with analyzing your appearance and behavior to avoid unfair visual judgments when others meet you for the first time or interact with you in social or business contexts. It also involves specific strategies that, once learned, will serve you well both socially and professionally.

> People like to associate with those who appear successful.

You want the opportunity to exhibit the positive qualities you possess and to develop good business relationships. Make sure your image is working *for* you.

The Language of the Soul

Morris E. Goodman

When people hear the word "networking," they usually think of word of mouth or verbal communication skills as the main tool of success in this arena. However, I have discovered another method that is a very effective way of getting business. I have been using this method for about twenty years now with some amazing results. It works like magic — yet it is overlooked by most people.

Before I tell you about my discovery, let me take you back to when I first became aware of its power. On March 9, 1981, I purchased my own single-engine aircraft. A private pilot for almost ten years, I loved flying, and I planned to use my new airplane in my life insurance and financial planning business, which spanned Virginia and eastern North Carolina. As a member of the Top of the Table and the Million Dollar Round Table, I had built my entire business on strong centers of influence and referrals. I hung pictures of my top clients on my office wall. I set up a board of directors — a banker, an attorney, an accountant, and other top professionals — that met regularly to exchange referrals. I was a master at networking. Business was booming, and I was on top of the world. But all that changed the next day.

On March 10, 1981, I left home after lunch to take my new airplane for its first flight. While trying to land I crashed into some electric wires. I ended up in the hospital, paralyzed from the neck down. I had broken or destroyed every muscle, nerve, or bone in my body. My neck was broken at the first and second cervical vertebra and my spinal cord was crushed.

I lay in the hospital for four days as the doctors tried to figure out what to do. Everyone in the medical field thought I would be dead in twenty-four hours, but after I hung on for four days they decided to try an operation that had never before been attempted. My neck was cut open, filled with special plastic, wired together, and fused. My chance of survival was said to be less than one in a million; my family were told that even if I survived the most they could hope for was that I might one day sit in a wheelchair and blink my eyes.

But I did survive, and for the next eight months I went from being hooked to a respirator, unable to do anything but blink, to walking out of the hospital. No one in medical history had ever made such a recovery. I was nicknamed the "Miracle Man" by the medical profession.

Now let me tell you about this amazing way of networking that I discovered while I was in the hospital. When the doctors and nurses came around, they would spend very little time with me; they assumed I would soon be dead. I knew I had to win them over to my cause if I were to have any chance of survival. But I couldn't talk or communicate. It seemed hopeless. Then I thought: If I can't communicate verbally, why not nonverbally?

And so I began with just my eyes and a smile to let them know I really appreciated what they were doing. I let them know with my attitude — my inner man — that they were important. Did it work? Like magic. I could hear them talking about me at the nurses' station, and they began spending more time catering to my needs. They were telling the doctors about this man at death's door — in excruciating pain — who was always smiling and happy. I became a topic of conversation throughout the hospital. Specialists and rehabilitation people were called in to take a look at my case.

I learned that all people are hungry for recognition, and if you give them genuine recognition and thanks they will be attracted to you like bees to honey. When you have an inner gratitude for everything and everyone and see the best in everything and everyone, this feeling reaches out, touches, and permeates everything and every person it comes in contact with.

> When you expect the best in everything and everyone, you reflect that attitude, and the best in everything and everyone is attracted to you.

It's what I call positive expectation. When you expect the best in everything and everyone, you reflect that attitude, and the best in everything and everyone is attracted to you.

So adopt this attitude, and begin to live and apply it toward everything and everyone you encounter. You will see amazing results, not only in your business but in every area of your life. Whenever the topic of your business comes up in a conversation, your name will be mentioned first by members of your nonverbal network. Greet every new day as a day filled with opportunity. Don't stop networking and asking for referrals verbally, but add nonverbal networking to your arsenal.

For twenty years now I have been doing this, and I end my morning prayer by asking not for opportunity equal to my ability but for ability equal to the opportunity that will come my way today. Try it — and get ready to reap a bountiful harvest.

The above excerpt from The Miracle Man *is used with permission.*

Nonverbal Networking

Darrell and Donna Ross

Those of us with experience in the business of selling our products or services have learned that much of what we communicate to our customers, colleagues, contacts, and networking partners takes place before we ever utter a word. We say a lot about what we're thinking and feeling without being aware we're saying it. How does this happen?

There's a lot we don't know yet, but in at least three areas we can make an educated guess. As a networker, you should be aware of the signals you send out just by entering a room, and you should learn to make these signals as clear and persuasive as possible in order to build rapport and trust.

INTUITION

Human resource professionals tell us that they usually know within the first two to three minutes of an interview whether the candidate is right or wrong for the job. The rest of the sixty-minute interview is taken up with confirming the first impression. Similarly, upon meeting someone for the first time, most of us form a reasonably accurate assessment of his or her personality within the first few minutes, starting even before the first word is uttered. It's obvious that humans form these first impressions intuitively, not rationally. We don't say to ourselves, "That person is wearing a pinstriped suit and carrying a cane. Therefore he is fastidious about his appearance, likely to be flamboyant in manner, a perfectionist in dealing with details, etc., etc." We don't think these things; we just feel them instinctively, almost instantaneously.

Of course, our experiences and our rational minds tell us that our first impressions can be off the mark and that we must be ready to change our assessment in light of new evidence. But our "working model" is driven by intuition, at least in the beginning of a relationship.

How does this intuition work? What is it based on? Studies have shown that we communicate with each other in many nonverbal ways. These forms of communication tend to be faster than a spoken language, because they don't require us to pay conscious attention to and interpret a string of words that is being directed at us or others.

> Nonverbal communication tends to be faster than spoken language, because it doesn't require us to pay conscious attention to and interpret a string of words that is being directed at us.

One familiar example is body language. For years professional communicators have studied and described how we communicate by our posture, gait, gesture, head position, eye movement, and other actions. The signals we send are mostly about mood, emotion, and attitude, but more explicit messages, as well as more subtle ones, are routinely sent and received without the use of words. Communication at this level can be controlled and managed if we are aware of what we are doing.

Another kind of message is chemical. Like most animals, we emit pheromones that tell others of our species, and in some cases our friends in other species, a great deal about our current emotional state, our fears and desires, our attraction to or repulsion from others. These messages are largely out of our conscious control. Different people react differently to these signals; some react strongly, others not at all. If we are conscious of their influence, we can choose to react to them or we can ignore them.

Can these known forms of nonverbal communication account for all the knowledge and behavior we refer to as intuition? Some popular authorities, such as currently fashionable spiritualists, hypothesize about mysterious, undetectable "forces" and "fields" that somehow fall outside the known laws of physics. It is true that there are many aspects of human psychology that we have yet to fully understand. But the history of scientific discovery shows that human nature, while mysterious, is accessible to the tools of science and that supernatural explanations are ultimately unnecessary.

What we do know is that we communicate with people constantly even when our mouths are closed. The secret is to become more aware of our unspoken communications so the messages we send are true reflections of who we are and how we wish to be perceived.

INTENT

All great teachers assert the importance of having intent and purpose in our lives. According to Benjamin Disraeli, "The secret of success is constancy of purpose." Before you go into a networking scenario, make sure you know your purpose. If your underlying purpose is to exploit the group, you will communicate differently, both verbally and nonverbally, than if you intend to give to the group. You expect an eventual return, of course, but a good networker goes in with the immediate benefit of others uppermost in mind.

We are, at most times in our lives, a dynamic mixture of intentions. We seek to do good for others, and at the same time we seek personal benefits in many different forms. When we attend networking events, our attention instinctively and constantly jumps from situation to situation, searching for opportunities that favor us. To fix your intention firmly on benefiting others, it is useful to organize your thoughts before the event by formulating, in writing, a clear statement of your main purpose — a mission statement. Focusing on your number-one priority helps you push your many other impulses into the background.

With your attention and intentions thus focused, you will communicate clearly and unambiguously your willingness to help others solve problems and satisfy needs. You will be more self-confident and open to the messages of others, and they will sense it and be attracted to you. Your message will foster trust and rapport with your networking partners, enabling you to establish and strengthen mutually beneficial relationships.

INTEGRITY

Integrity — "wholeness, soundness, uprightness, honesty," according to the Oxford English Dictionary — is the crucial feature of nonverbal communication. It is where our intuition meets the other person's messages and intentions and tells us whether he is trustworthy.

We've all found ourselves trapped by the fellow who is all smiles, handshakes, and concern about our business and health, but who in other ways communicates such a profound lack of sincerity that we can't wait to get away from him. He's obviously on the prowl for personal benefits, and his body language and attitude tell us clearly that his intentions don't match his words. He's like the telemarketer who calls you at dinnertime and greets you with a cheery, "How are you this evening, Mr. Smith?"

Just as we are repelled by the person who comes at us with mixed messages, we form an instant rapport with someone who approaches us with integrity and authenticity. For the networker, the most authentic message of all is this: "I would like to be your friend, and for you to be my friend. I think we will both benefit from it. And I want to start this friendship by doing something for you." If you communicate this orientation toward others in all possible ways, with integrity, you will easily form valuable, rewarding, long-lasting networking relationships.

11

Listening to Learn

IT'S IMPORTANT TO COMMUNICATE TO OTHERS WHAT YOU DO AND HOW THEY CAN benefit from your actions, products, or services. But in networking, it is perhaps even more important to learn all you can about your networking partners. By doing so, you learn how you can best give them the benefit of associating with you. In the following four articles, Debby Peters and Deanna Tucci Schmitt distinguish between three levels of asking questions and listening; Alice Ostrower describes how you can focus your listening skills to serve as a two-way conduit for information; Bob Burg outlines ten questions that will make you an expert in serving your networking partner's interests; and Mark Sheer spells out the best way to ask for referrals.

Getting to Know You

Debby Peters, with Deanna Tucci Schmitt

Imagine a big, hairy spider hanging out in the corner of the room, waiting for an unlucky insect to blunder into its web. This is how many view the "networker" — as a predatory menace lurking in a room full of businesspeople, ready to pounce and paralyze its prey with a torrent of sales talk and self-promotion.

This is exactly the image the networker must avoid projecting. Masters know that every good networking relationship, the kind that brings mutual benefit, begins with the discovery of common interests. And if you approach the relationship with the idea that what's most important is for the other person to learn everything about you as quickly as possible, you'll find yourself alone in the corner, perched on your web, waiting to snare anybody that hasn't been warned about you.

Master networkers turn the situation around. They look for situations in which they can be the listener. They start conversations by asking questions, one after another — not as interrogator, but as an interested listener. If they are asked questions, they answer, but quickly steer the conversation back to the new acquaintance. They have noticed something interesting about people: the more they talk — and the more you listen — the more they like you and trust you.

Master networkers have learned the secret of "active listening" — the art of hearing the inner voices and feelings of another person. Practiced by great counselors and psychotherapists, active listening creates trust. There's a more common phrase for this style of listening: "Getting to know you."

Since 1992 I have developed a fledgling company into a thriving business solely through networking and word of mouth. Until the fifth year of operation I did not engage in print advertising. My informal marketing plan was to meet new people every week. I set a goal: five days a week, when I ate breakfast and lunch, I would do so with someone new each time. I did not do this to gain customers or business, just to make new business friends. I would try to find that small commonality that could link us. Rarely did I fail.

THREE LEVELS OF BUSINESS CONVERSATION

Not only did I make many new friends, I learned a great deal about communication. Over hundreds of business breakfasts and lunches, I began to discern three levels of business conversation. It became clear to me that the objective for every networking meeting is to get to the third, most significant level of communication.

Level 1: Elevator Talk

Think of it! Ten or twelve people crammed shoulder to shoulder into a five-by-five closet for a minute that seems to go on forever. What do we observe? Strangers uncomfortable with the silence and trying to break the tension with strained words: "How's the weather?" "Do you think the Lakers are going to win?"

This perfunctory dialogue seems at first like noncommunication. But what elevator partners are saying is "I wish no one was here and boy is this a slow elevator. I can't wait till you or I get off and out of here!" Personal engagement is nil. Since there is little networking exposure or investment, there is also little return on the investment. You will probably never see this person again.

Level 2: Innocent Questioning

Finding yourself in conversation with a person you don't know very well, you engage in a bit of polite probing to show interest: "How's business?" Since you've not yet established a trusting relationship, you may receive a pro forma answer: "Just fine."

A year from now, you see him in the grocery store. You say hello to each other. You won't feel comfortable referring business or contacts to him, because you don't know him well enough. He probably feels the same way about you. Your relationship is the same as it was a year ago. Although you recognize each other on sight, you've shared no interests or experience upon which to build trust.

Level 3: Common Ground

You're engaged in conversation with a recent acquaintance and suddenly, to the surprise of both of you, you discover common ground. It might be a shared interest — you both fill your basements with model railroads. Or it might be that you have both been in Cancun during a hurricane, although not the same one. Unconsciously you both relax. No longer are you searching for something you can agree on; this thing you have in common makes it much easier to talk. Your confidence and trust in the other person grows.

> Eventually almost any two people can find a shared interest or experience on which to base a growing trust.

This kind of communication can bring great benefits to both of you. You can never plan how it's going to happen, but if you keep asking questions, it becomes more and more likely that you'll find common ground. It may happen immediately, or it may take a long time, but eventually almost any two people can find a shared interest or experience on which to base a growing trust — and perhaps, eventually, a solid and mutually supportive networking relationship.

Master networkers know that such commonalities are not rare, and that finding them need not be left to happy accident. They ask questions. They listen. Sooner or later they find the key that leads to a rewarding relationship and, not incidentally, abundant referral business.

Friendly, casual conversation is such a natural activity that envious colleagues and competitors sometimes don't connect it with the master networker's success. Business just "drops into his lap"; he's "just lucky." What they don't see is that the master networker has worked unobtrusively for years to engage people in Level 3 conversations and turn them into friends and networking partners.

When I network, I know my objective is to get to know the other person. If the two of us leave lunch feeling that we've made a connection, I never have to sell her my services. This new friend will come to me when she needs my services or wants to refer her friends to me. Friends do business with trusted friends.

Five years ago, I was inviting people to lunch. Today I get several lunch invitations a week from people interested in my sales coaching. I never have to cold-call anyone; I never hang out in corners waiting for victims to entangle themselves in my web. Now I just relax, enjoy my meal, and "get to know" my new friend.

Listening and Being Heard

Alice Ostrower

Networking is a process of connecting people who can help each other meet their objectives. Because networking relies so heavily on establishing and maintaining relationships, the two most basic skills you need to master to be an effective networker are listening and communicating. They are equally important skills — two sides of the same coin, really. The trick is to polish them to a high degree of perfection, then use them appropriately.

LISTEN AND LEARN

You listen to learn as much as you can about everybody you meet. You listen to find out what needs you can help fill for a fellow networker. You listen for opportunities to match the needs of one person with the products or services of another — sometimes your own. The more you listen, the less you talk about yourself, and the more you will be considered a wise and thoughtful person.

But listening is a lot more complicated than it seems at first glance. You listen differently in different situations. Your attention can drift languidly from one sound to another, as it might when you're relaxed and listening to nothing in particular but enjoying the sounds of a party — the music, the tinkle of glassware, the murmur of overlapping conversations. Or your attention might be focused like a laser beam, as when you're driving down the freeway at seventy miles per hour and your car starts making an unusual noise that grows louder and louder.

You even listen when you're asleep. Unlike your eyes, which you can close to shut off your vision, your ears stay open for business twenty-four hours a day, seven days a week. So when you're sound asleep, you hear the refrigerator running, crickets humming, traffic noises on the freeway in the distance — even a television program or a conversation between two people you know in the next room. You hear, but you remain asleep.

But if the baby whimpers, you're suddenly awake. Your unconscious mind, even in deep sleep, knows what's important to hear and switches on your conscious mind so you can take care of the situation. This skill, selective hearing, is an ability that comes naturally to you but that you can develop to an even higher level and use effectively in your wide-awake daytime world.

Let's say you're attending a meeting and, during a break, you are standing in the lobby, among a group of eight or ten people, comparing notes with a colleague. You're not paying much attention to the conversations going on around you until you suddenly hear the word "composite." You stop talking with your colleague and begin to listen more attentively. The person is talking about her business, manufacturing light aircraft. She's someone you met just yesterday, so during a break in the conversation you reintroduce yourself: "Donna, I recall being told you're bringing out a new plane. I've had my license for five years now, although I haven't flown anything but single-engine Cessnas. Can you tell me more about your new light twin?"

The reason you responded to the background conversation is that you've trained yourself to stay alert and listen to what is going on around you. Your mind then puts together fragments of information you hear that relate to each other — that is, it looks for patterns and matches. The word "composite" caught your attention because you have a friend in the business of manufacturing composites.

> Train yourself to listen to conversations that you might ordinarily tune out, and to evaluate every issue you hear with an eye to how it fits into the pool of talent, expertise, and resources your network represents.

Now you concentrate all your attention on your conversation with Donna. You're using a second facet of the skill of listening — shutting out all background noise to concentrate your attention on a matter of immediate concern, in this case an interesting conversation that you believe may lead to an important networking connection. This is "selective hearing," the wide-awake counterpart to what your sleeping mind does when it ignores unimportant nighttime sounds.

COMMUNICATE TO INFORM

This is where your second basic skill comes into play. You need to inform your new networking partner that you have important information for her — an opportunity that may be the answer to her problem.

"Donna, it's interesting that you're running into difficulty with your new assembly method. I think I know someone who can help you. His name is Frank Johnson. He's got a Ph.D. in chemistry from MIT, worked for Monsanto for ten years, and three years ago he started his own business in high-tech bonding agents. For two and a half of those years he's had a huge developmental contract with NASA, and now he's looking for ways to expand into more commercial lines. He may have just the thing you need to solve your assembly problems. Here's his card. May I call him and tell him you're interested in talking?"

Become an Information Exchange

To become a master networker, start by listening to everything. Train yourself to listen to conversations that you might ordinarily tune out, and to evaluate every issue you hear with an eye to how it fits into the pool of talent, expertise, and resources your network represents. One way to enhance this skill is to write down a list of your networking contacts and their products, services, and special capabilities. Read the list every day, keep it up to date, and respond quickly when something you hear connects up with something on the list.

Learn as much as you can about the special terminologies of your contacts' businesses. When you're referring someone with a problem to someone with a possible solution, it adds to your effectiveness and credibility to speak the language of both. It also helps you recognize the connection. But speak simply and clearly, in plain language whenever possible. Keep the message short and relevant. End with your offer to help.

Make the Connection

Here are four standard techniques that will help you get your networking message across effectively and encourage a positive response:

1. Get the person's attention. Show interest by asking questions: "How are you?" "Where are you from?" "What do you do?" "Have you heard about . . . ?" "Did you know . . . ?"

2. Add interest. Respond to the answer but don't move the conversation to you; elicit more information from the other person.

3. Involve. Use the "feel felt found" formula ("I know how you feel, I felt the same way, and this is what I found") to involve yourself in the other person's message before you deliver your own.

4. Network. Tie it all together by connecting one person's needs or goals with the resources, needs, or goals of another person. For example:

"I felt the same way until I met John Jones. He really helped me accomplish my goals. Why don't I have him give you a call? Is tomorrow evening convenient?"

This is networking at its best. Your new acquaintance finds a solution to a problem, your referral gets new business, and you gain a reputation as a friendly, reliable, knowledgeable person who seems to know everybody. Your name and reputation will become familiar to more and more people, and your business will automatically benefit in the long run.

The Networker's Best Ammunition

Bob Burg

Networking opportunities occur almost every day, practically anywhere and any time. We might expect to network at business functions, at chamber of commerce functions, on the golf course, in association meetings, or in organized networking or lead exchange groups.

That's just the beginning, however. Opportunities to meet new networking contacts and prospects also occur in places and at times we may not realize. Or we may think the situation is not appropriate for networking.

What are some examples? A PTA meeting, the racquetball court, night school class, shopping mall, airplane, casual introduction by a third party — the list goes on and on. How many times have you found yourself in one of these places and you were certain there were some potential business contacts waiting to be discovered? But you also felt that networking would definitely be frowned upon, that it would be considered . . . well, *tacky* by some . . . maybe even yourself? Please keep this in mind:

If you are networking correctly, the other person will enjoy the conversation even more than you will.

The first thing you do is simply introduce yourself to a person you want to meet. Of course, you don't do this in an aggressive, intimidating, turn-off fashion. You don't walk over with your arm stretched out and business card extended. That's important to keep in mind when meeting this person for the first time.

You tell him your name and offer a firm but nonaggressive handshake. He will respond reflexively by telling you his name. Then ask what he does for a living. He'll tell you and ask you the same question. You tell him briefly, but go right back to showing interest in *his* business.

Now ask him for *his* business card. He'll give it to you. *If* he asks for your business card, give it to him. Realize, however, that your card will be thrown out at the person's earliest convenience. More correctly, either it will be thrown out directly, or it will travel through a never-ending dimension of time and space, lost forever in The Rolodex Zone, never to be seen or heard from again. But, as we learned earlier, the main reason for having your business card is not to give it to someone else but *to get the other person's card.*

The next step is very important.

After the introduction, invest 99.9 percent of the conversation asking that person questions about himself and his business. Do not talk about you and your business.

Why? Because at this point, contacts don't care about you or your business. Let's face facts: your business and my business are probably two of the things in this world that person cares least about. That's just the way it is. He wants to talk about himself and his business. Let him! This is known as being you-oriented. Most people, of course, are I-oriented.

Will this get you off to a good start with your networking prospect? Let me answer that question by asking you a question: Have you ever been in a conversation with someone who let you do practically *all* the talking? If so, did you say to yourself afterward, "Wow! What a fascinating conversationalist!" Sure, we've all done that. Isn't it true that the people we find most interesting are the people who seem most interested in us? You bet!

TEN NETWORKING QUESTIONS THAT WORK EVERY TIME

I have ten questions in my personal arsenal. They are absolutely *not* designed to be probing or sales-oriented in any way. You'll notice that they are all friendly and fun to answer and will tell you something about the way that person thinks. You'll never need or have the time to ask all ten during any one conversation. Still, you should internalize them. Know them well enough that you are able to ask the ones you deem appropriate for the particular conversation and time frame.

Here are the ten questions.

1. How did you get your start in the widget business?

People like to be the Movie of the Week in someone else's mind. "I worked my way through college, then started in the mail room, then blah, blah, blah, and finally began the fascinating career of selling widgets." Let them share their story with you while you actively listen.

2. What do you enjoy most about your profession?

Again, it's a question that elicits a good, positive feeling. And it should get you the positive response you're seeking. By this time you've got him on a roll.

3. What separates you and your company from the competition?

I call this the *permission-to-brag question*. All our lives we're taught not to brag about ourselves and our accomplishments, yet you've just given this person carte blanche to let it all hang out.

4. What advice would you give someone just starting in the widget business?

This is my *mentor question*. Don't we all like to feel like a mentor — to feel that our answer matters? Give your new networking prospect a chance to feel like a mentor by asking this question.

5. What one thing would you do with your business if you knew you could not fail?

This is a paraphrase of a question from noted theologian and author Dr. Robert Schuller, who asks, "What one thing would you do with your *life* if you knew you could not fail?" We all have a dream, don't we? What is this person's dream? The question gives her a chance to fantasize. She'll appreciate the fact that you cared enough to ask. And you'll notice that people always take a few moments to really ponder before they answer.

6. What significant changes have you seen take place in your profession through the years?

Asking people who are a little bit more mature in years can be perfect because they love answering this question. They've gone through the computer age, the takeover of fax machines, the transition from a time when service really seemed to matter.

7. What do you see as the coming trends in the widget business?

I call this the *speculator question.* Aren't people who are asked to speculate usually important, hot-shot types on television? You are therefore giving them a chance to speculate and share their knowledge with you. You're making them feel good about themselves.

8. Describe the strangest or funniest incident you've experienced in your business.

Give people the opportunity to share their war stories. That's something practically everyone likes to do, isn't it? Don't we all have stories we like to share from when we began in business? Something very embarrassing happened that certainly wasn't funny then but is now? The problem is, most people don't get the chance to share these stories. You, however, are actually volunteering to be that person's audience.

9. What ways have you found to be the most effective for promoting your business?

Again, you are accentuating the positive in this person's mind, while finding out something about the way he thinks. However, if you happen to be in the advertising field, absolutely *do not* ask this question. Why? Because right now, it would be a probing question, and it would be perceived as such by your networking prospect. Eventually you will get to ask that question, but not now.

10. What one sentence would you like people to use in describing the way you do business?

Almost always, the person will stop and think really hard before answering this question. What a compliment you've paid him. You've asked a question that, quite possibly, the people who are closest to him have never thought enough to ask.

It's How You Ask

You may be wondering if a person will feel as though you are being nosey asking these questions during a first meeting. The answer is no.

Remember, you won't get to ask more than just a few of these questions during your initial conversation anyway. But more importantly, these are questions people enjoy answering. If you ask them the way I have them worded, you won't come off like Mike Wallace conducting an interrogation for *60 Minutes*. We wouldn't want that. These questions are simply meant to feel good and establish an initial rapport.

There are also *extender questions*, which can be utilized effectively when the person's answer needs lengthening. For instance, the words, "Really? Tell me more." The person will usually be only too happy to accommodate you.

Then there is the *echo technique*, taught to me by my friend and fellow speaker, Jeff Slutsky, author of *How to Get Clients*. According to Jeff, you only need to repeat back the last few words of a networking prospect's sentence in order to keep him or her talking. For instance:

NP (Networking Prospect): " . . . and so we decided to expand."

YOU: "Decided to expand?"

NP: "Yes, we thought the increase in our revenue would justify the cost."

YOU: "Justify the cost?"

NP: "Yes, you see, if the amount of . . ."

As Jeff warns, however, we must every so often adjust the phrasing of our echo, or eventually the person is going to look at us and say, "What are you anyway — an echo?"

THE ONE KEY QUESTION THAT SEPARATES THE PROS FROM THE AMATEURS

This next question is key in the process of getting this person to feel as though he knows you, likes you, and trusts you. It must be asked smoothly and sincerely, and only after some initial rapport has been established. The question is this:

"How can I know if someone I'm talking to is a good prospect for you?"

Let's discuss why this question is so powerful. First of all, just by asking the question, you have separated yourself from the rest of the pack. It is the first indication that you are someone special. You are probably the only person he has ever met who asked him this question during the first conversation.

During my live seminars, where I often address audiences numbering in the thousands, I'll ask for a show of hands from those who have ever been asked that question or even one similar by somebody they have just met. Seldom do more than a few hands go up. Often, none!

You have also just informed that person that you are concerned with *his* welfare and wish to contribute to *his* success. Most people would already be trying to sell their own product or service, but not you. You are wondering out loud how you can help the other guy.

You can be sure that your prospect will have an answer. I was recently talking to a person named Gary, who sells copying machines, and asked him the question. He suggested that the next time I walk by a copying machine in an office, I take a look at its accompanying wastepaper basket. "If that basket is overflowing with tons of crumpled-up pieces of paper," he said, "that's a good sign the copying machine is not working well. That's a good lead for me."

Don't we all have ways of knowing when someone may be a good prospect that the general public does not know? People you meet from now on will be glad to share their knowledge in that area with you. And don't you think they'll appreciate your sincere interest? You bet they will!

Again, that question will be the first indication that you are somebody special and different — a person worthy of doing business with, either directly or by way of referrals. My advice is to learn that question word for word until it becomes part of you and you could ask that question, as the saying goes, "in your sleep."

That question will serve you profitably throughout your life.

The above excerpt from Endless Referrals *is used with permission.*

THE Phrase to Use to Ask for a Referral

Mark Sheer

"**I**'m expanding my business and I need your help. WHO DO YOU KNOW WHO ... ?"

You must NOT alter this phrase. It has been tried and proven successful. Other phrases have been tried and have not produced the desired results — so don't waste your time using them. Once you become comfortable with this new phrase, it is very easy to ask your contact for a referral by simply saying:

"Who do you know who ... ?" Does that sound awkward to you? Would you feel uncomfortable saying that? That's okay. I understand how you *feel*. Many of my students have *felt* that way and wanted to change the phrase, but they soon *found* that it worked like magic, and they decided it was better to be a little uncomfortable at first, kept using the phrase until it became second nature, and then they didn't feel uneasy anymore.

"Who do you know who ... ?" is an open-ended question. If you are presently asking for referrals and are not getting positive responses, you are probably asking close-ended questions. Stop now and think for a moment of how you presently ask for referrals. Do you use a close-ended question such as "Do you know someone who needs to refinance their home loan?"

Using this close-ended, limited approach encourages the contact to respond with minimal thinking.

"Well, no one has said that they need to refinance so I'll say — NO."

You respond,

"Oh, okay. Thanks anyway."

And the conversation is over.

To bypass the automatic *no* response you must use an open-ended approach. Salespeople must get into the habit of always using open-ended questions, allowing the human computer to work *for* them. Open-ended questions are those that begin with: who, what, where, why, which, and how. It is more difficult to answer a simple *no* to these kinds of questions. They require a longer response, which is what we are looking for. The brain will automatically search for an answer.

"I'm expanding my business and need your help. Who do you know who . . . ?"

This open-ended phrase suggests several possibilities. First, it will make the person you are speaking to consider *themselves*, without having to ask directly if *they* are in need of your services. Then, if they do not fit into this category, the question will help them to think about people they know who may qualify. Besides, it's fun to use a different phrase. People are surprised — they pay attention and really try to think of someone they know who . . . *needs your service.*

Ah, but wait, you are going to help them along just a little more. So the conversation might go like this:

"By the way Sally . . .

"Who do you know who has recently had a baby?"

"Who do you know who has mentioned how high their insurance rates are?"

"Who do you know who is getting ready to retire?"

"Who do you know who mentioned that their retirement plan may not be adequate and are worried about it?"

"Who do you know who has been complaining about their tax bite?"

Now help them even more. Be *very* specific. Suggest people they know and use the *exact* words and phrases someone might say that would require using your product or service.

"Maybe someone you work with or a relative or friend? Someone who mentioned that they would be moving soon; perhaps one of your neighbors or someone at church?"

What you want to do is be more "generic" with your questions. Use less rigid questions that are free of constraints. Questions that help the contact *think*, that will include your service but may just as well cover your networking partner's service so you can exchange referrals. Help them out with your client profile, and *always* begin each question with, "Who do you know who . . . ?" Go down your entire client profile until you hit on a question that generates a spark.

"Who do you know who may be retiring?" (May need a smaller home, financial counseling, refinance.)

"Who do you know who recently had an accident?" (May need a chiropractor, attorney, auto repair.)

"Who do you know who mentioned their house is in disrepair?" (May need paint, carpet, remodeling, drapes.)

"Who do you know who mentioned that their taxes are a mess?" (May need a tax consultant, bookkeeper.)

"Who do you know who has been talking about their back yard?" (May need yard maintenance, spa, pool.)

"Who do you know who complains about having too many bills?" (May need refinance, debt consolidation, tax planning.)

"Who do you know who recently moved into the area and may be looking for a hairdresser, barber, dentist, draperies, carpet . . . ?" (May need your service or product.)

If someone has recently mentioned these things to your contact — bingo — you've got a referral. Most salespeople's questions are too general and they don't produce positive responses. You want to help people along with suggestive questions that make them think. Asking a close-ended question instead of an open-ended question, as we said earlier, relieves the person from having to think and encourages an easy *no* answer.

The above excerpt from Referrals *is used with permission.*

12

Establishing & Managing Contacts

CONTACTS ARE THE CURRENCY OF NETWORKING. YOU SEEK CONTACTS TO HELP YOU achieve your goals; you provide contacts to help achieve your networking partners' goals so they will remember you and wish to reciprocate. The art and science of acquiring and managing contacts is the subject of the next four contributions. Robyn Henderson outlines a systematic approach to managing your network activities; Don Morgan describes modern high-tech tools for keeping track of your contacts and activities; Ian Pendlebury makes clear the important distinctions between three kinds of contact information; and Robyn Henderson returns with advice for making the best use of the business cards you collect at meetings.

A Daily Networking Plan

Robyn Henderson

Successful networkers are organized. Thirty minutes a day spent on networking is a valuable investment of time. You can't spare thirty minutes a day? Ask yourself:

What am I doing that doesn't really have to be done?

What am I doing that could be done by someone else?

What can I delegate today?

What am I doing that could be done more efficiently?

What am I doing that wastes the time of others?

What can I do today to reduce this time wasting?

When you are looking at the effectiveness of your time management and wondering where you are going to find that additional thirty to sixty minutes per day for networking, get a second opinion on the questions listed above. You may like to ask some of your fellow workers to answer those questions on your behalf. Often they see things quite differently. . . .

Remember to focus your networking time — 50 percent of the time on old customers and 50 percent on new business. We need to keep both sides in perspective to grow our business to its full potential. Some progressive companies today also use this principle with their advertising dollar — 50 percent showing their current customers how much they value them and 50 percent looking for new business. Unfortunately, companies and professions only focusing on new business and not valuing their current and past businesses will ultimately end up out of business. . . .

Time management tips for your 15- to 60-minute networking time:

1. Allocate uninterrupted time. (If you were with a VIP client this would happen.) Networking must take a high priority because you are the most important person in your life. If you aren't, why not?

Date: _____ Day: _____
DAILY PLANNING SHEET
Today's priority jobs: Time allocated:
1. _____   _____
2. _____   _____
3. _____   _____
4. _____   _____
5. _____   _____
Today's phone calls:

_____
_____
_____

Tomorrow's calls and projects:

_____
_____
_____

2. Utilize your "on hold" time on the phone, arrive early for appointments and spend a few extra moments in the car to write a few notes. Stolen minutes here and there add up to hours. The more recognition you give to your customers, the more your business will grow.

3. Allocate a set day for writing birthday cards for that month. Place a small pencil mark on the envelope indicating the day the card has to be mailed to arrive on time.

4. Have your Christmas cards printed earlier in the year. Start writing personal messages on the cards rather than just your company name. It's the little things that count. The personalized reference to a golf handicap, planned Christmas holiday, or house renovation will make your card stand out from the dozens of impersonal cards landing on the desk.

5. Carry thank you notes in your diary or briefcase. After leaving a client's office, take a moment to write a short "thank you for your time" note and drop it in the mail on the way back to your office.

6. Make your job easier by employing effective networkers — headhunters are well aware how important networking skills are to a company's growth. There are only two sorts of people in the world — those you know and those you don't know yet. Some of your staff may already know the people you are wanting to meet. Ask them.

7. Start to take note of things that impress you with service and customer satisfaction. When you experience great service, write a note to the company and, of course, include your business card.

8. Include your business card with every item you send by mail — your credit card bills, electricity, orders, thank you cards, etc. Remember, your business cards are your silent salespeople. Make sure your cards are working for you.

9. Buy stationery in bulk. Having cards on hand is critical. If you have to go out and buy a thank you card every time you need one, you will never do it. Most printers are happy to provide a personalized range of stationery to suit all your networking needs.

10. Read daily newspapers and send letters of congratulation to people who achieve things you admire, whether you know them or not. Business is often done with people new to a position or location (sporting or political transfer) purely because you take the time to acknowledge their achievement.

11. Send a thank you card when you don't get the business. I repeat, send a thank you card when you don't get the business — you will certainly stand out from your competitors. Okay, so you did not get the business now, but maybe the successful provider fails to deliver. Who will more than likely get second choice? The one who stands out from the crowd for doing exceptional things.

The above excerpt from How to Master Networking *is used with permission.*

Managing Contacts in the New Millennium

Don Morgan

Not long ago, after giving a talk about the power of networking, I met a massage therapist who was having considerable success using a structured business network organization to get more referred business. However, now she wanted to create a national support organization for stepparents — a new role she was finding both rewarding and challenging. What, she asked, was the best way of creating such an organization?

I suggested that she use her business network to help her get the names of people across the country who shared her interest. This would be surprisingly easy, I told her. Through her current business network, she was only a step away from an enormous number of contacts. And anyone could afford the technology that would make the process fast, efficient — even fun.

Getting contacts is the easy part, I told her. It's after you get the names that the real work begins. It's the same for everyone who networks. The challenge is always to organize the names into a program that addresses your concerns.

It's basically a four-step process:

1. Organize the contacts into logical categories for easy retrieval.

2. Create a follow-up system to keep key contacts up to date.

3. Create a system to upgrade your contacts into potential partnering relationships as needed.

4. Assemble these new network partners into a primary network designed to help with a current project or set of activities.

You can use what I call the "ABC" method to catalogue your contacts. "A" contacts require immediate *action* as potential clients or hot referrals. "B" contacts are those with whom you wish to *build* long-term strategic relationships. And "C" contacts are those you wish to *connect* with others in your network for mutual gain.

The good news is that, over the past ten years, the art of contact management has evolved into a science. There are systems designed for managing and cultivating your contacts that will give you a competitive edge and let you harness the latent power of your networks — for almost any objective you can think of. There are also nationwide and international networking organizations to help you in this effort.

Several new contact management technologies now make this process efficient, affordable, and even fun. Everyone who seriously plans on becoming a master networker needs the following:

1. Fax. This can be a stand-alone unit or a fax capability built into your computer. It's best to have both. Use the stand-alone unit for receiving or backup, the computer fax for broadcasts. Install a dedicated line to make it easy for people to contact you.

2. E-mail. Beginning in 1997, it became virtually impossible to interact as a master networker without e-mail. The globe is shrinking, and networks are expanding. E-mail (along with broadcast e-mail) is the communication vehicle of choice for modern networkers.

3. PDAs (personal digital assistants), hand-held electronic contact managers that integrate and synchronize with computers and give you instant access to hundreds of contacts. The newest hand-held units recognize your handwritten notes, appointments, and contact information and can upload them to your computer for further work. The PDA is quickly replacing its low-tech predecessors, such as card indexes and appointment calendars, with combined capabilities that would have been considered science fiction a couple of decades ago — huge data capacity, graphics, handwriting recognition, phone and fax capability, even wireless Internet access.

4. Voice mail. People now expect a quick response, even when you're away from the phone. Face-to-face is always best, and live voice is next best, but when you or the other person can't answer the phone, voice mail is useful for both sending and responding to messages. Learn the art of leaving succinct messages.

5. Mobile phone or electronic pager. Depending on your responsibilities and duties, it may be important for people to be able to reach you instantaneously or within a couple of hours. Make sure you understand the value of access to good communication.

6. Internet site. Having your own website is a great way to advertise. You can post information about your goals, accomplishments, interests, networks, and skills. Potential clients who hear about you through word of mouth can get details from your site and send you information about themselves. Online chat rooms offer a unique new form of global communication.

New technologies bring new tools to help you network more efficiently and effectively. Why spend hours writing a guest list or follow-up letters when your contact manager can, faster and more effectively, input the names, categorize them, easily retrieve them, and integrate them through mail merge to a letter, fax, or e-mail format? Use the hours you save to do something else — to gain the competitive edge.

Tips, Leads, and Referrals

Ian Pendlebury

The central idea behind good networking is the expectation that if we bring new business opportunities to others, we will eventually receive new business opportunities in return. Many people find this sound business concept frustrating because opportunities they share are often handled poorly, and the recipients don't convert the opportunity into actual business.

You can ensure better results if, before passing a business opportunity to a contact, you consider two key questions:

- Is the opportunity a tip, a lead, or a referral?
- Can or will the recipient deal effectively with the opportunity?

Different Strokes for Different Folks

Three kinds of business opportunities are passed from one networker to another: tips, leads, and referrals. All are valuable, and all have a place in the networker's toolbox. But each must be handled differently, and not everyone knows how or is inclined to deal effectively with all three kinds. So if you are considering passing along a business opportunity, you need to be aware of what kind of opportunity it is and who would best be able to handle it.

Tips are the most basic, minimal information about a new opportunity that may exist. You may learn of it by rumor or hearsay or through limited public or confidential sources. The recipient needs to research the tip to confirm its validity, then follow up and establish contacts to turn it into a real business opportunity. Usually the subject of a tip is not aware of your involvement, so the recipient must make contact on his own. Therefore, give tips only to those who are willing to do the necessary research.

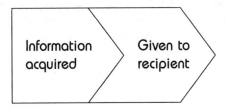

Leads are like tips, but more detailed. They are also known opportunities. You have advanced information to pass, such as specific products, pricing, and timing, as well as names to contact. The subject of a lead may or may not know that you've passed along information about her, and the lead may be passed to more than one prospective provider, so a cold follow-up is usually required. The person you've given the lead to should learn as much about the subject as possible and be ready to compete.

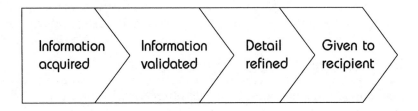

Referrals are the most valuable type of new business opportunity; they are what makes word-of-mouth marketing a good business strategy. A referral is a personal recommendation and endorsement from someone known to the subject of the referral. It is also exclusive; you don't refer more than one person to a given subject. There's no cold-calling, because the subject expects the recipient of the referral to call. The selling work is minimal. Referrals are warm, trusting, personal arrangements between three parties — referrer, subject, and recipient — all of whom are fully informed and aware of the opportunity to do business. These factors make referrals very likely to be converted into new business.

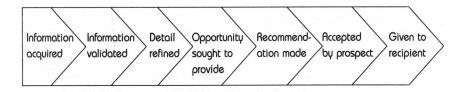

Referrals are developed from opportunities that started out as potential tips. This is what makes referrals much more valuable than tips and leads: you do most of the basic research yourself and pass that information along as part of the referral. The skill and dedication with which you do this directly influences the value of the relationships you build. And relationships are the capital of networking — they are the machinery that generates benefits for everybody.

LOOKING FOR A PERFECT FIT

It's frustrating to refer business to someone only to see the opportunity wasted. This can easily be the case when you don't understand the capability of the person you're referring — for instance, whether that person has the time and inclination to research a tip or lead and close the sale, or the training and resources necessary to take advantage of a good referral. One skilled tradesperson may not be comfortable trying to sell her products or services; another who is good at sales may not have the time to start at ground zero and dig up the information. In either case, a tip would be wasted.

When you pass along a lead, which is less of an unknown than a tip, you need to know that the person you're passing it to has the ability and desire to prospect what is probably a solid opportunity, can make a professional presentation, and has the time to follow up to convert the lead into a business transaction. As with tips, the recipient's willingness to do the work is something you must judge.

When you give a referral, you've already done most of the basic research. You know it's a real opportunity, and you know what the business deal will probably involve. You know the subject's needs in some detail, and this information is part of the referral. But it's especially important for you to know the person you're referring well enough to judge her ability to address those needs. Does she have the necessary skills, tools, or products?

> When you give a referral, you've already done most of the basic research. You know it's a real opportunity, and you know what the business deal will probably involve.

Does she have the will and energy to follow up on the referral? Will she do an honest job for a fair price? Is she trustworthy?

The success of the referral depends on all of these factors, as does the benefit that you may eventually realize from it. If you pass referrals that result in either the recipient or the subject ending up dissatisfied with the result, your value as a networker will drop. Rather than referring opportunities to you, others will avoid you. So, in the end, when you recommend one person to another, it's your reputation that's on the line, and your future success as a master networker. Do the work, make it good, and keep the trust others have in you.

Taming Your Business Cards

Robyn Henderson

Don't just throw [all those business cards you've collected] in the drawer and forget about them. Not only have you given up three or four hours of your valuable time tonight, you have also made twenty-five brand new contacts.

As soon as possible after the function do something with the business cards. First write the name of the function and the date it was held on the back of each business card. This will jog your memory when you start to get a large collection. Carefully go through the cards and create two piles — one for people who may be interested in your product or service and one for people who you believe have no need or interest at this time.

On a "With Compliments" slip, handwrite a personal note:

Hi Maria,

I enjoyed meeting you at the Australian Executive Women's Network function. You will remember my mentioning that I was in the office equipment business and I have enclosed our latest brochure. The contents may be of interest to you now or some time in the future.

I recall you wanted to know the name of a good builder. [This is something you did discuss with that person — remember how you made a note of everything you talked about on the back of their card?] John Jones is a friend of mine. You can reach him at 555-1212 and please feel free to mention my name.

Hope to see you at the next function.

Regards, Robyn

With this communication you have achieved the following:

- You have now made direct contact with a person you met.

- You have reminded her of the business or service you can offer.

- You have given her the information she wanted.

- You have mentioned when you may next meet.

- You have shown that you value her.

It is important to action your business cards within seven days of making contact with the new person. If you are a person who attends a lot of functions, networking will take up a large part of your time. I assure you the results will justify the efforts.

Now, let's go back to the business cards and look at pile number two — those who you think do not have a need for your product or service at this time.

On a "With Compliments" slip, handwrite a brief note:

Hi John,

Hope you enjoyed the Australian Executive Women's Network function as much as I did. You will remember I mentioned that I run a child-care center. I realize you may not have a need for my service, John, but please feel free to refer me to any of your friends or associates who may have a need in this area, either now or in the future.

I have enclosed an invitation to another group that I belong to — the National Speakers Association of Australia — you may be interested in coming along to one of our meetings. If so, give me a call.

Robyn

Send this without a brochure, but include a business card. With this communication you have achieved the following:

- You have made contact with a person you recently met.

- You have reminded him of the business or service you can offer.

- You have issued an invitation to attend another group that may be of interest to the person or one of his associates.

- You have shown that you value him.

Whenever you send any form of correspondence, always enclose your business card. People may throw away the correspondence but they won't throw away your business card. Of course, if you are in constant contact with this person (more than twice a month by phone or letter) don't worry about the business cards — the person already has a collection.

Remember: there are only two sorts of people in the world, those we know and those we haven't met yet.

Use the people you know to introduce you to those you haven't met.

The above excerpt from Networking for $uccess *is used with permission.*

13

Cultivating Contacts

IF IT IS TRUE, AS DR. MISNER HAS SAID, THAT NETWORKING IS MORE ABOUT FARMING than hunting, then contacts are the individuals plants in the crop that you cultivate. The care and nurturing of contacts to grow them into healthy, productive, two-way relationships is what the authors of this chapter have uppermost in mind. Dr. Misner and Robert Davis discuss the three stages a relationship goes through as it is cultivated into a close, mutually beneficial association; Marjorie Cowan tells you how to apply Dale Carnegie's principles to the nurture of your networking relationships; and Norm Dominguez joins Dr. Misner in a fable about the incalculable value of trust.

Three Phases of Getting Acquainted

Ivan R. Misner and Robert Davis

The key concept in referral marketing is relationships. The system of information, support, and referrals that you assemble will be based on your relationships with other individuals and businesses. Referral marketing works because these relationships work both ways: they benefit both parties.

A referral marketing plan involves relationships of many different kinds. Among the most important are those with your referral sources, with prospects these referral sources bring you, and with customers you recruit from the prospects. These relationships don't just spring up full grown; they must be nurtured. As they grow, fed by mutual trust and shared benefits, they evolve through three phases: visibility, credibility, and profitability. We call this evolution the VCP model.

Any successful relationship, whether a personal or a business relationship, is unique to every pair of individuals, and it evolves over time. It starts out tentative, fragile, full of unfulfilled possibilities and expectations. It grows stronger with experience and familiarity. It matures into trust and commitment. The VCP model describes the process of creation, growth, and strengthening of business, professional, and personal relationships; it is useful for assessing the status of a relationship and where it fits in the process of getting referrals. It can be used to nurture the growth of an effective and rewarding relationship with a prospective friend, client, co-worker, vendor, colleague, or family member. When fully realized, such a relationship is mutually rewarding and thus self-perpetuating.

VISIBILITY

The first phase of growing a relationship is visibility: you and another individual become aware of each other. In business terms, a potential source of referrals or a potential customer becomes aware of the nature of your business — perhaps because of your public relations and advertising efforts, or perhaps through someone you both know. This person may observe you in the act of conducting business or relating with the people around you. The two of you begin to communicate and establish links — perhaps a question or two over the phone about product availability. You may become personally acquainted and work on a first-name basis, but you know little about each other. A combination of many such relationships forms a casual-contact network, a sort of de facto association based on one or more shared interests.

The visibility phase is important because it creates recognition and awareness. The greater your visibility, the more widely known you will be, the more information you will obtain about others, the more opportunities you will be exposed to, and the greater will be your chances of being accepted by other individuals or groups as someone to whom they can or should refer business. Visibility must be actively maintained and developed; without it, you cannot move on to the next level, credibility.

CREDIBILITY

Credibility is the quality of being reliable, worthy of confidence. Once you and your new acquaintance begin to form expectations of each other — and if the expectations are fulfilled — your relationship can enter the credibility stage. If each person is confident of gaining satisfaction from the relationship, then it will continue to strengthen.

Credibility grows when appointments are kept, promises are acted upon, facts are verified, services are rendered. The old saying that results speak louder than words is true. This is very important. Failure to live up to expectations — to keep both explicit and implicit promises — can kill a budding relationship before it breaks through the ground and can create visibility of a kind you don't want.

To determine how credible you are, people often turn to third parties. They ask someone they know who has known you longer, perhaps done business with you. Will she vouch for you? Are you honest? Are your products and services effective? Are you someone who can be counted on in a crunch?

PROFITABILITY

The mature relationship, whether business or personal, can be defined in terms of its "profitability." Is it mutually rewarding? Do both partners gain satisfaction from it? Does it maintain itself by providing benefits to both? If it doesn't profit both partners to keep it going, it probably will not endure.

The time it takes to pass through the phases of a developing relationship is highly variable. It's not always easy to determine when profitability has been achieved — a week? a month? one year? In a time of urgent need, you and a client may proceed from visibility to credibility overnight. The same is true of profitability; it may happen quickly, or it may take years — most likely, somewhere in between. It depends on the frequency and quality of the contacts, and especially on the desire of both parties to move the relationship forward.

Shortsightedness can impede full development of the relationship. Perhaps you're a customer who has done business with a certain vendor off and on for several months, but to save pennies you keep hunting around for the lowest price, ignoring the value this vendor provides in terms of service, hours, goodwill, and reliability. Are you really profiting from the relationship, or are you stunting its growth? Perhaps if you gave this vendor all your business, you could work out terms that would benefit both of you. Profitability is not found by bargain hunting. It must be cultivated, and, like farming, it takes patience.

Visibility and credibility are important in the relationship-building stages of the referral marketing process. But when you have established an effective referral-generation system, you will have entered the profitability stage of your relationships with many people — the people who send you referrals and the customers you recruit as a result.

The above excerpt from Business *by* Referral *is used with permission.*

Winning People Over for Your Network

Marjorie Cowan

One of the most important parts of an effective networking plan is the ability to develop close relationships with other people who are significant to the achievement of your goals. The way you talk with people will determine your success in developing these critical relationships. A man who epitomized the ability to build relationships, and who subsequently taught the skills to develop a positive environment for building relationships, was Dale Carnegie (1888–1955).

In 1937, Carnegie wrote the first notable modern book on the art of human relationships in answer to what he saw as the overwhelming need of humans to be liked, appreciated, and valued. Carnegie was one of the first people to state that the biggest problem in business is dealing with people. All businesspeople, whether in sales or management, need not just relevant technical skills and knowledge but also leadership skills and the ability to understand and get along with people.

Relationships, whether personal or business, have a mystical quality; they are hard to understand, explain, or predict. It's easy to make someone dislike us, but we cannot force someone to like us or be our friend. We can, however, develop specific skills that will make it more likely that people will want to know us better, and even appreciate and trust us. Carnegie suggested thirty principles and techniques for inter-

> It's easy to make someone dislike us, but we cannot force someone to like us or be our friend.

acting positively with others toward this end — and all of them are important in networking, where people deal with each other on more than just a superficial level.

When I was director of career development for a major real estate firm in Atlanta, I gave a copy of *How to Win Friends and Influence People* to every new agent in the firm. I saw proof of the value of Carnegie's advice. Agents who read the book and practiced the principles were more successful than those who didn't.

I recently met a printer who told me enthusiastically how Dale Carnegie had just saved her a bundle of money. How had that come to pass? She had heard an accountant give an interesting presentation and had arranged to meet her the following week. The brief appointment turned into a long conversation, and the two women formed a close professional relationship. Before long the printer's new accountant had found a previously invisible $2,000 the IRS owed her.

But what about Dale Carnegie? It was his principles that had made the difference. The printer had shown appreciation and genuine interest in the accountant; she encouraged the accountant to talk about her interests; she listened attentively and made the accountant feel important.

The accountant reciprocated by asking questions. Without criticizing the printer's current accountant or making the printer feel foolish for employing her, she created a desire for change in the printer, who was pleased to have her return audited.

If you plan on becoming a powerful networker, you will be called upon to master a wide range of human relations skills. Doing so will pay you more dividends than any investment you can make. Reading and applying Dale Carnegie's principles will enrich both your business and your personal life.

A Legacy of Trust

Norm Dominguez and Ivan R. Misner

Alan had a nagging desire to run his own business. He wanted to call the shots, control his future, and make all the decisions that would affect his career. Spending six years as a junior executive in a medium-sized company had only made the desire stronger.

Alan was inspired by Jerry, a CEO who had spent more than thirty years building an organization with A-plus credibility, a leader whose management style, marketing expertise, and willingness to "share the magic" made experienced business owners and novices alike seek him out for advice. Alan decided he needed to meet Jerry. But how?

He remembered hearing about the "six degrees of separation" — the concept that you could make a connection with any person on the planet through no more than five other people. He thought, Who do I know who can connect me with Jerry?

It took a few weeks and a lot of inquiries, but Alan discovered that his connection was a lot shorter than six degrees. Alan had been an all-state forward on his high school basketball team; the coach, it turned out, was now the fitness trainer for Jerry's company. He called his coach, who arranged a meeting.

The first thing Jerry said was, "I saw you play in the state championship game nine years ago. Do you still get out on the court?"

"I play a couple of times a week," said Alan. "It helps me stay in shape and relax."

After a bit of sports talk, they were soon discussing Alan's entrepreneurial ambitions. Jerry answered Alan's questions one after another. He spoke fondly of his early days in business, and about one person in particular to whom he owed much of his success.

"My mentor taught me, among other things, how important it is to build and maintain good relationships. Having a network you can rely on makes all the difference. But a network is only as good as the relationships, and each relationship is built on trust.

"Most important of all, he told me his six secrets of business success. I still use them, every day, twenty-five years later. Whatever I've accomplished, I owe mostly to my mentor's six secrets of success.

"Now, just between you and me, they aren't really secrets. They're good, common-sense business principles that people tend to forget and have to be reminded of from time to time. I post them everywhere, I tell everyone, I hand them out at meetings. I probably make a nuisance of myself, but most people seem to like to hear me list them every so often. They say it helps them stay focused on what's most important in their business.

"But I'll save them for another visit, when we'll have time to discuss them. Right now I want to invite you to attend a business mixer with me next week. I think you'll find it useful. You'll get a chance to meet some pretty big names. I'll introduce you to some people who can help you in various ways. If you'll agree to attend, I'll give you the first secret now."

"I'll be there," said Alan.

"Fine. Here's the first secret:

"Always display a positive and supportive attitude.

"In other words, avoid the negative. Don't be cynical or pessimistic. It drives people away. When your attitude's right, the rest tends to fall into place.

"See you next week."

The next day, Alan called his coach and thanked him for the introduction.

"Did Jerry tell you his six secrets of success?" asked the trainer.

"He gave me the first one."

"When I met Jerry fifteen years ago, I was struggling with a decision, and I didn't know how much I should tell the people I was working with. Jerry told me his six secrets, and the second one really hit home. He said,

"'Be truthful with your associates and the referrals they give you.'

"He said that clear, open, and honest communication was the only way to build a sound business relationship. I never forgot that, and it's been a big factor in my success.

"As for the rest, I'm sure he'll tell you in due course. Good luck."

Six days later, Alan arrived at the mixer and found Jerry there already, busily mixing. Jerry introduced him to several of his associates, including a general contractor who had built two plants for him. The conversation brought to light the third of Jerry's "secrets":

Provide the quality of products or services promised at the prices quoted.

"Living by this rule," said the contractor, "has helped me build many solid relationships over the years."

"I can vouch for that," said Jerry. "His clients come back, again and again. He always delivers. If trouble occurs, he makes it right."

After a warm conversation with a leading investment professional, Jerry told Alan his fourth secret:

"Build goodwill and trust with members of your network and their referrals.

"I think you've already seen this one in action, but I bring it up here because that investment broker was a tough sell at first. I have an accountant friend who's been with me more than twenty years. My books had become totally messed up, and this number-cruncher straightened them out and saved me from disaster. Well, I referred him to the broker, who was skeptical but hired him on my say-so. My friend helped the broker save tens of thousands of dollars over the next three years. Since then, the broker has been an especially valuable source of referrals for me."

Jerry introduced Alan to his team's marketing executive, then left to take a phone call. The woman immediately told Alan Jerry's fifth principle, "because it's the one that I live with every day. I started as a customer service representative nearly twenty years ago. I learned right away that it all depends on the customers. If they're happy, we're happy. If not, we have to fix it quick. Whether it's good or bad, customer feedback is a gift, and it's important that we follow up. And referrals from other customers are a special gift. We especially need to thank those customers by rewarding them."

Jerry had returned. "And what's my fifth secret, Alan?"

"It would have to be,

"Follow up with all customers and referrals.

"Right?"

"Right," said Jerry.

"Okay, can you come to my office tomorrow at ten? We'll go over these points, and I'll give you the final piece of the puzzle."

On the drive back to his office, Alan found himself thinking how great it would be to have Jerry's mentor. But that wise man was gone now, and there was no bringing him back. Then it occurred to him: the mentor's wisdom still lived — and now Jerry was his mentor! Perhaps, if he achieved the success he envisioned, he would become somebody's mentor and play a part in passing along the wisdom.

The next day, on a framed plaque like the ones found throughout his corporate offices, Jerry revealed the sixth principle:

Always live up to the ethical standards of your profession.

"I would be glad if you would consider me as your mentor," he told Alan. "Business success is one thing, but I think most mentors feel more satisfaction in helping others follow their path to success. I'm happy to have a new friend and networking partner."

Alan was reminded of a phrase he had encountered several times in the business mixer: "Givers gain." This was intriguing; it sounded like a rephrasing of the Golden Rule. And it was something Jerry had not included among his mentor's six principles. But it was a principle that Jerry was demonstrating by his actions: the idea that those who give of their time, knowledge, and experience gain much more in return. It was a topic for his next meeting with Jerry.

Note: The story is fiction; the six ethical secrets come from BNI's Business Code of Ethics.

14

It's Not What You Know...

THE VALUE OF KNOWLEDGE AND INFORMATION IS MEASURED MAINLY IN TERMS OF ITS usefulness to people. This is why networking is primarily the science and art of relationships, not simply a way to exchange information and expertise. The six articles that follow exemplifly this focus on the individual. Jack Canfield and Mark Victor Hansen show you how to go about meeting anyone you want to meet; Herb Kay tells you how to find and cultivate contacts who can help you finance your startup; Wes Holsapple recounts how meeting a key individual opened a whole series of doors for him; Art Radtke likens the art of matching needs by bringing people together to the solving of a puzzle; Bill Becks recounts how the people he knew, both inside and outside the organization, furthered his professional career; and Jerry Schwartz describes how chance encounters and being alert led to new opportunities for business success.

It's Who You Meet That Counts

Jack Canfield and Mark Victor Hansen

The people you meet should excite you, inspire you, make you grow. That's why you should endeavor to constantly add to the number and variety of people you meet. Each one will polish a different facet of your mind and stimulate you in ways you may not anticipate.

One of the people I always wanted to meet was Red Skelton. One day I was waiting at an airport in a lounge and I saw Red sitting there.

Knowing that he was a superstar, I might have been intimidated and might not have found the courage to go and speak to him. . . . But Red Skelton was one of the people I had long ago determined I was going to meet someday. I had written his name down on a list. So in my mind I *knew* that sooner or later I was going to meet and learn from him. Consequently, I had no trouble walking up and introducing myself.

"Mr. Skelton," I said, "you don't know me, but I'm a fan of yours."

"It's been a hot day," he replied. "I need a fan."

At first I was taken aback by his humor. Then I played to it. I said, "Mr. Skelton, is it true that you have a photographic memory?"

He said, "Yep, it's underdeveloped."

Within a few minutes we were laughing and talking like old pals. I spent an hour and a half with him. We talked about a lot of things, one of which related to broadcasting. I explained that I had been asked to do a couple of TV pilots for Public Broadcasting.

Red said that was great, but that when it came time to sign the contract, I should always hold out for the broadcast rights. They might not be worth anything immediately, but in the future they could be of sizable value.

I subsequently did the shows for Public Broadcasting. And when I signed the contract, I made sure I retained all broadcast rights. Soon after, PBS discovered that it had lost all the money it thought it would have for those shows because Ronald Reagan pulled the plug on $160 million of its funding. But because I had retained the rights, a quarter-million dollars worth of filming was turned over to me . . . for no charge!

Now I use that film as invaluable promotional material.

You see, it wasn't that I was any particular kind of smart guy. It was my meeting with Red Skelton that gave me an insight based on his experience. It allowed me to grow and profit in the future.

Write It Down

It's one thing to think about meeting someone. It's quite another to write it down. As we've seen, writing down makes it a commitment. It tells our conscious mind what we want to do and puts the subconscious on notice that it had better get started figuring out how. (To further stimulate our subconscious, we can write out ten questions that we plan to ask the people we intend to meet.) . . .

Write numbers sequentially from 1 to 200 on a blank piece of paper. Begin with any name that enters your head. Perhaps you'll jot down celebrities from TV, movies, or music. You may add a who's who from local or national politics. Later, . . . other names will start looming up — people you'd like to meet in your own field of endeavor or areas of special interest. . . .

Remember, your purpose here is to enrich and enliven yourself with what you learn from meeting the people on the list. You'll learn their goals, values, beliefs, doubts, and fears, and this will awaken you to new levels of previously undiscovered potential in yourself. Your imagination will come alive with possibilities, and a new sense of excitement will pervade your thinking. You'll find yourself saying "If they did it, so can I!"

Meeting Those on Your List

The law of attraction states that you will experience whatever you are thinking about long enough and deeply enough. If your goal is to meet someone, he or she will be there for you to meet. The law will bring you together; what you do with the opportunity is up to you.

The above excerpt is from Dare to Win, *by Jack Canfield and Mark Victor Hansen, copyright © 1994 by Mark Victor Hansen and Jack Canfield. Used by permission of Putnam Berkley, a division of Penguin Putnam Inc.*

How to Meet Rich People

Herb Kay

Now that I've said where not to look for start-up capital, let me tell you where you can look. You're going to have to raise the money from rich people who are, at the beginning, total strangers to you. But no one in his right mind is going to hand over a wad of cash to a complete stranger. You have to develop relationships.

On Your Mark . . .

How, you might ask, do I develop relationships with people I don't even know? Simple. You hang out where rich people hang out.

Here's a short list of ideas to consider:

1. Your church, temple, or mosque.

2. Your kid's sports team. Volunteer to coach a Little League team. Rich guys dote on their kids.

3. Local politics. This generally works only if you are a conservative or live in a large city such as Los Angeles or New York.

4. Charities and fundraising. This is the best place to meet rich guys' wives!

5. The "right" health club. This must be in the best section of town, and you must be in seriously good shape.

There's no one place that will do it for you. Be inventive. Out here in Tucson the absolute best place to start is the old, local country club. The bad news is that, to afford the entry fee, you may have to do without food or electricity for a while. The good news is that most country clubs offer junior or associate memberships. In Tucson, the most established country club has a $30,000 initiation fee, but this fee is waived until you reach the age of thirty-five. You can join, pay a monthly fee as a junior member, then jump it up later. If you can possibly, in any way, shape, or form, get into a country club environment, I highly recommend that you do so.

Here's what you do. Start showing up at the club and get thrown into a golf foursome. (Important tip: Take golf lessons and get good!) You never know who you're going to end up playing golf with. It doesn't matter — the other three players will all have more money than you.

Actually, you don't have to join a country club. Just put yourself into a nonwork environment where wealthy people hang out. Everybody has hobbies, especially rich people. Get involved in tennis, fly-fishing, sailing, flying. That's where you'll meet rich people. Be logical; if you were filthy, stinking rich, what kind of hobbies would you pursue — a brewsky with the boys down at the bowling alley, or a cocktail on the 19th hole?

Get Set . . .

Once you find yourself in the country club (or on the tennis court, or knee deep in a trout stream), do not, under any circumstances, talk about money. You're the new guy or girl. The established members are naturally going to be suspicious of you at first. Bringing up the subject of money with them would be business suicide. Of course, what you're secretly saying to yourself as you wet your pants is, "Oh my God, I'm playing golf with the rich guys!" But you have to be nonchalant.

If the subject of money comes up, jokingly avoid it. When I was first starting out and people asked me what I did for a living, I would never answer seriously; the fact that I managed money would have immediately put them on guard. I would say, "I'm in organized crime." And they'd laugh and say, "No, really. What do you do?" "I'm a professional golfer." Now, if you had been on the golf course with me then, you'd know just how funny that is. Put them at ease. If they really want to know about your career, make them pry it out of you!

You have to be patient. Take your time; build your relationship. I don't mean days; I mean months. A year, maybe. Would you give a large sum of money to some guy you've played golf with two or three times? Of course not! You have to establish trust. The time it takes to do this is exactly why, once you have a great business idea, you need to act on it immediately. As soon as you think of a workable

> You have to establish trust. The time it takes to do this is exactly why, once you have a great business idea, you need to act on it immediately.

idea, begin looking for potential investors. While you're taking the time to gain their friendship and trust, you can be drawing up a solid, realistic business plan to show them — when the time is right.

But the time isn't right yet. First you need to ingratiate yourself with the group. How? The best way is to do a lot of selfless things and follow through on what you say you'll do, every time. The quickest way to piss off a person is to make a promise you have no intention of keeping. So if John Rich Guy offhandedly mentions to you that he needs something, and you have a connection that may help him get it, then get it for him, no matter what lengths you have to go to. Take advantage of any opportunity to help a rich person.

Keep in mind that anything you do for John Rich Guy is a favor; it's free. When he tries to thank you by giving you something in return, turn it down. No matter what. Don't take money, don't take gifts, don't take gratuities, don't take anything. If he insists, just say something like, "Don't worry about it. Friends help friends." You're trying to establish credibility. You need to be unbelievably decent, unbelievably honest, unbelievably straight, someone who never, ever takes money for a favor.

So if you sell cars and you can get one of these potential investors the car his kid wants at invoice, do it. Don't take a single nickel on the markup. If he's thrilled that you were able to help him get it and wants to give you a couple of hundred bucks' worth of gratitude, you tell him, "Nah, we're friends. I'd feel stupid taking money from you."

If a potential investor mentions that she and her husband would like to go out of town and get away for a weekend and you know they have a couple of kids, volunteer to watch them. Whatever you can do for them, do it. But never, ever profit from these people early in your relationship.

You need to be as honest as possible about your history. Got something embarrassing in your background? Don't be ashamed. We all do. Bring it out in the course of friendship. It is far better to tell them yourself than to have it come slithering out from under a rock somewhere down the road. Did you go broke in the pet store business when you were twenty-one? Confess. Flunked out of college? Don't manufacture a degree. You were a screwed-up drug addict who turned your life around through Buddha? Tell them. If you get out ahead of it, you can wear it as a badge of honor. They will respect you if you are honest and willing to admit your mistakes, because they've made them, too. You want them to feel completely at ease and safe in your presence.

Go for It!

All right, you've been patient. You've behaved yourself long enough. Now you can begin to reap the rewards. Once you've become friendly with these people and they've deemed you trustworthy, the transition is so easy that it's almost invisible. In the course of conversation, turn to your new rich friend and say, "Bob, I've put together this great business plan. I hate to bother you with it, but I need to raise money for it and I was wondering if you could suggest the right people to talk to. Would you mind reading it and giving me any helpful hints? I would really appreciate your input because you're successful, and I only want to take advice from successful people."

Rich Friend Bob will be more than happy to help you out, since you've been such a good friend and helped him whenever you could. Remember that Rich Friend Bob is rich for a reason: he's a good businessperson. If you've really got a solid business plan with potential, Bob's going to jump at the chance to invest. And even if it's not the right time for Bob, you can bet the farm that Bob will know who to refer you to.

It sounds obvious. It is. Filthy, stinking rich is easy. All it takes is a little initiative and a little common sense. No one is going to make your success happen except you. So get out there and get started!

The above excerpt from How to Get Filthy, Stinking Rich and Still Have Time for Great Sex *is used with permission.*

Open-Door Selling

Wes Holsapple II

As an outsider in a business community, you have tremendous hurdles to overcome if you want new customers. Learning how to build meaningful relationships with key businesspeople allowed me to network within a new business community that I didn't know and that didn't know me. Making my task as a newcomer more difficult was the challenge of looking for new customers in small towns in Mississippi where I was an outsider.

In January 1985, I joined the Dale Carnegie training organization in Jackson, Mississippi. As a sales representative and trainer, I was assigned to travel into nearby towns to sell the Dale Carnegie sales courses.

On one occasion, I had an appointment with an individual in Columbus to discuss the impact our courses might have on his business. I arrived on time and asked to speak with him. The receptionist said that he had not yet returned to the office. His father, Earl, who was the owner, invited me to sit in his office while we waited for his son to return. The next fifteen minutes' conversation proved more productive than the entire three weeks I had spent in the territory. The life lesson I learned has stayed with me to this day.

Our conversation started when I asked about the relationships he had built during his twenty-eight years in business. As Earl talked about his experiences with the local business owners and decision makers, he would occasionally pause in thought and add, "You know, he'd be a good person for you to contact for your school." By the time his son arrived for our appointment, I had a list of seven Columbus business leaders to call on.

What was most surprising was what he did next. After my brief meeting with his son, which resulted in my enrolling him in a course, Earl met me in the hall. He told me that he had called each of the seven prospects and talked personally with them or left a message that I would be calling them for an appointment. He had recommended me to each one.

The influence of one respected businessman had a far-reaching effect on my image and success in his business community.

From that point on, selling seemed easy for me. My entire attitude about selling improved. When I called to schedule appointments with the businesses on my referral list, the decision makers had an attitude of positive expectancy. They were sincerely interested in what I had to offer and gave me their undivided attention. I found that my closing ratio went from 24 percent to 70 percent when someone influential in the community referred me. Even those who didn't currently need my services offered to refer me to others who might be better candidates. The influence of one respected businessman had a far-reaching effect on my image and success in his business community.

Most amazing to me was the unusually positive attitude of those who had been referred. They missed fewer sessions, completed more assignments, and were more enthusiastic than those who had been cold-sold the course.

When I returned the next year to promote another class, I scheduled meetings with the previous year's graduates and their supervisors. These meetings regenerated their enthusiasm, and the referral process began all over again.

The lessons I learned in Columbus about how to sell a course have benefited me throughout my thirteen years in the industry. The lesson is simple. If you don't have a strong selling center of influence in your target market, borrow someone else's by asking them to refer you to their influence group.

Here are some other lessons I've learned about network selling:

1. You have to let people get to know you. Before they commit to your vision and follow your lead, savvy businesspeople must see in you something they admire and want for themselves.

2. Sharpening your public speaking skills is an effective way to make a favorable impression and get the attention of people who might help you later on.

3. We are all in the people business. Learning how to deal with people effectively is as important (or more) than the technical skills you bring to the table.

4. We all go through phases in our careers and our personal lives. Some of these phases are

   • Excitement about the possibility of a new opportunity

   • Worrying about the correctness of our decision (sometimes called buyer's remorse)

   • Blaming everyone but ourselves when things go wrong

   • Looking for the excitement and optimism of starting something new — a new job, a new car, or a new relationship. But we must guard against taking our old problems with us and simply repeating the same mistakes.

One way to avoid a cyclical life pattern is to follow three simple strategies:

1. Set realistic goals or objectives. Celebrate the goals you have achieved, then move on to setting new ones.

2. Learn how to build personal and business relationships of high quality, upon which the quality of your life depends.

3. Develop the habit of learning, and adapt your way of thinking to new ideas and information.

P.S. We filled our classes through word-of-mouth referrals.

The Rubik's Cube of Business Success

Art Radtke

Since Hillery Schanck discovered referral marketing through networking he no longer wrestles with boredom on tedious commuter flights. Instead he initiates conversations with his fellow travelers in hopes of connecting them with clients or other referral group members.

"It's like a Rubik's Cube to me," says the thirty-two-year-old investment manager. I just keep thinking how I can connect people. I love it when the pieces fall in place. I never knew marketing could be so much fun!"

In fact, networking has been so profitable for Schanck that he now devotes all of his marketing efforts to creating "strategic alliances" with other professionals who can refer him business and for whom he can return the favor. Gone are painfully frustrating cold calls and fruitless hours spent pounding the pavement in search of one or two good leads.

Now, instead of picking up the phone book, Schanck thumbs through his growing stack of business cards and calls people he knows. He also receives direct leads from people who understand his business and his own unique way of handling clients. He belongs to a structured business referral network, which he treats as a board of directors for his business and a place he can try out new strategies and make direct pitches for exactly the kind of customer he wants.

"Cold calls are so ineffective," Schanck says. "They waste your time and drain your energy. With the law of averages in cold-calling, I'd have to make a hundred calls before I signed ten new clients.

"Networking puts me immediately in the inner circle, with people who need my service and who actually want to buy from me because someone they trust recommended me. That means more sales in less time with less effort. Networking is a dynamite marketing tool!"

This new way of marketing, focusing more on servicing the client's needs than on making the sale, shifts the entire sales paradigm into a win-win situation that creates a sale, keeps the customer longer, and geometrically multiplies sales volume. Turning grateful customers into referral partners creates many new sales.

The business networking group Schanck belongs to passes an average of two referrals a week per person, which quickly translates into sales. For instance, recently one member, Eddie Drescher, distributed a client "wish list" indicating the specific contacts and companies where he needed an introduction. Contacts that would normally have eluded him, such as the CEO of a Fortune 500 company and the head of a large regional contracting firm, were handed to him in a matter of minutes, thanks to connections already established by other members of the group.

> "Networking puts me immediately in the inner circle, with people who need my service and who actually want to buy from me because someone they trust recommended me."

"In business, you're trained to look out for yourself and forget the other guy," says Drescher, "but this kind of sales approach is completely different. My job is to get referrals for other members so the principle that 'Givers gain' can come back to me.

"Most people I do business with will refer me to someone whether they're in a referral group or not. With my business network referral group, I have a team of more than thirty people on the lookout for business for me. I have a nonstop, enthusiastic, dedicated sales force working for me all the time. Who can beat that?"

Shanck says, "I love it when I hit the jackpot." Recently, on a flying trip, he applied his networking training and struck up conversations with a few of his fellow travelers in hopes of linking them with existing clients or other referral partners. Within minutes he had connected two of the people on the plane and realized that two of his current clients needed the use of his new traveling friends.

For me it goes back to that jigsaw puzzle of putting people together. That's the fun of it. The circle just keeps getting bigger and bigger. If I'm spending my time looking for contacts for you and giving you good trustworthy people to do business with, I'm going to earn your loyalty. We all know that's what getting and keeping customers is all about.

Networking Inside and Out

Bill Becks

Networking is such a natural part of life that we sometimes don't realize how much it contributes to our careers. Looking back, I now see that most of my jobs came to me through networking, often without my even being aware of it at the time.

- My first job, a paper route, came about when a friend told me there was a route available.

- My high school job at a service station came through a tip from a friend who was working there.

- All of my summer jobs during college were brought to me by networking contacts.

- After graduation, I got started in social work through a friend who worked in a psychiatric hospital and with whom I later attended graduate school.

- I got interested in drug addiction work after visiting an innovative psychiatric hospital program, whose directors later helped me get jobs in the field.

Outside contacts helped me move easily from one job to the next, accumulating valuable skills and experience along the way. My emerging skills in networking brought me yet more opportunities to advance in the health care field, where I learned about networking within the organization.

THE INSIDE NETWORK

In my first postgraduate job, I reported through an advisory board to administrators of three separate institutions. In another job, I was paid by one institution to administer a program within another institution. These positions all involved keeping several bosses happy, a real challenge in my organizations, which had different treatment philosophies. Wearing several hats and reporting simultaneously to different bosses with different expectations was invaluable in teaching me how to network effectively within each organization. It eventually brought me to the job of senior division director of research and development in a crown corporation of Ontario, Canada.

Why do some people survive and progress within an organization while others stagnate, regress, or leave? Those who advance understand the organization's power structure and develop strategic alliances with key players. Many of them volunteer for extra assignments, helping others in their network. A willingness to go the extra mile often brings rewards — and trust.

Trust

Your reputation and success depend on whether you are considered trustworthy. This is as true within the organization as it is outside. No one gets a promotion (or more contacts or referrals) if his superiors (or networking partners) feel he can't be trusted. No promotion opportunities equals stagnation and early departure. Can you be counted on to do your job? Do you support the organization's basic philosophy? You may not agree with everything the organization does, but do you offer constructive criticism and suggest improvements?

Whether within an organization, within a community, or within a group, all networking depends on trust. How do you earn that trust? One way is by volunteering for extra duties or taking courses for self-improvement; supervisors value people who show initiative and communicate well with them. Another way is to seek out a mentor or colleague who can help you develop a successful game plan.

> Whether within an organization, within a community, or within a group, all networking depends on trust.

Being seen as a team player and offering your support to other players will create additional rewards. Being flexible and adaptable are essential elements for survival and progress. Remember, bosses have an interest in maintaining their positions on issues of status quo. If your intent is to make changes, do it constructively to support your boss. You look good when you make your boss look good, and your boss will remember you when it is time for promotions.

I am pleased to say that networking is still getting me jobs. I now own a fast-growing franchise business that fits my specialty, an opportunity that came my way from a colleague in addiction treatment just as I was thinking about retiring. I want to stay busy, so I've volunteered for new assignments. I'm developing a new mentoring system and am coauthoring a book about it. Networking has served me well from the beginning of my career to this day.

The Knock on the Door

Jerry Schwartz

All my life I have worked well with people, but only recently did I realize the full potential of purposeful networking. I became a direct sales consultant because I wanted the extra income and thought it might be fun. Never did I imagine that it would lead to major life changes.

When opportunity comes knocking, sometimes it doesn't knock very loud. One day I volunteered to pick up some people who were flying in to conduct a sales seminar. I thought that if I drove slowly I might pick up a few pointers on how to make more money in direct sales.

What I got instead was a new business, one that is growing rapidly and that I am perfectly suited for.

The couple I picked up at the airport became my good friends. Eventually they asked me to become their partner in a new business. I was skeptical at first; I thought that they simply needed help developing their business in my city. After only two years, however, the business has grown into a significant enterprise, one that is in the top 10 percent of the industry and has won major awards. I have become a leader in the field of business networking and have made guest appearances in local radio and television shows.

In networking, it is important to learn as much as possible about everyone you meet. Once you know the range of skills, knowledge, and resources around you, you can work out ways to help achieve each other's goals.

At the first company conference I attended, I sought out people who I felt might help me expand my business. I met Art, my counterpart in a neighboring territory. When I got home from the conference, I followed up with a phone call and suggested that we meet and get to know each other a little better. During our first scheduled meeting, Art and I hit it off nicely. We had fun brainstorming new ideas for our businesses. As a result of this relationship, I improved my customer service program and doubled the size of my business.

How do you learn about others? You listen. Hear what they say about their business, their techniques, their preferences, their goals, and especially their needs. Listen especially for things you have in common — key issues, problems, directions, goals. Dig deeper; learn how you can work together to help each other.

I discovered that Art wanted to move his family to a resort area to the south. I agreed to help him think of ways to accomplish this goal. Since his sales area bordered my own, we worked out a plan that would allow me to buy his area and him to purchase the area he wanted, farther south. We created a proposal that the corporate head office could not refuse. We both got what we wanted. I bought Art's area, and he bought his dream territory. The outcome was so successful for both of us that we were honored for our networking at a later annual conference — a recognition that has helped me form new relationships with other key individuals.

> In networking, it's important to learn as much as possible about everyone you meet. Once you know the range of skills, knowledge, and resources around you, you can work out ways to help achieve each other's goals.

I have continued to build relationships with key people — other directors in my business, local business associates, new colleagues who help me grow my business. These experiences have taught me valuable lessons. Two in particular stand out:

- Listen carefully to learn about others.

- Seize every opportunity to achieve mutual goals.

If you keep these principles firmly in mind, you won't miss even the most subtle knock on the door.

15

Myths, Mistakes, & Misconceptions

IN NETWORKING, AS IN ANY OTHER ENDEAVOR, THE ROAD TO MASTERY RUNS THROUGH many junctions, any of which can present you with wrong turns. In the essays and stories that follow, Anne Baber and Lynne Waymon list ten good ways to ruin a potentially valuable business relationship before it even gets started; Ron Sukenick outlines ten common myths about networking and how to avoid falling victim to them; Steve Lawson shows how people sometimes think they're networking when they're not; and Patti Salvucci and Tom Fleming tell a story about helping a business owner understand the true nature of word-of-mouth marketing.

Avoid Turnoffs

Anne Baber and Lynne Waymon

The classic definition of a bore is someone who, when you ask him how he is, tells you. Being boring, though, also entails committing a variety of other small talk "sins." Here are the top ten. Can you think of others? It will be easy for you to recognize other people's "sins." The question is, are you guilty of any of them, and, if so, how can you change your ways to be a more attractive conversation partner?

1. Telling Too Many Details

The person who insists on telling everything will soon lose his audience. We've all had the experience of being infuriated with people who wonder out loud, "Let's see, was that in October or November?" Don't include everything; sketch in the broad outlines. A companion "sin" is making your comments or stories so long that they become monologues.

2. Bragging

Storyteller Will Rogers once said, "It ain't braggin' if you've done it." Notice that Rogers was talking about achievements, not possessions. He didn't say, "It ain't braggin' if you own it." Bragging about "things" — "toys" — is certainly more obnoxious than telling people what you actually have accomplished.

Focusing too much on yourself can turn people off. Zsa Zsa Gabor (so the old story goes) was talking on and on about her favorite subject — herself. Finally, she stopped short and turned to her partner. "But dahling," she purred, "we must talk about you for a change. . . . How do you like my dress?"

3. Interrogating

Persistence is usually counted as a virtue. However, good small talkers know when to stop probing. The interrogator doesn't. She says, "You should . . . " It's one of her favorite phrases. "Why don't you . . . " runs a close second. "Surely you know that . . . " ranks right up there. Long after a topic has run out of steam, the interrogator is still battering her partner with it. The interrogator generally has strong feelings about the topic and pushes her partner for agreement.

Tone of voice has as much to do with interrogation as does the wording of a question. The interrogator uses a harsh tone of voice rather than a mild or questioning one. Her questions are delivered in an accusatory tone, often belittling or demeaning her partner.

If you are getting put on the spot by an interrogator about something, say, "Why on earth would you ask me about that? I never talk about. . . . " Or, "Are you comfortable talking about that? I'm not." Depersonalize the topic. Move the question from one that makes you uncomfortable to one that is appropriate and energizing.

4. INSISTING ON ONE-UPMANSHIP

The person who always has a better story than yours to tell or a better deal to relate is committing one-upmanship. He can never merely accept a comment or story; he has to top it with one of his own. These people use small talk to make themselves look wonderful — sometimes at the expense of others. They always seek to demonstrate that they are better than the person they are talking to. If you have closed a $1 million deal, they've got a $5 million one to tell about. If you went skiing at Keystone, they went to the Alps.

5. SEEKING FREE ADVICE

This kind of bore always wants to get something for nothing. She corners doctors to ask about her physical symptoms, lawyers to ask about planning her estate, computer systems consultants to get detailed advice on setting up her computer system. She abuses her small talk partners by asking questions she should be asking in a more formal situation. She wants free advice, when she should be paying for it.

6. INTERRUPTING

This bore never lets you get a word in edgewise. He trounces your comments with nonstop verbiage of his own. He insists on having the first, the middle, and the last word. He especially likes to interrupt subordinates and women to show who's more powerful. He ignores questions and insists on directing the conversation himself.

7. REFUSING TO PLAY

Some people were told too often as kids, "It's not polite to talk about yourself." Concerned that they'll appear self-centered, they never tell you anything about themselves. They always toss the ball back in your direction. This isn't being polite — it's refusing to play.

Others downplay what they've done, leaving you to feel quite foolish when, later, you discover the facts. An executive tells about a conversation with his CEO. "I said, 'How was your weekend?' He said, 'Not bad ... played a little golf. How was yours?' Later I heard he and six other CEOs had flown to the Virgin Islands for a weekend golf retreat. I felt out of it. I wish he'd told me the whole story up front."

8. Trying to Make Converts

These people have all the answers and merely want to make converts to their way of thinking. They want confirmation of what they've already decided. When you're listening, keep an open mind to gain understanding, and sometimes, as a result of talking with others, you may even change your point of view. People do expect to be comfortable as they small talk. It's not about trying to change someone's mind or force opinions down their throats.

9. Giving Advice

If you evaluate your own life, you reveal yourself — not a bad thing to do in small talk. But if you evaluate others' lives, you may offend them. Know the difference. Never say, "Why don't you ... " Or even worse, "You should ... " Or "You should have." If you feel that your experience might be helpful to someone else, ask permission. Say, "Would you like to hear about what I did in that kind of situation?"

10. Coming Across as a Bigot

Jokes or comments that refer to race, religion, gender, age, or national origin have no place in today's diverse business world.

You may be saying to yourself, "Well, I'm not guilty of this sin!" But watch out! Insensitivity to others comes out in subtle ways. Ben was discussing potential new hires. "She's a woman, but her references all say she's very committed and decisive." No wonder his comment drew more than a few raised eyebrows from his female colleagues.

When someone you're with makes an out-of-place gesture or statement, practice your assertive skills and simply say, "That's not appropriate." When Art's boss said something that was disparaging of older workers, Art said in a firm but friendly voice, "Let's be sensitive to how that might sound to someone who doesn't know how you respect everybody's input." Tact is the knack of making a point without making an enemy.

The above excerpt from Great Connections *is used with permission.*

Ten Networking Myths

Ron Sukenick

There seem to be certain misconceptions about the networking process, and because of this, many people either don't follow through successfully, or they just don't take the networking process seriously. I thought that I would take a few moments and list what I feel are the ten most common networking myths that many have about the process and give you some ideas about what you can do about them.

MYTH #1: IF YOU DO A GOOD JOB FOR PEOPLE, THEY WILL ALWAYS COME BACK TO YOU.

Not necessarily so. What I mean is sure, they'll come back to you only if they're not starting to build relationships with someone else. Let's say that you feel your long distance telephone carrier is the right choice, you get your bill in the mail each month and with no hesitation you pay it. No big deal, you have other things to think about and you just go right on with everything else you have to get done. Then all of a sudden you meet someone at a chamber of commerce Business-After-Hours. They seem friendly and over a period of a few weeks you get together to discuss what each of you do for a living, actually have lunch once, pass a business lead or two, and the relationship-building process is picking up quickly. Oh, by the way, this person that's your newfound business networking buddy works for a competing long distance carrier. Even though your current long distance carrier is doing a good job, if you made the comparison and everything was equal, would you consider, if asked, switching to the new company? Of course you would if you truly believed in the "Givers gain" philosophy.

Myth #2: If you do a good job for people, they will tell others about you.

If this was true you can only imagine the amount of business leads and referrals you would have. What is true is that the only way you're going to really, and I mean really, kick in word-of-mouth marketing is to far exceed their expectations. It's called going into legendary status with the people you do business with. A great story that has been around for years that exemplifies what I'm talking about is the one where a lady brings a set of automobile tires into the famed Nordstrom department store and requests a full refund. Within minutes, the cashier returns her money, thanks her for the visit, and the customer walks out satisfied. Now you're asking what's so legendary about that and the answer is that Nordstrom doesn't sell tires. You see, the point I want to make is that if you want people to talk about you, you have to far exceed their expectations. I'm certain that you agree with me that Nordstrom had done just that.

Myth #3: If I give to others, I can expect that it will come back to me in a short period of time.

Sure, this is possible if the person that you're interacting with is in a position to fulfill your need at that time. This is not the rule but the exception. What really takes place is that you start to build what I call "Net Profits" — building equity in your networking system in that what goes around will come around. It may not come around at that very moment but when you eliminate the unfulfilled expectations, good things start to happen and the process of giving and receiving provides a pretty solid foundation for building relationships with others. A quote that I always enjoy repeating is one by the English poet William

Blake that says to "Always give without remembering, always receive without forgetting." It is a great rule to live by, in my opinion.

Myth #4: Networking Takes Too Much Time and Energy.

If you include it as a part of your marketing strategy, it isn't. Networking is not a place that you're going to but a place you're coming from. Instead of walking up to the fireplace and getting warm, think of yourself as though coming from being the fire. By doing this, you'll bring your whole self to the meeting and people will be impressed with your presence. Don't confuse it with something that you have to spend a lot of time preparing for. Why not just have it be a part of everything you already do? Remember, it's a process for developing and maintaining contacts and it's a passion that one develops from the work that they do. So don't just think of networking as something that you do sometimes and some places but as something that you can do with ease all the time and everywhere.

Myth #5: You Can't Have Your Cake and Eat It Too.

Of course you can if you really want to. People all over this world are sharing ideas and their resources, discovering that it makes sense to help others. Because people are sharing, they enjoy a sense of self-confidence, higher productivity, and a feeling of belonging. They're building bigger and stronger relationships with others. With networking, you feel secure and proud that you know people that can get things done.

Myth #6: I Won't Bother Following Up On This One — It'll Never Pan Out.

It is so often that we underestimate the opportunities that present themselves, that we fail to take the steps that are so necessary in reaping life's biggest rewards. Follow-up is a constant process that must be adhered to. Never underestimate the power of opportunity that someone can provide to you or one of your networking buddies. Sometimes a business lead can take months or even years to pan out.

There are times when the person you followed up on is not in a position to help you today, but down the road they may be and their remembrance of how you followed up, took an interest in who they were, and your willingness to help them will be long remembered after the deed has been done. Whatever you do, follow everyone through as though your life depended on it.

Myth #7: But I don't really know anyone.

Who said that you needed to know anyone in order to start the networking process? I sure didn't. What do you do during your normal work day? Do you work with others? Whom do you speak with on the phone during the normal course of your job? What social activities do you like and are you participating in any now? Do you practice any religious beliefs? Where do you go shopping? There are so many opportunities to meet people and the good news is that they're just as interested in meeting you.

Myth #8: What you don't know can't hurt you.

In the highly competitive and impersonal world that we live in, there's no substitute for facts, information, and knowledge. In fact, one of the greatest challenges for people in business today is gaining access to the information they need when they need it. We're in the information age and if what everybody is saying is true, then the flow of information that will be coming to us in the next twelve years will more than double. How can you expect to keep up with the times all by yourself? We're living in a specialized society and there are so many people becoming experts in areas you know very little about. Why not consider tapping into their resources and expertise? Others will help to keep you informed. Remember that others are more than willing to put their experience and knowledge to work for you.

Myth #9: You only go around once.

You have a whole world of possibilities at your fingertips and you go around as often as you like. Not all networkers network the same way. Some are aggressive and will go to any networking opportunity that they hear about. Others are more targeted and focused in their efforts. You can attend chamber meetings on a monthly basis and affiliate with organizations that meet weekly. By listening for the opportunities and being clear on what you and others want to accomplish, the variety is endless and so is your networking experience.

MYTH #10: PEOPLE TAKE ADVANTAGE OF YOU WHEN THEY CAN.

Sure, there are people that will try to do that from time to time, but in the long run, if you maintain integrity and stay focused, you'll make more good decisions than bad. Don't go out blindly and fail to safeguard your most important trade secrets or prized possessions. You still have to pay attention to whom you're associating with and you should check references when appropriate.

The above excerpt from Networking Your Way to Success *is used with permission.*

Lip Service Is Not Enough

Steve Lawson

Why is it that two people of the same profession, in two different but similarly structured referral networking groups, following the same program, can sometimes receive vastly different amounts of referral business? If I ask both people whether they are following the system — which I, as a professional trainer, teach to the groups — I usually get the same answer from both: Yes, I joined the group, I go every week, and I follow the program!

At this point I try to sit down with the person having problems generating referrals, and dig deeper into her perception of "following the system." Invariably, this is where the problem lies. Her interpretation of "following the system" is often very different from the more successful member's. I usually discover that unsuccessful networkers are only paying lip service to the system — going through the motions at a minimum level. Quite often they are simply unaware of the depth of commitment and the amount of work that's required to realize good referral results.

Next, I try to ascertain why the person isn't doing the necessary work. Is she a "can't do" or a "won't do" type of networker? If she's a "won't do," then I know she is not going to be a successful networker. Whatever I tell her, I know she won't do it. More often than not, this type of person is looking for a quick, easy fix, and is not prepared to invest the time and effort needed to make the networking system work.

On the other hand, if she is a "can't do" type, then there is some potential for success. The "can't dos" often simply don't know what they need to be doing to generate great results.

Here, then, is what I try to teach the "can't do" networking student who wants to do more than just pay lip service: To be successful at networking and thus increase your referral business, you must do four things:

1. Participate

This is the hard part, because it's where the work starts. Great networkers don't mind going to networking meetings, even if they start early in the morning. They consider weekly attendance requirements not a chore but a golden opportunity to expand their contacts, build relationships, and promote their businesses.

Participate fully in your networking group. Attend all meetings, on time, with a positive attitude; support all other members; introduce visitors and new contacts to the group. If your group is following a tried and tested system that generates results, don't modify the program to suit yourself, but adapt yourself to the program.

2. Communicate

Networking is primarily a matter of building relationships. You can't network effectively just by attending weekly meetings; to develop strong, lasting relationships, you must constantly interact with your associates outside the regular meeting environment.

Not long ago I met a man who had been a member of the same networking breakfast group for over eight years. He amazed me by telling me that never a week went by that he didn't meet with at least one person in his group. When asked why, his answer was quite revealing: "I can't afford not to. I need to keep stimulating my associates to find business for me!"

3. Educate

Not only must we communicate regularly, our message must be clear and deliberate. This is where many people's networking effort often fails: most of their hard work and effort is wasted because they are not educating while they are networking. In the thousands of presentations I've witnessed, far too many people have effectively communicated nothing at all.

I watched a travel agent stand in front of twenty-five business associates and say, "I guess you all know what a travel agent does, so if you are going on holiday call me." I could almost hear her audience thinking, Nope, can't take a vacation this week. How much more powerful and effective it would have been if the travel agent had said, "Last week our agency bought a large block of Caribbean cruise tickets at a ridiculously low price. If you're talking to friends, clients, or business associates, and they complain of being overworked and tired, tell them you know of a travel agency that has some unbelievable three-, four-, or five-day cruises at amazingly low prices! Listen for two key phrases this week: 'I'm tired,' and 'I'm overworked.' When you hear those phrases, think of me." By saying this, she would have both educated her associates and got them looking for a specific kind of referral for her.

If you're a member of a referral group, treat the other members as your sales team, with yourself as the sales manager. Each week, give them specific instructions about the kind of business to look for. This will bring you results!

4. Reciprocate

Networking organizations thrive when the members all subscribe to the "Givers gain" philosophy: "If I help you, you will help me, and we will all gain." This is the cornerstone of all successful networking. Without it, the system breaks down. Why would anyone want to go out of his way to look out for business opportunities for you, if he did not feel you were helping him?

You must participate in your networking group with the sincere intention of helping the other members become successful. Always network with a spirit of sharing, and try honestly to help each other. Don't just say you care — show them you care. Lip service is never enough.

A Thousand Mahalos

Patti Salvucci, with contributions from Tom Fleming

A colleague complains: that great downtown print shop that delivers free is moving out to the suburbs because they weren't getting enough business to pay the rent. A neighbor tells you that her favorite sandwich shop — the one that opened at six every morning — has closed and now she has to make her own lunches. You think: I wish I had known about these places.

Why do excellent business like these, businesses that offer five-star service and top-quality products, so often fail? Why do we hear about them, about their special attributes, only after they've been around many months or years, or when they are forced to move or close?

I believe it is because too many business owners work *in*, rather than *on*, their businesses, as Michael Gerber explains in his book *The E-Myth Revisited*. Many small-business owners are so focused on the technical aspects of their business that they fail to see the overall picture — that building a successful business involves much more than just the basic productive skills of the owner. Among other things, the business owner who offers a uniquely valuable product or service must take action to get the word out to potential customers. That's where my role as a networking consultant comes into play. I teach would-be entrepreneurs that building a strong referral-based system of marketing is one of the best ways to work on their business.

I often see businesses that are achieving half or less of their desired or expected business volume. The owners are very adept in the operational aspects of their businesses, but they have little money available for advertising and no clue as to how to get their products or services before the public. As a consultant with extensive experience in referral marketing, I tend to see such cases from the perspective of both a professional and a customer.

Recently, while visiting a friend in Honolulu, I wanted to experience a real gourmet meal, so we asked my friend's neighbor to suggest a top-quality restaurant. The neighbor recommended a small establishment called Tai Pan and told us to "ask for Ernesto," the owner. We called and made reservations.

When we arrived, we were surprised to see only two other diners in the restaurant. We were puzzled. The atmosphere was relaxed and pleasant; the decor was simple but elegant. Why were there not more customers? Could it be that the food was, after all, disappointing?

Ernesto arrived with our menus and, in a low-key way, described in detail the evening's specialties. They sounded impressive — and difficult to choose between.

Before long our appetizers arrived, and we began to understand why the neighbor had recommended the restaurant. They were perfect — artfully arranged, and every bit a food lover's dream. Our entrées then confirmed our opinion that this was a special place.

So why, I wondered, were we the only two diners left in the restaurant at this early hour? Such a fabulous restaurant, and no customers! Perhaps it was too new, and word hadn't had time to spread. I ventured this idea to Ernesto.

"Yes," said Ernesto. "We are only three years young!"

Now I was intrigued. How did he advertise himself? What was his marketing strategy?

"Word of mouth," he answered. "We do not advertise." He explained that, if he continued to run a high-quality establishment, word would spread.

Was he a member of the local chamber of commerce? No, he said. He didn't have the time.

After I flew back home to Boston, I wondered how I might help this man. One of the best restaurants in Honolulu, and hardly anyone in the community knew he was there! I wrote him a letter telling him how much I enjoyed the meal and how wonderful I thought his restaurant was.

I went on to suggest that he shouldn't take it for granted that word of his great business would spread on its own — that visibility, as well as the development of relationships within the community, were crucial in bringing financial success and longevity. Get to know your neighbors, I wrote. Start an incentive program to encourage your regular patrons to pass the word to their clients, customers, and friends. I enclosed a copy of Dr. Ivan Misner's book *The World's Best Known Marketing Secret: Building Your Business with Word-of Mouth Marketing.*

Several weeks passed. Then I received a rather large package in the mail. Inside it was a box of chocolate-covered macadamia nuts (which were delicious and which disappeared within hours) and a note thanking me for the book and for my interest in his business. "A thousand mahalos!" ("Mahalo," he explained, was "Thank you" in Hawaiian.)

Did I have an impact on Ernesto's business? I hope so, at least a small one. I want Ernesto, and thousands of small-business owners like him, to understand that simply being great at what you do is not enough; that to make a business successful you must relinquish some of the technical and managerial work and become a marketer as well; and that a systematic pursuit of word-of-mouth marketing means spending time establishing relationships with other people by joining a business networking group.

> Simply being great at what you do is not enough; to make a business successful you must relinquish some of the technical and managerial work and become a marketer as well.

What's different about your business? How are you better than the competition? Who are your target customers? This is what you have to tell the world. And the best place to start is face-to-face, through stable, long-lasting, mutually beneficial relationships. That's what referral-based marketing is all about.

16

The Instinct to Help Others

DEEP WITHIN EACH OF US LIES AN URGE TO HELP OTHER PEOPLE WHEN WE RECOGNIZE a need. This is a social instinct, and it is part of what makes us human. In the next three articles, the authors demonstrate how that need can manifest itself and how we can put it to good effect. Victor Blumenthal tells of how his daughter recognized his business networking talents and gently pushed him to develop them in a referral network setting; Bill Cates exhorts us to focus on finding different ways to help others with referrals; and Don Morgan analyzes the giving aspect of networking and finds within it three major components.

Networking for Networking's Sake

Victor Blumenthal

It was my daughter who told me, "Dad, networking is you!"

At first I wasn't sure what she meant.

"Look at your Rolodex!" she said. Yes, after thirty-five years in key executive positions with major corporations, I had acquired quite a list of contacts.

"And the way you're always helping people solve their problems or fulfill their needs by providing a phone number and telling them, 'Mention my name. I'm sure they can help you.'"

I agreed that I enjoyed solving problems by putting people in touch with each other. It was the process that fascinated me, the idea that no matter the problem, there was someone out there who, if you could only get in touch, could provide a solution.

Matching needs with resources was a process I had learned and refined over my years as an executive. It was based on two acquired abilities:

1. The skill of listening to people and identifying a need.

2. The art of building trusted relationships with resourceful people.

I have also long felt that helping others, a key component of successful networking, is one of the most rewarding personal goals you can achieve. Finding that satisfaction again and again reinforces the skills you need to become a master networker. The other reward — the business that is referred to you by people who like and trust you — becomes secondary.

Over time, networking to help others becomes an automatic, almost instinctive response to life around you. As a lifelong, habitual networker, you make two friends every time you make a connection: the person whose problems you've helped solve by putting him in touch with someone who can solve the problems, and the person to whom you've brought the opportunity to solve the problem. Both friends will seek to reward you for your actions — but having made friends is the best reward of all.

> Many people are hesitant about getting into networking, unsure of their ability to help others with useful contacts, and uncomfortable about the possibility of receiving referrals but not being able to return the favor.

Many people are hesitant about getting into networking, unsure of their ability to help others with useful contacts, and uncomfortable about the possibility of receiving referrals but not being able to return the favor. It's normal to feel this way. It takes time, focus, and practice to master any skilled activity, especially the very human skill of networking. But if you keep in mind the very basic principle on which networking is based — "what goes around comes around" — you'll get the hang of it quickly and find yourself automatically helping people with your network of contacts. Then, when you see the good a simple referral can do for a friend, you'll feel very comfortable with the benefits you'll find yourself receiving in return.

"So why don't you join this networking group?" asked my daughter. It was BNI she was talking about. Thus I found myself, for the first time, being encouraged to attend a networking program in the community.

So I joined the local chapter of about a hundred members, all from different professions, none of whom I knew. At my first meeting, the speaker talked about his product, hardware and software that linked personal computers with LCD overhead projectors. After the meeting I introduced myself to him and mentioned a good friend of mine, a university professor who was looking for exactly this kind of software. I gave the speaker my card and my friend's phone number and suggested that he call. Before long he was invited to demonstrate his products to a group of professors, and he ended up selling them more than $40,000 worth of equipment.

For an experienced networker, making this kind of referral is unconditional. I expect no direct benefit from my actions. But I know that when I help others I am ultimately helping myself — that, in the end, "Givers gain."

Be a Referral Giver

Bill Cates

Since building a referral business is not just a set of techniques but a mind-set, you must become an expert at giving referrals. Serve your referral alliances, your customers, and your friends as best you can by *helping them with referrals* as often as you can — not just by finding prospects for them, but by helping them meet people and businesses that will serve them, whatever their need. There is no better way to send the message (or should I say plant the seed) that you work from referrals than to practice the giving side of it.

Let's say you meet someone at a business event who might become a good referral alliance. The next time you get together, do whatever you can to serve him. Try to find a way to refer him either a prospect or someone with a product or service that will help solve a problem.

GIVE REFERRALS FROM YOUR CATALOG

We talked so much earlier about having your own "personal catalog" of products and services. It's important that you develop two types of catalogs. One is a network of companies and individuals with services related to your product or service. When you learn that prospects and customers have a need you can't fill or a problem you can't solve, you're ready to refer them to someone who can.

The other catalog is more general: it contains companies and individuals in a broad range of categories that you can refer on occasion — car mechanic, graphic artist, dry cleaner, or specialty advertising company, for example.

PRACTICE THE GOLDEN RULE OF REFERRAL GIVING

When you give referrals to other salespeople and entrepreneurs, make sure you give them in the way that you'd like to receive them. Let's say you run into someone who might be a great prospect for one of your referral alliances (or even a customer). Here are a few reminders on how to pass on this referral:

1. Get permission from the new prospect to give his or her name to your referral alliance. This way your referral alliance can be proactive and not have to wait for the prospect to call her.

2. Demonstrate enthusiasm to the prospect about who will be calling them. Tell the prospect about how this salesperson has served other customers.

3. Upgrade the referral as much as you can. Have plenty of information to give to your referral alliance. Make certain to represent the information accurately.

4. Don't sit on hot referrals. Pass them on as quickly as possible.

5. Don't give the same referral to more than one or two referral alliances. If you do, make sure that all parties know.

When people ask me for referrals, I do my best to accommodate them. After I give them the names and numbers, I upgrade the referrals. Then I volunteer to warm up the prospects — to say good things about the salesperson before they call. Once someone has earned my trust and respect and has served me well, I do all I can to give him or her high-quality referrals.

The above excerpt from Unlimited Referrals *is used with permission.*

The Trilogy of Network Leverage

Don Morgan

There are three ways to increase the power of your network and improve its ability to help you achieve goals. Fortunately, anyone can create this leverage by understanding three fundamental characteristics of human nature. However, only those dedicated to becoming master networkers will commit to mastering the arts of (1) friendship, (2) generosity, and (3) character. A person who creates this trilogy of leverage will be on the road to unlocking the full power of networks.

FRIENDSHIP

Friends like to help friends. At some point in your life, you've helped a good friend do something you might not have enjoyed doing — painting a bedroom, helping out with a move — just because he was your friend. You really couldn't avoid it. If you make good friends of your networking associates, you gain the same kind of leverage.

How do you turn network associates into good friends? There's nothing complicated or mysterious about it. Think back about how you and your best friend became best friends. You went places together, did things together, and suddenly one day realized that you had been best friends for some time without even thinking about it.

That's what you do with your networking partners. Go places with them, do things with them, help them when they need help. Soon you'll discover that associates have become good friends. Not all of them, of course, but the more effort you put into it, the more friends you'll make. And the more powerful your network will be in helping you achieve your goals.

GENEROSITY

You're at a party. You're handed several presents. You don't have anything to give in return. How do you feel? A little less than wonderful, right? It's human nature to want to give a gift in return.

The same holds true in networking circles. When you give something to a network associate — a business referral, assistance with tax returns, emotional support — she will want to give you something in return. Perhaps you won't get a return gift immediately. However, the more you give to your networking partners, the more inclined they will be to reciprocate.

A true gift is an unconditional gift; you give without expecting anything in return. However, you usually get something back anyway. First, you gain the satisfaction of having helped a friend. Second, human nature dictates that you will probably get something in return. When you least expect it, you may receive a gift worth far more to you than the time and effort you expended.

CHARACTER

The most lasting impression others have of you is their first impression: the way you looked and behaved when they first met you. If that's a bad impression, it may take a long time to overcome and others may be reluctant to get involved with you. A master networker understands this and puts a lot of effort into creating a good first impression by dressing and behaving appropriately at all times.

However, your long-term image goes well beyond how you look at first glance. Equal in importance are three character attributes: responsibility, reliability, and readiness. When the group needs some task done or problem handled, do you take responsibility? Can you be counted on to come through whenever the need arises? Are you quick to volunteer your services?

Above and beyond the first visual impression you make, your responsibility for, reliability within, and readiness to participate in group activities become the most important aspects of your image in the long run. If the group sees you as an asset by virtue of your character, individuals in the group will trust you, rely on you, and enjoy associating with you. And they will feel comfortable referring their friends and associates to you — and your business.

In the end, this trilogy of networking leverage comes down to an old principle, known in some parts of the world as the Golden Rule. Networkers just phrase it a little differently: "Givers gain."

17

The Law of Mutual Benefit

PEOPLE NETWORK IN PART BECAUSE THEY WANT TO BE HELPFUL. BUT THAT'S NOT THE whole story, of course. They also network because they expect to reap benefits in return. And that is why good networking is so successful: the good effort you expend on behalf of others comes back to you multiplied. George Fraser tells how the helping hand he gave a promising young businessperson was repaid many times over in the form of a valuable business opportunity; and Leslie Taylor compares the mutually beneficial nature of a close networking partnership to the buddy system used by swimmers.

Make Networking Work for You

George Fraser

While working at a Black Expo in Cleveland recently, I ran into Lynn Feaster, a young woman who had come to me about five years ago with several other eager young African-American entrepreneurs seeking advice on starting their own businesses. Lynn was starting her own travel agency. I had attempted to support her in her business and she, in turn, had supported my SuccessSource endeavors. She and I had maintained contact over the ensuing years.

When we happened to meet again recently, she reminded me of how I had encouraged her in the early days of her business. And since I had a booth at the Black Expo, she purchased some of the products we were selling and asked if we could get together soon so she could bring me up to date on a new opportunity that she was involved in that I might also find interesting. I happily agreed to meet with this go-getting, natural-born networker.

Just a few days after our chance encounter, she called to set an appointment. On the telephone, she was charming and quick to the point. "George, it was great seeing you again — you have grown more successful each year," she said. She had my attention. "I have come across a significant opportunity that could result in thousands, if not millions of dollars for my business, your business, and the city of Cleveland." She continued to have my attention. "But I need some help and advice. Would it be possible to see you soon to discuss it?"

With an approach like that, could there be any doubt that I would meet with her? "Of course," I said, and of course, I meant it. We met, and as it turned out, she had not overstated her case. The opportunity was as important for me as it was for her. She brought a group of close friends — her support network — to the meeting and outlined her immediate needs to me. Once a television-commercial writer, she had been awarded a multimillion-dollar contract to start a pilot program for a black-oriented home shopping network. She needed an office space within two days so that she could meet some critical deadlines. I listened carefully to her proposal and then agreed to help.

On Lynn's behalf, I went to Saad Khayat, a prominent attorney who owns several small office buildings and apartment complexes. I had not known Saad long, but I was helping him put together a group of African-Americans for another business venture. We had an established networking relationship that I wanted to expand to include Lynn. When I called, Saad was pleasant and open. I explained the situation briefly and simply asked if he could meet with Lynn to hear her proposal and possibly help her meet her immediate needs. He thanked me and offered that he had been looking for a tenant for a small office building that he owned. Saad said that if I recommended Lynn as a tenant, then that was all he needed. He and Lynn met, and several days later, she was moving into her new office space in his building.

As soon as she was set up, Lynn called to thank me for my assistance in establishing her new business. I then called Saad and thanked him for helping Lynn and he, in turn, was grateful to me for helping him find a reliable new tenant. By the way, I had mentioned how her proposal eventually would prove to be nearly as rewarding for me as for Lynn. Well, she has offered me twenty-five minutes of free time to advertise my products. Now, that is how effective networking works! Everybody felt good about the process. Nobody was asked to do something beyond his or her means. Everybody gained something. In this case, it was win-win, and win again!

Networking works when you fully understand that there is *inherent value* in every human being and every human relationship regardless of title or position. Only when we mature enough to stop *prejudging* people as to their worthiness of our assistance can we truly give without expectation. When you give first, without expectation, you are networking for the benefit of others, and therefore the law of increasing returns will reward you tenfold. There are no exceptions to this law. Had the people in my life prejudged me because I lived in publicly subsidized tenement housing or because I mopped floors at La Guardia Airport, I would never have had the assistance I needed to fully blossom and maximize my full human potential. At some point neither would most African-Americans. This is the spiritual and philosophical underpinning of effective networking.

> Networking works when you fully understand that there is inherent value in every human being and every human relationship regardless of title or position.

Networking works when you understand that there is very little that you can do or have in life without working with other people. Therefore, you work diligently on building and developing your infrastructure of human resources.

Networking works when you understand that the whole is greater than the sum of its parts. Networks must be built upon a foundation of established relationships, first of all, but they can extend beyond. Building that essential foundation, however, takes time. You must have an established rapport with your key core of networking contacts.

Networking works when you can comfortably and successfully match needs and resources. Creating the win-win situation is the optimum, and although it may not always be exactly an even exchange, often things work out that way in the long run.

The above excerpt from Success Runs in Our Race *is used with permission.*

The Buddy System

Leslie Taylor

When I worked as a swim instruc-
tor and lifeguard during high school and college, I taught a cardinal
rule of swimming: Never swim alone. People who swim alone run a
high risk of getting hurt. Instead, use the "buddy system." Always
swim with another person, and watch out for each other.

The same rule applies to business. Too many businesspeople are
swimming alone out in the business world and running a risk of
getting hurt — and many do.

How can we implement the buddy system in our businesses?
Here are several innovative ways.

BRAGGING BUDDIES

Although most of us like to receive compliments, we may find it
awkward to respond to them. Someone praises you, and you say, "Oh,
it was nothing," or, "It was all Joe's good work that made the difference." You may make a point with Joe by saying this, but you're
cutting your own throat, because people may believe you and go
directly to Joe for their next job. It's better to accept the compliment
gracefully and say, "Thank you."

We don't usually like to brag on ourselves, either — but to succeed
in business, you have to. Most businesspeople brag by buying ads
and think nothing about it; it's just business. But the best way to
brag, and to receive compliments at the same time, is to have a
bragging buddy — someone who sings your praises to others at
strategic moments, and about whom you brag to others. Smart
businesspeople cultivate bragging buddies through their network.

When attending a contact social or business event, take someone
with you who knows your business and background and whose

business and background you know. Act as though your buddy is a visiting dignitary whom others need to meet and know. As you approach people, first introduce yourself, then ask whether they have met the person you are with. Follow up with a testimonial about your buddy. Take turns introducing each other to different people, and by the end of the function you will have had more fun than anyone else in the room, and you will probably have made at least one contact on which you can follow up for future business or other benefits.

COLD-CALLING BUDDIES

I know of a CPA, with virtually no experience calling on businesses, who went cold-calling with a sales professional in the payroll processing business. Every time they buddied up and cold-called together, they both came away with new clients. They introduced each other, answered questions about their profession, and expanded their business. And they had fun!

NOMINATING BUDDIES

The Small Business Administration, chambers of commerce, and most volunteer organizations give awards. Ever wonder who nominates the people who get them? Often it's a client or a business friend. Wouldn't you like to be nominated? Find out about local awards; research the qualifications. Nominate someone you feel is qualified and deserving. Ask a client or business associate — a buddy — to nominate you. Winning such an award is great advertising.

TESTIFYING BUDDIES

Have you observed someone giving leadership, direction, time, or energy to a business or volunteer organization? Has someone helped you solve a problem? Send her a thank-you note or write a testimonial letter; be specific about the value she's added. Send a copy to her boss. Offer your services as a reference.

What about yourself? Has someone — a satisfied customer, a grateful vendor — given you testimonials or praise? Ask him to write it out, or write it yourself and ask his permission to use it in advertisements, flyers, or brochures to market your business. Or invite him to attend a business mixer with you or nominate you for an award.

Educational Buddies

Here's a great way to meet new contacts and win clients: ask a buddy to team up with you and create an informational marketing seminar. This approach is used successfully by CPAs, attorneys, retirement planning professionals, skin care consultants, and many others. Share the costs with your buddy, and you'll have fun sharing the information and the clients.

As you can see, the buddy system can be very useful in marketing yourself to the community or your target market. The only limits are your imagination and resolve. But don't try it alone!

18

What a Little Networking Can Do

BY NOW YOU PROBABLY HAVE A BETTER UNDERSTANDING OF THE GENERAL PRINCIPLES that lie behind good networking and the basic reasons why a strong network is a good thing to develop and nurture. But maybe it's time to get more specific. Exactly what goals can good networking help you attain? In the next two pieces, Harvey Mackay tells you ten specific ways a good network can help you, and Paul and Sarah Edwards, along with Rick Benzel, describe three types of business objectives that networking can help you achieve.

Harvey's Top-Ten List

Harvey Mackay

It's not enough for me to convince you that you need a network. I want you to know *why*. Here are ten reasons:

1. A NETWORK REPLACES THE WEAKNESS OF THE INDIVIDUAL WITH THE STRENGTH OF THE GROUP.

. . . If I had written this book five years ago, I would have suggested that people wanting to connect with a particular kind of group could find what they were looking for at only one place — the library.

But now you have the option: the library or the Internet.

You can be on line instantly, communicating with people in whatever network you're interested in.

The benefits of this kind of networking have been hyped so much already, the only thing left is to sound a cautionary note.

Groups, be they the old-fashioned, meet-for-lunch-every-Wednesday types or the Internet variety, are ready-made for the group, not custom-made for you.

Like ready-made suits, they're not tailored to fit you individually but to fit some basic group prototype. If you're looking for a scholarly analysis of nineteenth-century Guatemalan postmarks or a rent-a-car discount, there's a ready-made group for you. If you're looking for the best urologist in town, or trying to find out whether your department is going to get axed in the next downsizing, you need your own personal custom-made group. . . .

2. MIRROR, MIRROR ON THE WALL.

A network is the magic mirror that can show you how the dress *really* looks on you before you wear it to the party.

Does the big report you've been sweating over the last two months make sense?

People who write or sell for a living, whether it's called "marketing planning" or "copywriting" or "just plain peddling," need to know if their stuff works. Who is going to tell you before you go out and make an ass of yourself?

Your network.

Get a network going to read your copy or listen to your presentation — in return for which, of course, you do the same for them.

Your network can identify what's unclear or confusing or simply wrong.

They'll catch the typos and grammatical errors you never dreamed you made. They'll tell what's funny, what isn't, what's perceptive, what's offensive. . . .

Asking for a raise. Interviewing for a job. Presenting a report. Whatever it is: Your network can be your sounding board to learn what works and what doesn't. You'll avoid mistakes. You'll be helping others with the same needs as yours. . . .

3. KNOW THINE ENEMY THROUGH THINE NETWORK.

. . . [A]s everyone in business knows, you have to know what the competition is up to.

Who will tip you off if a key employee may be ready to jump ship to the competition?

Who can you count on to help you counteract someone circulating negative gossip about you or your company?

Who will tell you when others are making inquiries about you? . . .

It's always smart to have some pipeline, however informal, into the enemy camp.

Suppliers. Bankers. Lawyers. Customers. Former customers. Employees. Former employees. Salespeople. Truck drivers. Spouses. Girlfriends. Car dealers. Bartenders at the cross-town factory's favorite watering hole.

PEOPLE LOVE TO TALK! . . .

4. MY NETWORK CAN HELP YOU EXPAND YOUR NETWORK.

. . . One of the big mistakes you can make when you're starting your career is being afraid to use your network to ask for help.

Where to start?

There's Dad. There's Mom. But all their well-meaning career advice gets jumbled up with the other stuff about brushing your teeth and eating your broccoli. You need a fresh eye.

Whose?

Best bet: a family adviser, particularly a lawyer or a banker, a rich relative, one of your parents' bosses at work — anyone old, experienced in business, with a wide range of contracts and some personal or professional connection to your family.

Why? Because most so-called gurus and old fuds like me are downright flattered when someone asks their opinion — on anything.

We have fewer axes to grind. It no longer seems like every kid who walks through the door is trying to take your job away or waste your time.

Whether we've formally inscribed it or not, we have a network, and inevitably, it's going to evaporate along with us, and we know it.

Still, we like being a player, and one way to do that is to pass along our time-honored war stories and offer a little godlike advice to whoever will listen. . . .

5. A NETWORK CAN ENRICH YOUR LIFE ANYWHERE IN THE WORLD.

How many non-Americans are there in your network?

With phone rates, e-mail, and faxes measured in pennies these days, it's hardly any more costly to build a global network than a local one.

It's not tough to learn about customs and holidays abroad. Most places where you can find a greeting card will also sell you a global calendar so you know when to send it. I'll start you off with a couple of freebies: In Holland, St. Nicholas Day is December 6. In Hong Kong, Chinese New Year is always celebrated between January 21 and February 19.

One of the most powerful global networks is Guanxi, or overseas Chinese. There are 50 million people in this network, and they control huge wealth because of the importance that the extended family has to Chinese business.

In France, a huge percentage of the corporate bigwigs are graduates of the École Nationale d'Administration or the Polytechnique. . . .

And then there's that wonderful old-boy network in Russia — the Communists. They're just itching to stop reminiscing and start giving each other high-buck government jobs again. . . .

6. A NETWORK CAN PROVIDE YOU WITH NEW EXPERIENCES AND KNOWLEDGE.

I know a fellow who manufactured waffle irons. He sold his company for more money than he ever thought possible and retired at the age of fifty. By age fifty and three months, he was climbing the walls. He'd been a racing fan all his life, so he decided to go into the horse business.

The first horse he bought never made it to the track. The second and third were a little better. They earned modest sums before they too broke down.

The fourth horse was the charm. While he didn't actually make money on it, he entered it at several of the better tracks in the country, where it won a few races and lasted for several seasons. . . .

Horse owners are a unique subculture. Many couldn't tell a hock from a stock. They compete with each other for goals that are essentially meaningless. Ninety percent lose money, and those who make money generally don't need it to begin with.

But still, you have only to look at the beaming faces in those winner's circle pictures to realize that the satisfaction of owning a racehorse has nothing to do with anything that makes economic sense.

It comes from being momentarily successful in a slightly glamorous, slightly naughty, enterprise far removed from the world of waffle irons.

"A good horse will take you to places you never dreamed of," Mr. Waffle Iron told me.

True enough.

Thus it is that even for those of us who stamp out waffle irons while fantasizing of rubbing elbows with the Willie Shoemakers of the world, there are networks to match our dreams.

7. NETWORKING CAN HELP YOU HELP OTHERS.

Networking can be very rewarding for people who work the system on their own behalf. It can also be rewarding for people who work it on behalf of others. . . .

Charitable and civic organizations are desperate for volunteers, especially fundraisers. The best fundraisers are people willing to call their friends and associates and ask them for money — particularly if those friends and associates are wealthy and beholden to the callers in some way. . . .

There's a creative way to combine your efforts on behalf of individuals with your fundraising duties.

When I'm asked for a favor, I'll often tell the caller, "I'll be happy to make a 'best efforts' attempt on your behalf — on one condition."

"Uh-oh. What's that?"

"If I deliver, then I want you to make a donation for $_____ to _____ charity." (I fill in the blanks based on the difficulty of the task at hand and a kind of seat-of-the-pants rotation among the United Way, the American Cancer Society, the American Heart Association, and a few others.) . . .

8. Job security? Don't rely on the corporation. Rely on your network.

. . . Your network can be formal or informal. That is, you can (1) dream up a company-approved team project that operates through standard company procedures, that will put you into a close working relationship with people in other departments; (2) establish a "buddy system," a back-channel network of people who people will watch out for possible slots in their area for which you may train or qualify in return for your doing the same for them; or (3) do both. . . .

9. A network can make you look good.

No salesperson who knew the names of his customers' kids ever went broke.

Knowing the spouse's name, unfortunately, is no guarantee.

You haven't seen your old buddy, Buddy, in a couple of years. You call him for lunch.

"How have you been, Buddy?"

"Great."

"How's Budette?"

"Budette ran off with her psychiatrist. They're living in Anchorage."

"Oh. Well, how's that terrific dog of yours, Squat?"

"Squat died. I have a new dog now, Grunt."

"Oh."

Not a pretty sight. I know. It's happened to me too. A name and a few scribbled notes on a 3 x 5 card do not constitute a network. You have to keep it fine-tuned or you're going to run into a lot of Buddy-type situations. Two years is too long between tune-ups. . . .

To keep your network up and running, freshen up each entry at least once every six months. . . .

10. A network expands your financial reach infinitely.

So far we've talked about networking among individuals.

Barter, sophisticated modern barter, is networking among corporations. What makes it different from personal networking is that barter is networking stripped down to the bare essentials, cold-blooded tit-for-tat exchanges. . . .

Let's say you run a United States–based chemical producer doing business in Africa. We'll call it the Chemco Company. You've agreed to take locally made sheets and pillowcases as well as a certain amount of production time at a weaving mill to satisfy an obligation. You have no use for 100,000 sheets and pillowcases, nor for the production time, nor do you have a clue as to how to market them.

Enter the barter company.

They happen to handle several hotel chains for clients interested in bartering.

Hotel company A winds up with Chemco's sheets and pillow-cases. Hotel company B wants towels, and they want them with their monogram on them. Hotel company B winds up with the production time at the mill, where towels are made according to B's specs. Chemco winds up with room, food, and beverage trade credits for its sales force to use at hotels.

The above excerpt from the bestseller Dig Your Well Before You're Thirsty *is used with permission from Harvey Mackay, author of this and two other New York Times bestsellers,* Swim With The Sharks Without Being Eaten Alive *and* Beware the Naked Man Who Offers You His Shirt.

Networking Three Ways

Paul and Sarah Edwards and Rick Benzel

Perhaps networking can best be summed up with the expression "You help me, and I'll help you.". . . As a teaming-up activity, however, networking goes beyond being a convenient way to make contacts and get business leads. A network can become a team of individuals who actively work together for one another's success in any combination of the following three ways.

1. Networking as a Marketing Team. Many networks are, in fact, or could be, highly effective marketing teams in which each person takes on the responsibility of learning as much as she or he can about the businesses of other members and each actively works to promote and sell the others' services. In some networking groups . . . members are required to bring referrals to each meeting and actually carry a business card case containing one another's cards. Such groups are essentially mutual-referral networks, and they consider one another to be extensions of their own businesses. . . .

The key to making networking a marketing team effort lies in joining networks or linking up with others in a network who are willing to view networking activities as more than a quick chance to meet new business prospects. When a group takes a longer-term perspective of working to build one another's businesses, there are multiple mutually beneficial marketing activities they can explore. The Seattle Chamber of Commerce, for example, offers an annual business expo as part of its member services. These annual business expos provide a way for members to jointly market their businesses. And as we mentioned before, several members of the San Diego–based Secretarial Association Services have taken the initiative to link their marketing efforts by taking out a collective yellow pages ad under the name of the association.

> The key to making networking a marketing team effort lies in joining networks or linking with others . . . who are willing to view networking activities as more than a quick chance to meet new business prospects.

2. Networking as a Support Team. Networks can also become highly effective support teams in which members view one another almost as "family," helping one another in whatever ways are needed. Networking associations can become a source of encouragement and feedback on new ideas, a problem-solving arena for finding answers to sticky business questions, a source of advice from experienced individuals, and a chance to belong to a community where you can get the support you need as well as contribute to the success of others.

When Peggy Glenn started her own secretarial service, she felt isolated and cut off from colleagues and associates, so she decided to create a network for herself. As she told us, "I called a few other people who ran secretarial businesses and invited them to lunch, Dutch treat. Six or seven of them came, and right then and there was the birth of what has become a great network. We support one another. We help with overload. And best of all, there is somebody to call on a bad day (or on a good day), somebody you can learn from if you've just received a job that is something you've never done before, somebody to refer others to if you don't want to take the job."

When an Oakland wildfire destroyed Sue Rugee's home and her home-based information research company along with it, colleagues from the professional association she'd been active in sent her gifts and pitched in to help her get started again. When a major account pulled their business back in-house, Chellie Campbell's bookkeeping service almost went under. But by joining a mentor program sponsored jointly by the National Association of Women Business Owners (NAWBO) and the Small Business Administration, Campbell was assigned to a successful woman business owner who provided specific direction and emotional support to help Campbell rebuild her business.

Networking as a support team is a two-way street. Not only do you benefit, but you also are able to provide advice, encouragement, referrals, leads, and introductions to everyone else within your network.

3. Networking as a Springboard to Other Generative Relationships. Networking is probably the most effective way to create, discover, or stumble upon a wealth of other serendipitous opportunities. Networking provides a doorway to meet interesting people to team up with, a low-risk platform for exploring and testing the potential of new relationships, and a way to hear about projects and activities you can engage in. In other words, networking is a way to find relationships that will lead to other relationships and to become involved in activities that evolve into still other activities you would never otherwise have known about or been included in.

For instance, Chicago business consultant Jordan Ayan . . . met his teaming-up collaborator, Deanna Berg, when he was attending a conference for professional consultants in the Boston area. Their meeting was actually a fortuitous occurrence, because Jordan had just lost a very important bid on a major contract. While networking that evening with people at the conference, Jordan met Deanna and began telling her about his plight. Much to his surprise, it turned out that Deanna was the person who'd won that very same contract. Since winning the bid, Deanna had decided that she needed help on the contract, so she invited Jordan to join her in doing the project, while splitting the fees. After that project, Jordan and Deanna have continued to do workshops and consulting jobs together, pooling their complementary strengths and expertise. While they are not formal business partners, they work together as frequently as they can.

The above excerpt from Teaming Up *is used with permission.*

19

Networking to the Max

NETWORKING CAN BE INTIMATE OR GLOBAL; IT CAN BE SIMPLE OR SOPHISTICATED; IT CAN be nuts-and-bolts or strategic; in any case, the same basic principles apply. In the four articles that follow, Bruce Elliott explains how, though networking has evolved from its original community scope to its present-day worldwide reach, the basics have not changed; Cynthia Greenawalt explores the relationship between complexity and functionality in networking; James A. Fontanella describes how a major high-level networking organization matches corporate needs and resources; and David Bullock tells the story of finding capable executive talent through international networking.

Marketing through Millennium Networks

Bruce Elliott

The technological advances in electronic information storage and retrieval have led to changes in marketing that most businesspeople have barely begun to think about, much less understand. Our business community or target market used to be oriented to a neighborhood or territory stretching only a few miles. In days past, we might have kept in touch with our community by virtue of service clubs, religious organizations, or sports programs, and this would have been sufficient to stay on top of our business. We knew that it was important to maintain a sense of current affairs, but our perspective was to our geographic community.

Now virtual communities of like-minded people communicate regularly across the region, the nation, and even the globe. This expanding sense of community is possible through the ever more powerful information technologies. Proof of this is found in the global corporations and, at the other end of the spectrum, the many live chat rooms where networking relationships are maintained on line. Those who appreciate and understand how to make use of these new millennium network technologies will become masters of their craft and of their life.

Sociologists used to estimate that each of us knew 250 people. This was our primary network. Today, many of us have access to thousands of names through client lists, friends, and associates we meet in transnational and transglobal travel. More important, we have facial recognition with many of the thousands of people we meet at trade shows, business mixers, conventions, conferences, and video conferencing, not to mention our normal excursions into the workday world.

> It's common for a seasoned businessperson to have accumulated hundreds of business cards over years of traditional contacts. Now, millennium technologies can expand contact sources by an order of magnitude.

Getting more contacts is never a real problem. All you have to do is go to intensive networking arenas, such as business-to-business events or specialty trade shows, or join one of the many community networking groups. It's common for a seasoned businessperson or a well-traveled individual to have stacks of hundreds of business cards that have accumulated over years of traditional contacts. Now, with millennium technologies, we are expanding our source of contacts by an order of magnitude.

To get effective results from networking, however, the task is still the same. Names alone are just the start. The essence of networking is everything that comes after: the systematic conversion of names into relationships of lasting value — business as well as personal value — for both you and the other person.

The process is simple. First, to the name, attach contact information: mailing address, telephone number, e-mail address. Use this information to establish follow-up contact with the person, to create mutual recognition by name and face. This follow-up might consist of phone calls, e-mail correspondence, chat-room participation, face-to-face visits, thank-you cards or gifts for favors received, or an offer of useful referrals.

Next, make the contact a networking partner by meeting regularly with him or her in sports, business, or civic group activities, working on joint tasks, or sharing common goals. By doing this, you establish a personal familiarity. When your networking partner discovers a need for your products or services — his own need or someone else's — your name and face will naturally come to mind.

As you acquire more networking partners, you will find that with some you have an especially valuable mutual relationship. Concentrate your time and energy on these; build them into strong, trusting mutual-support systems. This is where your network partnership becomes fully realized, with both of you exchanging referrals, client lists, and personal introductions and recommendations. On line, this can be a virtual partnership, but a true business partnership may be the eventual result.

> Your common interests, contacts, information, assistance, support, referrals, and recommendations can be shared just as readily over the World Wide Web as in a meeting hall.

The difference with millennium networking is that your base of contacts is far larger than it ever could have been in the past, and that it can include people on the other side of the world. Your common interests, contacts, information, assistance, support, referrals, and recommendations can be shared just as readily over the World Wide Web as in a meeting hall.

To create lasting relationships of value, you still need the traditional face-to-face meetings and word-of-mouth referrals. With videocams and teleconferencing, however, your meetings can be virtually face-to-face. The only thing you cannot easily do is shake hands — not yet, at least. But airline travel is getting faster and more economical every year.

You can create networking partners through formal networking groups or by direct or online encounters. Whether contact occurs in business or social settings, formally or informally, others will assess you and your ability to provide customer service. Make sure you do your level best with everyone, every time.

The Power of Complexity

Cynthia Greenawalt

Master networkers are often admired for their ability to achieve remarkable results with little apparent effort. The secret of their success is the complexity of their networks. Masters view networking not as a one-on-one, one-thing-at-a-time activity but as a complex linking of all possible needs with all possible resources at all times. They constantly look for ways to put people in their network in touch with other people in their network, and in other people's networks as well, to achieve the greatest benefit for all. They are heavily invested in the power of complex teamwork.

How is this mastery achieved? It is useful to look at the process in terms of levels of networking complexity. All three levels are stages though which the typical networker might progress as she develops her skills, her perceptions, and the size and extent of her own network. Each level satisfies at least the basics of what networking is meant to accomplish, from the initial recognition of a problem or need through the actual delivery of a solution — a product or service to satisfy that need.

Level 1

Networking at this level of complexity means an individual providing a single product, service, or resource to another individual or individuals — such as a transaction between a salesperson and a buyer, or the same transaction with several unrelated buyers. This networking relationship is relatively shallow and transitory. The buyer may refer others with similar needs to the same vendor, but both the buyer and the vendor will typically look elsewhere to satisfy other buying needs. In Level 1 networking, there is no communication of potential tie-ins for other products or services.

LEVEL 2

Suppose a caterer, in the course of contracting to supply refreshments for a wedding reception, mentions a florist he knows who could help solve a problem the client is having with flower arrangements. By doing so, the caterer helps both his client and a potential networking partner, but receives no direct benefit. However, the client forms a better impression of the caterer's service and expertise, and is more likely to refer other business to him. And the florist, who is grateful for the referral, is in a position to refer many future clients to the caterer.

Thus a single transaction — a catering job for a wedding client — produces the potential for multiple referrals as the result of a single timely referral. The florist is well positioned to discover the catering needs of many kinds of events that use flowers: wedding parties, birthdays, entertainment events, celebrity receptions. This leveraging of a single transaction into multiple referrals is typical of Level 2 networking complexity. It is the mainstay of most referral organizations and can sometimes produce as much business as the client can handle.

LEVEL 3

World-class, black-belt master networkers develop the kind of networks that are multiply connected in all directions with other networks. The result of this Level 3 complexity is the ability to satisfy multiple needs via multiple resources simultaneously. This can come about in several different ways.

One kind of complexity involves circular referrals, sometimes called "round robin" referrals. Suppose Contact A is in the business of wiring offices for computer networks, Contact B sells and installs carpeting, and Contact C designs web pages. The master networker, who views her contacts as a bank of products, services, and ideas and herself as a broker who matches needs with resources, might refer Contact A to Contact B for follow-up recarpeting services for Contact

> World-class, black-belt master networkers develop the kind of networks that are multiply connected in all directions with other networks.

A's clients; Contact B to Contact C to design web pages for Contact B's business; and Contact C to Contact A for rewiring its computer network after a planned office expansion. The more contacts the master networker has, the easier it is for her to discover needs and find ways to fill them. Her payoff? She becomes known as a person who knows how to get things done, and the beneficiaries of her efforts are likely to refer multiple clients to her — whatever her profession.

Another kind of complexity can be seen in multiple parallel networking. Perhaps the master networker knows of a group of office complexes that require extensive expansion and remodeling. He also knows several businesses that could work together, coordinating schedules and suppliers, to accomplish a large remodeling job more efficiently than if the remodeling were done by contractors working independently or in competition, with their attendant scheduling conflicts. The networker arranges for the contractors to work together to design a remodeling package that will save time and money, then refers the potential client to the virtual consortium. The result? A happy client — and grateful vendors who will surely refer business back to the "can do" networker.

> The master networker understands and applies John Naisbitt's concept of "six degrees of separation": the idea that every person on earth is connected to every other person through no more than six other people.

The master networker understands and applies John Naisbitt's concept of "six degrees of separation": the idea that every person on earth is connected to every other person through no more than six other people. The trick is finding the connections, and the more people you know, the easier it becomes to find the path from one person's need to another person's resource.

Master networkers recognize the inherent power of people working together toward a common goal. Martin Luther King Jr., who described this process as the "interrelated mutuality of life," said, "I cannot be who I ought to be until you are who you ought to be, and you cannot be who you ought to be until I am who I ought to be." In essence, the master networker satisfies her own fulfillment by fulfilling the interests and needs of her entire network.

Intercorporate Network Mindstorming

James A. Fontanella

Renaissance Executive Forums is an organization that brings together top executives from similar-sized but noncompeting companies around the world in an advisory board environment. The process is designed to address the opportunities and challenges executives face as individuals and as leaders of their organizations. Here are a couple of examples of how members have benefited from the networking.

During a break at one of our monthly meetings, the CEO of an international corporation with headquarters and staff in the United States and factories in Mexico mentioned to our chairperson that his people were redesigning the firm's entire computer system. They were determined to link all their facilities seamlessly, but the design team was not meeting objectives on time and within budget. Our chairperson recommended introducing the topic later in the meeting. When the CEO did so, he received excellent advice from other members with experience in similar projects. Our chairperson also introduced him to a new member in another group who had expertise in the same area; out of this contact came a business arrangement. The project was soon back on schedule. The CEO now feels as though his company is well on its way to meeting its information management objectives.

Another member told an executive session she was unhappy with a supplier who refused to increase manufacturing capacity to meet her company's projected needs. The member was reluctant to abandon her vendor because she had been doing business with them for a long time and other sources were uncertain. Other forum members offered advice on how to persuade the supplier to meet her production requirements. After the meeting, another member offered more substantial help. His factory, although set up to make other products, had excess capacity that could be used to supplement her primary vendor's output — and both their companies would benefit.

Thus, through intercorporate networking, two organizations solved two big challenges. All it took was an environment that facilitated networking between large groups of people.

Your Personal Network of Trust

David Bullock

If you develop your personal network as a network of trust it can be enormously valuable years later.

A good example is a headhunt that I undertook from my home in the United Kingdom to find a marketing director for a large, multinational beverage company. I wanted someone with international marketing experience and knowledge of the Far East but who might be living and working anywhere in the world; someone who would have impressed key businesspeople in the Far East in recent years, especially expatriates working at the board level.

I had two candidates whom I already knew well. One was the former head of Guinness in Indonesia, and the other was former head of Carlsberg East Asiatic. Both were now managing directors of their firms in Hong Kong. I also listed people who would have seen good marketing people in action elsewhere in the Far East. Most of these were expatriates I had known and trusted when I had been head of a transnational company in Jakarta. Now most of these contacts were spread over the Far East, United Kingdom, and Asia. I faxed them a concise, single-page job outline with the simple request to please let me know of anyone who they felt either would be a strong candidate or would know people who could be.

Some quite naturally expressed their personal interest, and most sent suggestions by return fax. Over the next four days, I was faxed or called by people I had never met or had lost touch with, who had been sent copies of the job outline. This is why I had sent only a single-page fax, so that each person I sent it to could easily pass it on to others. They helped me because they, in turn, were helping a friend or associate of theirs by sending them my opportunity.

Within one week, I had a strong short list of people to interview in Hong Kong, Singapore, and Bangkok. For example, one candidate who was recommended to me had worked in Korea for a former managing director of K&J. Thus, I had a high-integrity referral to a strong candidate hitherto unknown to me, from a country I had never visited.

All this activity meant that I was able to brief my client and then fly to the Far East to conduct interviews. In the end, fate helped out (as often happens for those taking action): I bumped into the Guinness man in the British Airways lounge at Heathrow, then met the East Asiatic managing director of Carlsberg at Kai Tekko airport, Hong Kong.

Most of the people I interviewed I had not met or known previously. However, I was able to identify and contact them quickly because I had a good, diverse network of people and I used a fax machine to lead me to potential candidates or people who would know potential candidates. Because I was trusted by my prime network, they were able to assure prospects that they should make time to meet me in whichever country was most convenient. Thanks to this network of trust, my client was able to receive a short list of top-quality candidates, fully vetted, in an exceptionally short time span.

> Because I was trusted by my prime network, they were able to assure prospects that they should make time to meet me in whichever country was most convenient.

Sometimes it is important to expand your network of trust through other networks of trust. On one search, I was charged with finding potential joint-venture partners to start a new personal products business for a major transnational company. The location was Southeast Asia, and I was in the United Kingdom. To visit many countries in my investigation would have been slow and costly. Instead, I contacted people in my personal network and outlined what sort of business or local entrepreneur I was looking for.

My masterstroke came when I appointed one of them, a senior Singaporean, formerly chairperson of a leading British transnational in that country, as my local partner in the venture. He had his own huge network of trust throughout the Far East and, as an older man, commanded the respect the Chinese give to the older generation who have proven themselves. He was able to approach many leading local firms and entrepreneurs in Malaysia, Singapore, and Indonesia. He was also able to speak highly of me as a former head of a large and successful business in Indonesia, so that their trust in him was transferred to me.

Later, when I met for the first time with his referrals and contacts in Malaysia, I found a warm and trusting relationship. They had used their own network of family and business contacts to check up on my past and my reputation in Indonesia before I arrived.

I was using my own network, and trust in me was being transferred to valuable contacts through other people's networks — truly an expanding network of trust.

Let me extract a few master networking lessons from this:

1. Whether you like it or not, you do become part of a network, so make sure you leave a good impression.

2. Maintain and cultivate your network — even if only by sending holiday cards every year. Encourage people to visit and stay with you whenever they are in your area or country.

3. When seeking to use your network for information or advice, try to empower individuals in your network to feel that by helping you they are helping someone else.

4. Be prepared to quickly build rapport and reinforce the positive expectations people have been given by their contacts.

5. Be cross-culturally aware.

The value of having your personal network of trust applies wherever you operate. It is particularly valuable in areas such as the Far East, where the culture of the community requires that you take time to build a trusting and mutually respectful relationship first. Trust is equally important in western cultures, though it is usually won and lost more quickly than in the Orient.

In some societies, people are accepted or not for who they are, not for the name of the company on their business card. A leading Chinese entrepreneur who was being wooed by the giant British firm GEC once asked me in genuine desperation, "David, how can I trust them? Who is this chief executive Sir Arnold Weinstock? I don't know him. Who do you know in GEC that I can trust?"

In other words, he was looking to meet and develop trust with an individual first, and only then would he trust the huge multinational. Trust is transferable; since he trusted me, he would accept and trust someone I could introduce him to and vouch for.

Your network of contacts can be even more valuable if you have taken care to make it a network of trust.

20

The Skills of a Master

No matter how good we are at networking, we can always become better — and although we stand in awe of the true masters, networking mastery is not out of reach of most of us. But how do we get from here to there? The best way to start is to emulate the masters — watch them, and do what they do. In the pair of essays below, the authors enumerate the skills that are associated with mastery in networking. First, Frank De Raffele and Edward Hendricks list the ten skills they consider most important in networking; then, Mike Smith, with the help of Scott Simon, gives seven fundamental principles that lie behind the skills of a master networker.

Top Networking Skills

Frank J. De Raffele Jr. and Edward D. Hendricks

What are the skills required of a good networker? Networking gurus themselves have been discussing these attributes for years. Their conclusion is that there are common characteristics that tend to correlate with success in networking. Based on our interviews and our own experience, ten important networking traits emerge as important to being a successful networker.

1. Integrity. Giving and receiving referrals can affect the lives of many people, including employees, investors, and customers. With vested interests at stake, people will seek to influence your thinking and sway your recommendations. Your integrity must remain scrupulous to avoid losing objectivity when trying to cater to the demands of many people or groups. Diminish your integrity, and you may harm others besides yourself.

2. Salesmanship. The businessperson who waits for clients to beat a path to his or her door will soon be out of business. Regardless of the nature of your business, you have to sell your services. It is very easy to spend all of your time on a current project, only to realize that you don't have work once that assignment has ended. Wise businesspeople schedule assignments to avoid this feast-or-famine cycle. Selling begins with contacting a person who might be a prospect for your network. Selling is the focus of your discussions with the customer, from your first contact through the conclusion of the project — and beyond. Your satisfied customer may bring you further business or a strong referral. Successful salespeople maintain scheduled contact with all their former clients. They know the importance of keeping themselves in the top of their clients' minds.

3. Diplomacy. Networkers have little, if any, authority to make things happen. You must rely on your ability to persuade people to take action. Former business executives from large companies who become entrepreneurs often have difficulty making the transition from a decision maker to one who influences others to take action. Networkers are very persuasive, and they do it in such a way that others think it was their idea in the first place.

4. Communication skills. You may possess all nine of the other skills listed, but if you can't communicate effectively, your career in business will be very short-lived. Without good communication skills, you will not be able to develop a network, sell a proposal, gather accurate data from interviews, or have your ideas accepted.

Topping the list among communication skills are sharp listening skills. Being able to draw out information during an interview will greatly influence how a problem is perceived. Customers tend to judge you on your willingness to listen to them. A common mistake is to try to dazzle customers with the breadth of your knowledge by talking too much. An adage we often use with our clients is "Remember, we were created with two ears and one mouth — they should be used proportionately."

Cogent writing ability is the means by which you demonstrate that you listened and that you understand the needs of your customer. If your letters, marketing materials, or proposals are not clear, are poorly focused, or contain typographical errors, your chances of winning a client are diminished.

Oral presentation skills are vital. It is not enough to know the answers to customers' needs; you must be able to clearly respond to them. A response poorly phrased can cast a shadow over your credibility.

5. Flexibility. No two customers or members of your network are exactly alike. Even when you work within a specific industry, the culture of different people and organizations in that industry will test your ability to adapt. Dress codes, levels of formality and informality, decision-making processes, and the personalities of the people you have to deal with will be different. An ability to adapt and fit in is very helpful to gain trust. Sticking out like a sore thumb does not engender openness on the part of your networkers or your customers.

6. Problem-solving skills. Good businesspeople and successful networkers are problem finders as well as problem solvers. Rarely will customers accurately identify their problems or needs. More than likely you will have to ferret out the underlying issues. Being curious by nature helps you avoid superficial or simplistic explanations that lead to improper referrals.

7. Self-discipline. Successful networkers and businesspeople are generally very bright people. Yet it is the customer who is the boss — even if the customer is not well educated or sophisticated. It takes self-discipline to remember this and to stay in control of your emotions and physical well-being. Personal preventive self-care will help to avoid networking burnout.

8. Resourcefulness. If solutions to problems were readily available, your customer would find the answer without your help. Customers expect their consultants to have advanced knowledge of their field of expertise. They pay for your ability to access hard-to-get materials. You may not know all the answers, but you are expected to find most of them.

9. Self-confidence. As a networker, when things go wrong during a project — and they will — you will be blamed; when things go right, the customer will take the credit. If you must rely on the recognition of others to stroke your ego, you will not go far as a networker. When working in a network, you will often work "backstage." Successful networkers derive satisfaction from knowing that they are good at what they do. At times you may be called upon to defend the strength of your convictions and speak frankly on a subject even when others do not want to hear what needs to be said.

10. Creative time management. In addition to everything else, you must be able to juggle many demands for your time and attention. Successful businesspeople usually are also successful networkers who can focus on more than one relationship or one customer at a time. Along with business demands, you may be pulled by the demands of a family, a profession, civic activities, parental programs, and social activities with friends, as well as demands for maintaining your health and well-being. Successful networkers learn to manage their time effectively.

The above excerpt from Successful Business Networking *is used with permission.*

Seven Principles for Success

Mike Smith, with contributions from Scott Simon

Networking is an acquired skill. As with other skills, the secret to mastering networking lies in understanding its principles and putting them into practice, over and over again, until they become part of your life.

The seven principles below are a good starting point. Each is an aspect of your mastery of the skills and practices of networking.

1. Your Beliefs

Beliefs come in two flavors: yours and theirs. Networking brings your beliefs into contact with the beliefs of others, day after day. As you learn more about other people, you have to be flexible enough to deal constantly with change. Some of the changes you will have to make will challenge your beliefs.

The master networker knows where his own beliefs end and others' begin. He thrives on relationships that constantly bombard his reality with new thoughts, beliefs, and actions. The secret is to hold to your beliefs while respecting those of others — and to be ready to understand and to learn. As Norman Vincent Peale said, "Change your thoughts and you change your world."

To become a master networker, you need to believe one thing above all: To learn and refine complex networking skills, you must be a lifelong student and face constant discomfort and challenges — but the rewards will outweigh the effort.

2. Your Goal

What do you expect to achieve by networking? More business? New opportunities? Information? Emotional support? Before you can reach your destination, you have to know where to start and how to recognize it when you arrive. To avoid wasting time on false starts, you need to have a well-thought-out plan and the resources necessary to carry it out. Asked how he would devote his time if given just an hour to chop down a tree, Benjamin Franklin replied that he would spend most of the time sharpening his ax.

> Asked how he would devote his time if given just an hour to chop down a tree, Benjamin Franklin replied that he would spend most of the time sharpening his ax.

3. Your Commitment

Most of us will try something new for ninety days or so, then, if results are less than expected, move on to something else. This ninety-day syndrome doesn't work well with networking. Building the necessary long-term relationships takes much longer. By the end of ninety days, you're just beginning to remember people's names. You spend the first year of a business-networking relationship getting to know your contacts, the second year learning to like them. By the third year — if all goes well — you will have formed lasting relationships of mutual respect and admiration.

But there are several big, unspoken "ifs" in this process: *if* you resolve to help others with no expectation of immediate reward; *if* you commit to building the relationships; *if* you stick with your commitment. For a long time you may realize no tangible benefits for the time and effort you spend helping others. But if you have the patience and foresight to wait for the payoff, you will eventually be rewarded.

4. YOUR INTENSITY

Ninety days is not nearly enough time to establish solid, long-term networking relationships, but it's plenty for a high-energy, short-term effort. It's a widely accepted business period — as in quarterly earnings, sales goals, and advertising campaigns — and it's useful for establishing good habits.

To monitor the performance of your network, plan an intense ninety-day networking blitz: attend meetings faithfully, establish as many new connections as you can, be especially alert for needs that you can refer to your contacts, and follow up promptly and faithfully on every referral you give or receive. Don't expect to see the results immediately; instead, watch carefully to see if the next quarter's networking productivity increases. You'll be surprised at how much difference it makes.

5. YOUR RESULTS

It is important to think of results not as a final goal but as part of the networking process. Sales trainers teach that each sale begets the next sale. Similarly, business that you get through networking should be seen as a measure of how well your network is functioning and should point the way toward even better results down the road. Networking is a lifelong journey, a never-ending process of creating and maintaining relationships that serve not just your business goals but your life goals. Your results are signposts along an endless path to mastery.

It takes a lifetime to develop a network resource bank, and the deposits and withdrawals will constantly change. Keep asking yourself these questions:

- Am I getting back more in value than I am paying out?

- Are my results good enough to satisfy and strengthen my belief system?

- Have I devoted enough time to the task to achieve my desired result?

- Are my beliefs, my goals, my commitment, and my actions strong enough to let me achieve the results I want?

6. Your Personal Growth

The desire for increase is inherent in all nature. It is the fundamental impulse of the universe. All human activities are influenced by our desire for increase. Here are the areas you need to concentrate on in your journey to becoming a master of networking:

- Increase your awareness

- Increase your business

- Increase your exposure

- Increase your personal network

- Increase your networking skills

- Increase your possibilities

- Increase your knowledge of marketing

- Increase your public speaking skills

- Increase your membership in networking organizations

- Increase your service

In the movie *First Knight*, King Arthur (played by Sean Connery) says, "In service to others we are best served ourselves." Networkers shorten this to "Givers gain," the law of reciprocity that governs mutually beneficial relationships. Increase the quantity and quality of your relationships, and always be prepared to learn from and help others.

7. YOUR INFLUENCE

Jim Rohn, the "Master of Success," exhorts us to constantly ask ourselves these questions:

- Who am I around?
- What are they doing to me?
- What have they got me reading?
- What have they got me saying?
- Where do they have me going?
- What do they have me thinking?
- What do they have me becoming?
- Then ask yourself the big question: Is that okay?

You will become the sum total of everyone and everything that influences you over your lifetime. You can become the architect of your own future or you can live in the model someone else builds for you. Since the future is where you will spend the rest of your life, it makes sense to invest your time and effort wisely.

21

The Traits of a Master

SKILLS ARE THINGS YOU CAN ACQUIRE ON YOUR WAY TO NETWORKING MASTERY; BUT what kind of a person is a master networker? What character traits should you strive to develop? Elisabeth and Ivan Misner enumerate the ten traits found in a survey to be most important in good networking; Betsy Sheldon and Joyce Hadley list and describe what they consider the twelve most important traits; Dan Georgevich tells what characteristics a networking group should look for when recruiting new members; Connie Hinton, Bob Travis, and Carol Grebe describe the behaviors anyone wishing to become a master should emulate; and Elisabeth Misner returns with a lighthearted take on the worst and best kinds of networkers.

Top Ten Networking Traits

Elisabeth L. Misner and Ivan R. Misner

Recently, we conducted a survey of more than 2,000 people throughout the United States, United Kingdom, Canada, and Australia. The survey asked participants to rank a variety of traits in order of perceived importance to networking. The survey results were about the same in all four countries, which tells us that the principles of good networking transcend national and cultural boundaries. The chart on the next page shows the top ten networking traits they selected, with number one being the top choice.

Note the low priority of traits common in the stereotypical image of networkers as people who aggressively work their network. Strong networkers do, of course, work with their networks, but the highest-rated characteristics are the ones related to practicing good human relations and maintaining good relationships. This did not surprise us. We have always held that networking is more about farming than hunting.

Let's take a closer look at the top five traits.

1. Follows up on referrals. This was ranked as the top trait of successful networkers. It's no secret that if you present opportunities — whether a simple piece of information, a special contact, or a qualified business referral — to someone who consistently fails to follow up successfully, you'll eventually stop wasting your time with this person.

2. Positive attitude. Not too long ago, we added this value to the formal code of ethics and leadership qualifications for our business referral organization. A consistently negative attitude makes people dislike you and drives away referrals; a positive attitude makes people want to associate and cooperate with you.

TOP TEN CHARACTERISTICS OF A SUCCESSFUL NETWORKER

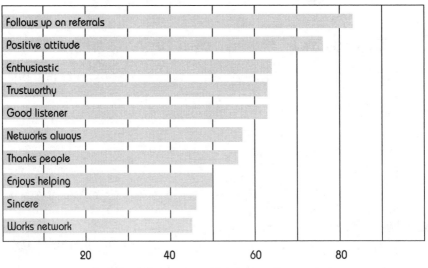

Percent of Respondents Mentioning Characteristic

3. Enthusiastic/motivated. Think about the people you know. Who gets the most referrals? People who show the most motivation, right? It has been said that the best sales characteristic is enthusiasm. To be respected within our networks, we at least need to sell ourselves.

4. Trustworthy. When you refer one person to another, you put your reputation on the line. You have to be able to trust your referral partner and be trusted in return. Neither you nor anyone else will refer a contact or valuable information to someone who can't be trusted to handle it well.

5. Good listening skills. Our success as networkers depends on how well we can listen and learn. The faster you and your networking partner learn what you need to know about each other, the faster you'll establish a valuable relationship. Communicate well — and listen well.

What Does It Take?

Betsy Sheldon and Joyce Hadley

Good bone structure, like many things in life, is something you're either born with, or you're not. But the beauty of networking is that it's *not* such a gift. True, some people are naturally adept at making connections, but having been born with the personality of a talk-show host is not a requirement for becoming a successful networker. Nor do you have to have a computer-like brain to store all the names of people you've ever been introduced to. With commitment and purpose, anyone can develop more effective networking skills.

And there's more good news: Many of the traits that experts identify as crucial to successful networking tend to be the characteristics typically identified as "female" — the qualities pinpointed by management pros as indicative of the new female management style.

So you may have more of an edge than you imagined. Let's consider some of the key characteristics that make a successful networker.

A successful networker is . . .

1. Committed. . . . Once you accept the premise that networking is a way of life, it's obvious that it requires a long-term commitment. Developing a web of relationships is an ongoing process. Not only is it necessary to commit to a networking philosophy, it's essential to devote a certain amount of time and energy as well. . . .

Will you make an effort to stay in touch with your contacts? Are you willing to set aside time to call people regularly, schedule lunches, send off quick notes, fax interesting articles, whip off e-mail messages, and focus on the concerns of your connections? If so, your network will flourish. If you let these relationships go, if you fail to be there for others, your network will eventually go to seed. . . .

2. More interested in *giving* than getting. Truth is, we're all in it — whatever it is — for ourselves. Most of what we do in life is somehow connected to "WIIFM": "What's In It For Me?" And that's okay. But in order to get anything out of networking, you've got to learn to put your personal interests on the back burner, and focus your energies on others' needs and goals as well. It's a sort of "Do unto others" philosophy found at the core of many spiritual beliefs.

A good networker can find hundreds of ways to give: referrals, informational interviews, encouragement, and feedback. As you graduate to more senior status through networking, you'll be able to give more. But wherever you are, you already have a lot to give. Too many women are willing to contribute, but don't believe they have anything of value to give. . . .

3. A good listener. Being a good listener is more than smiling, nodding, and interjecting an occasional "uh-huh" when others talk to you. Good networking requires real listening — reading between the lines. . . . Responding with enthusiasm when a former co-worker expresses interest in a local company is one level of listening. Faxing your friend a few recent news clips, or introducing her to the human resources director at that company, is a more advanced level. Fine-tune your listening skills for powerful networking: instead of simply acknowledging the problem, try to provide solutions.

4. Curious. When interfacing with others, a good networker — using her excellent listening skills — hears clues that stimulate interest and offer opportunities to explore further. Without the element of curiosity, your networking conversations may often drop with a thud after you establish what the individual does and where he or she works. But a curious networker will probe further. "You provide a gift-basket and flower delivery service targeted to businesses. What was it in your background that led you to this career path? What would you say really launched your business? What sort of company do you find makes the best customer for your service?" . . .

5. Ready to follow up. . . . [M]any of us have probably had the experience of running into a casual business acquaintance frequently, always to conclude a brief exchange with, "We really have to get together soon." And that's the last we hear of it. An important rule of successful networking is, if you say you're going to do something — do it. Whether it's scheduling lunch or passing on some information, follow through with your commitment, so that your networking connections come to know you as someone who does what she says.

At the very least, follow up with a call. "Ellen, I told you I'd let you know if I knew of anyone looking for a graphic designer. I thought I could come up with a couple of names, but it seems no one's looking right now. I'll let you know if things change." An addendum to this rule: Follow up when you say you will — if you promise you'll call tomorrow, be sure that you do. . . .

6. Able to ask for help. . . . The ability to ask others for help is crucial to successful networking. Whether it's requesting advice, information, or an introduction to an important contact, you'll need to be able to make your needs clear. You can't count on networking contacts to intuit what you need. If you merely "hint" to your co-worker that you'd really like to work in marketing, he may not guess what you *mean* is that you wish he'd introduce you to his pal, the director of the marketing department. . . .

If you've built relationships based on mutual support with your networking connections, it's entirely appropriate for you to *ask* for help. And most people are appreciative of the opportunity to help an individual they have a positive relationship with.

7. Able to brag. . . . A good networker *must* learn to be comfortable with sharing her achievements. No, we're not implying that you should monopolize every conversation with your exploits and bore everyone to tears with your success. But it is essential to let your networking connections know what you're doing and what you've accomplished. You may be a charming lunch companion, but if your fellow members at your professional association don't know you've (a) landed a prestigious account, (b) achieved record sales in your industry, or (c) won an important award, how will they know that you truly are an exemplary businessperson, one to recommend to others?

Take credit. Don't share your success, then blush and pass on the credit to your co-workers, boss or, worse, luck. Be proud, not pompous, about your achievements and spread the news. This allows your contact to learn not just about what you do, but how you do it — with excellence!

8. A consumer of knowledge. While networking is indeed about relationships, reading up on your profession, your community, and the business community in general is going to give you an edge in developing those relationships. By keeping abreast of events, you'll know where to seek out effective networking connections. If you haven't already, develop a voracious appetite for information. Read avidly. Hop aboard the Internet. . . .

9. Courageous. It can be scary to do something new — whether it's braving a bungee jump, changing your hairstyle, or walking into a room full of strangers. While networking situations aren't always ones that provoke sweaty palms or somersaulting stomachs, it does require occasional stretching — reaching out to new individuals, perhaps joining an organization where you know no one, or (shudder) speaking before a group of strangers.

It takes a certain amount of courage to network well. Recognize that discomfort may accompany you in some networking situations, but don't let it hold you back. . . .

According to Dr. Frank Farley, a University of Wisconsin psychologist who's studied risk-takers for thirty years, you define yourself and add to your self-esteem and self-confidence with every risk you take. With practice, you may surprise yourself at how easy it becomes to reach out to people you don't know.

10. Able to remember. Yes, remembering names is important to effective networking. But when you're forced to admit that you've forgotten the name of someone you know you've met, approaching him or her with a genuine smile can work magic and pave the way for forgiveness.

What's even more impressive than remembering names is remembering details about a conversation you may have had. Try approaching someone at a luncheon or event with a smile and comment reflecting a previous interaction: "Oh, I've been wondering since we last talked how your fundraiser finally turned out," or "Last time we met, you were getting ready to send your daughter to college. How are you coping with an empty nest?" Chances are the individual won't even notice whether you used his or her name. Remembering the details about an individual is one of the most effective ways to transform a casual introduction into a solid connection.

11. Patient. "What goes around comes around." "You never know what the future will bring." These are the mantras of successful networkers.

"It's not a quickie thing," emphasizes Lya Sorano, director of Atlanta Women in Business. "Coming to one meeting and then going home and saying, 'I never get anything out of it,' means you came with the wrong expectation. You really have to regard it as an investment that you are making. It takes a while to build up contacts." Andra Brack advises new members of BNI that they may have to put in a year of weekly meetings before they see a strong payoff in networking-generated business.

The above excerpt from The Smart Woman's Guide to Networking *is used with permission.*

The Ideal Networker

Dan Georgevich

A network grows in two ways. It extends outward, from person to person, as far as you can follow the chain of contacts for a given interest. And it grows at the center, as new members join the organization and thereby expand the number of professions or areas of interest represented in the central group. One of your responsibilities as a networker is to bring in new networking partners to increase the density and power of the network's core.

What's the most important qualification to look for when you're identifying potential networking partners? Your first thoughts naturally go toward attributes that might come up in a job interview: experience, knowledge, and skills. How much networking has this person done? What has she learned about networking that she can apply? How good a networker is she?

This approach, evaluating a potential networking partner as if you were hiring a new employee for your organization, overlooks the fundamental nature of networking skills. We humans are social beings, born with the rudiments of networking in our blood: cooperating, communicating, helping each other, referring friends and acquaintances to others for help. Most of us use networking skills in everyday life. Accomplished business networkers merely hone these skills to sharpness by constant practice directed toward a recognized purpose. So finding partners with networking experience is not necessarily the most efficient use of your time. Yes, you can find one readily, but you're looking for someone who is a devoted networker, whose skills and commitment can stand the test of time.

Well, then, surely a better approach would be to find highly motivated networkers — true believers who have studied networking, have strong ideas and theories about the principles of networking; highly educated, trained individuals who have devoted their careers to the science of networking and who perceive networking as a virtuous activity in itself. Yes, it's true, searching out networking scholars and specialists can lead you to individuals whose efforts are likely to bring predictably good results. But once you've found your candidate, will he be a practical soul like you, interested mainly in results, or will he be a professional networker, more concerned with networking for its own sake or for the thrill of the pursuit? Will he be more absorbed in the theoretical possibilities and ideas than in the bottom line?

Let's put ourselves in the expert's chair for a moment by getting theoretical and looking at our selection task scientifically. Think of our field of candidates as a large circle, big enough to take in everybody we know, casually or otherwise, whom we might consider recruiting into our network. How can we most readily identify a person, among all those we have met, who will make a good, reliable, long-term, effective network partner?

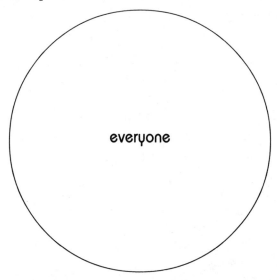

We first try to narrow down our selection by specifying those with known skills, knowledge, and experience in networking. This is the next smaller circle within the "everyone" circle.

Then we specify that we will look for the true believers, the individuals who have studied all aspects of networking and who perceive networking as a good in itself.

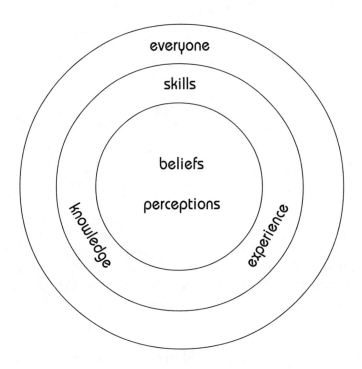

As you can see, we've been narrowing down our field of candidates by refining our selection criteria. Surely by this process we will find the best networker to bring into our organization, right? But we still haven't defined this individual in terms of character or personality. And, as any experienced employer can tell you, strong and honest character is, in the long term, the best predictor of an associate's value. Is she honest, responsible, and trustworthy? Can she be counted on in difficult times? Will she be there for the long term?

Most important of all, does she have the attitude that service to others is not only a good way to live one's life but a good way to ensure one's own success? It's this attitude — the intuition that "Givers gain" — that is the keystone of a great networking partnership. So the inside circle — the "bullseye" of the target we've been sketching — is attitude.

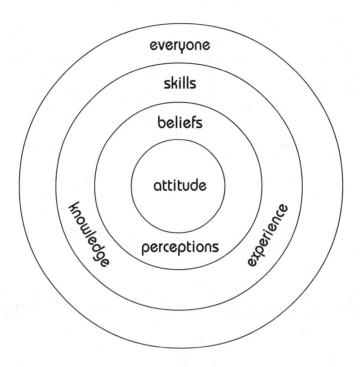

Now, here's the interesting thing about narrowing down our search to people with the right attitude toward others: our narrowing down is really a broadening of our search criteria. Why? Because when we search for networking partners with the right attitude, we are automatically ensuring that we will find people who fit in all the other circles. With the right attitude, a neophyte networker will soon discover how her philosophy of benevolence toward others — of behaving with people as she would want them to behave with her — fits the principles of good networking, where being generous with information, assistance, and referrals for fellow networkers brings in the long run an abundance of information, assistance, and referrals for oneself. Moreover, a person with the ideal networker's attitude will soon refine and enhance her innate networking skills to match the best.

Conversely, if you recruit someone who is cynical, selfish, or dishonest, whose primary concern is making money off the efforts and good will of others, you will soon find yourself beginning a new search. No portfolio of skills, knowledge, or experience will make this person a trustworthy networking partner; no theoretical beliefs in or perceptions of networking's effectiveness will change a bad attitude into benevolence. Such a person will do more harm than good for the network.

Your responsibility as a master networker is to find and recruit networkers of the highest potential — individuals who can be trusted and who will form long-term relationships. Look for good people who embody the attitude that is essential to the health and effectiveness of your network and that of your fellow networkers: "Givers gain."

How to Spot a Master

Connie Hinton, Bob Travis, and Carol Grebe

Do you know what's the fastest way to learn a skill? It's the same method we've all used since we were children: we imitate the person whose skills we admire.

We humans are born networkers, but some of us get better at it than others. When we recognize the benefits of networking for ourselves and our businesses, we begin to realize that the people who enjoy the greatest success are the master networkers. We begin to envy their skills, and we want to be like them and enjoy the same kind of success.

So — how do you learn to be a master networker? You copy the behavior of a master networker! All you have to do is find one you can watch and emulate. And that's not all that difficult. The master networker stands out in a crowd — especially in the same networker gatherings that you've been going to, where they're in their element.

Below, not necessarily in order of importance, are ten clues to the behavior of master networkers. Keep your eyes, ears, and mind open and see if you can spot one.

Masters keep their eyes open. They understand that an opportunity may present itself at any time and that they must be ready to seize it. They stay alert for information that can help them or their fellow networkers. They are observant; for instance, they notice that the carpet in the reception area needs cleaning and offer to introduce their host to their favorite carpet-cleaning specialist.

Masters maintain a positive attitude. You will notice, if you watch closely, that the master is one of the most positive people in the room — smiling, shaking hands, introducing people to each other. Masters believe in themselves and in others; they radiate confidence and optimism, qualities that attract people and encourage them to open up. Their excitement and energy establish the atmosphere in which creativity and cooperation take root and grow.

Masters bring people together. At a networking meeting, you may well think the master networker is the host, but the master simply likes to meet people and put visitors and new members at ease. In doing so, the master often finds an opportunity to put people in touch with one another where there may be mutual benefit. The more people a networker knows, the broader the network and the more opportunity for referrals.

Masters listen. They spend as little time as possible talking about themselves, because they know it is preferable to let others sing their praises. Instead, they listen. They ask questions. They focus on the person doing the talking, to learn as much as they can about others whom they might be able to help. They listen to the details of what is being communicated — including the body language — and keep careful notes for later reference.

Masters seek to learn. They use their networking tools to continually improve themselves, never assuming that they know all they need to know. They are information addicts, always reading books and periodicals, surfing the Internet, asking questions. They know that knowledge is power, and that staying abreast of major business trends increases their power both to compete and to network effectively.

Masters communicate. Their special attributes include the desire to pass along useful information and the skill to pass it along effectively. This includes, of course, information about themselves that others may find useful when they need help or when they need to steer a contact to a fellow networker. They are good at introducing themselves at meetings and describing their products or services; they carry business cards, pamphlets, and other literature that will keep them in others' minds when a need arises. They are also adept at providing similar information and materials about other network members.

Masters set goals. Most people network casually and unconsciously as part of everyday life. Masters network purposefully, to create a web of friends and associates who can mutually benefit by sharing information. This is the master networker's goal. Only by setting a goal and aiming for it can you be certain of achieving it. Being purposeful also brings others on board to help achieve your goals — and theirs. One important point: writing down your specific, well-defined goals multiplies your chances of achieving them.

Masters are committed. How much of yourself are you willing to put into networking to achieve success? Master networkers perform a leap of faith with every person they meet. They commit themselves to helping others with no expectation of anything in return. They know they will be rewarded eventually, in some cases by no more than the knowledge that they have helped someone. Such open-ended giving requires genuine commitment, even through the times when results seem nonexistent. Commitment transfers promise into reality.

Masters are good team players. They recognize that networking is by nature a team sport, and that each member of the network can accomplish far more by teamwork than by acting alone. The best networks are teams of teams — extended networks that connect with other networks, accessing all the skills and resources needed to reach any goal. If you are part of a marketing team, seek to extend your reach by sharing ideas with other marketing teams, such as civic or networking organizations.

Masters genuinely strive to help others. They live and breathe the "Givers gain" philosophy, but they act selflessly to benefit others with no explicit expectation of when or how they might benefit in return. They volunteer their time, energy, expertise, and resources for the benefit of other members or the community at large. They mentor new members and others who can benefit from their experience. They follow through on referrals and show their gratitude for referrals given. They don't just act as though they care about others — they really do care.

Becoming a master means becoming skilled or proficient at what you are doing; it means taking authority or control of your future and the future of your business. As networker Ray Cataldo reminded his colleagues at a networking meeting in Santa Rosa, California: "It's not who you are — it's who you can be."

The Wise Farmer

Elisabeth L. Misner

In my first job after college, I had a boss who I considered the king of networking. He knew everyone in the local chamber of commerce, was in several networking groups, and was active in his trade association. I began to model my own developing networking skills and style on his.

But I soon became aware he was not the master networker I had at first thought. Most of his connections were superficial and tenuous. He was not forging the long-lived mutual referral network that I hoped to build.

In the gatherings I attended, I began to notice different people had different networking styles, some of which were more effective than others. As I studied these styles, I resolved to avoid the least effective and strive to become the best. I even came up with my own pet names for the different kinds of networkers. They reminded me of people and creatures you might see out in the country, around a farm.

My boss, whose style was the first I became aware of, would flit from group to group — like a butterfly. The Butterfly goes from meeting to meeting, shaking hands, introducing himself to others, handing out lots of business cards, and mailing lots of follow-up notes. He has plenty of energy but doesn't stand still long enough to learn much about those he meets. He meets a lot of people, and so by sheer volume of contacts will reap some benefits from networking. But he doesn't form the strong ties that grow into healthy, stable referral relationships.

The Impatient Farmer is more focused than the Butterfly, but not by much. He joins a group, waits for something to happen, then gets tired of waiting and moves on to another group. It's as though he planted an apple tree in one corner of his farm, and when after a year it doesn't seem to be bearing fruit, he rips it out of the ground and replants it in another spot. No surprise that it doesn't yield a crop the next year, so he moves it again. The Impatient Farmer doesn't realize that the tree has to stay in one place long enough to establish a healthy root system before it can yield a bounteous harvest. The lesson? Stay put long enough to develop strong relationships.

Then there's the Big Game Hunter. He doesn't want to fool around with the little guys — he's out for bear. He wants to be introduced to the CEO. What he doesn't realize is that in the time it takes him to get in to see one big wheel, he could have made dozens of more valuable connections with lesser players. Every contact has the potential to put you in touch with many terrific prospects, some of whom are in a better position to help you than the most powerful executive. Don't ignore anyone. Get to know everyone in your network.

And watch out for the Vultures! You can usually spot them in time to avoid them. They're the ones who just hang around looking for whatever prey comes into view and stands still long enough to pounce on: "Hey, I'd love to have ten minutes of your time to show you my fantastic, money-making, quit-your-job-and-retire opportunity!" Don't risk turning into a Vulture. When you meet someone, resist the urge to tell her all about yourself; instead, try to find out all you can about her and her business. Ask questions; find common interests. Try to discover something you can do to benefit her. Then you will have a loyal networking partner you can count on for business and referrals in the future.

If you have great skill, focus, and patience, you can become an Angler. The Angler goes looking for a particular kind of fish; he knows where it is likely to be found and what kind of bait to use. He knows you can't just throw your line in any puddle and expect a strike. To be an Angler, you have to plan ahead, research your quarry, look in the right places, and shut out all distractions. Once he's found the fish he's looking for, the Angler reels it in patiently and carefully by practicing "Givers gain" — the cultivation of mutual benefits.

I saw quite early that it wouldn't be very rewarding to be a Butterfly, an Impatient Farmer, or a Big Game Hunter. Nor did I want people to think of me as a Vulture. I also knew I would never make a good Angler; I like to stay active, and if I don't get a nibble right away, I'm too eager to move to another part of the pond. So I made it my goal to become the best networker of all: the Wise Farmer.

Good networking is like good farming. You prepare the ground, plant the seeds, add water and fertilizer and time, then reap the harvest. The Wise Farmer knows that the more she puts into the effort — the more she gets to know her contacts and seeks ways to benefit them — the more she will realize in return. She knows that growing a crop takes patience and perseverance; you don't see the payoff right away, but if you work at it long enough you will be amply rewarded.

22

How Good a Networker Are You?

HAVING STUDIED THE BEST TRAITS AND SKILLS FOUND IN THE MASTERS, PERHAPS YOU would be interested in seeing how you rate as a networker. It's good to know where you stand when you're trying to figure out which way to go. Here are three articles that will help you rate your skills and knowledge. Lillian D. Bjorseth presents a self-test, based on personality type, that will tell you your personal networking style; Martin Lawson provides a tool to help you assess your confidence level — that is, the confidence other people have in you; and Donna Fisher and Sandy Vilas give you a way to rate your own effectiveness as a networker.

Discovering Your Networking Style

Lillian D. Bjorseth

Each of you is as unique as a snow-flake. Like snowflakes, you also have similarities, enough so that we can group behavioral characteristics into four major categories. Each of you exhibits varying amounts of all of them. Most of you have the tendency to show dominance in one or more categories, i.e., this is the behavior or behaviors you feel comfortable exhibiting.

Most of you also exhibit a low amount of certain behavioral characteristics, i.e., you prefer not to act in a certain way when you have a choice. It is not natural or comfortable for you.

Through knowledge of your behavioral style, you will get a better understanding of your strengths and limitations. You will know your hot buttons: what makes you tick and why you act, feel, and think the way you do. What is it that makes you "you"? How can you become a better "you"? In what situations are you most effective? In what environments are you least effective? With the answers to these questions, you can purposefully seek out personal and professional opportunities where you are naturally most effective and increase your chances for success and happiness. Conversely, you can seek to eliminate or lessen the amount of time you need to spend in environments least conducive to your communication style. . . .

Once you have improved your intrapersonal communication, i.e., you are comfortable with who you are and, preferably, really like who you are, you can use the same model to improve interpersonal communication.

What makes other people tick? Why do they act or react the way they do? What kind of environment motivates them? . . .

When you know more about why you have the tendency to behave the way you do than the other person understands about behavioral or communication styles, you will be ahead of the game. When you also understand more about why others behave as they do, you will be in charge of the situation.

The only person you can control is yourself. When you want/need people to behave differently — like getting them to close a sale or recommend you to another person — you need to change your behavior. When you know how to make other people feel more comfortable (people like being dealt with in their style), you can realistically expect better results. It will mean the beginning of more satisfying professional and personal relationships.

The model we will use to help you discover your networking style is *DISC*, which stands for

- Dauntless

- Indefatigable

- Supportive

- Careful

It's time to find out your networking styles(s). It will be fun — and rewarding!

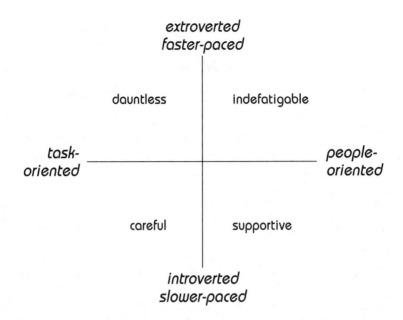

LEARN YOUR NETWORKING STYLE

1. In each of the sets of four statements, identify those behaviors that are typically *most* or *least* characteristic of you. Read the four statements under each heading, then rank them from 4 to 1, giving a 4 to the behavior most like you, 3 to the next most like you, then 2, with 1 being the statement that reflects your least typical behavior.

2. Beginning with the "A" statements, enter the number you assigned to each in the appropriate box. . . . Repeat the process for all "B," "C," and "D" statements.

3. Check your accuracy by adding the columns together; they will equal 150.

4. Look at the answer key . . . to verify your most prevalent networking style(s). If two of the numbers are the same, you have a tendency to use both of these styles equally.

Appearance

A. I always wear power suits and accessories when I attend any business function.

B. I usually wear suits; however, I like to deviate from the gray / navy blue syndrome and individualize with accessories that have panache. I have to be me!

C. I like to blend into the crowd. Gray or taupe slacks or skirt and a navy blazer make me feel comfortable.

D. I prefer conservative, tailored clothes and accessories and everything needs to be perfect, down to the last detail.

Business Card Filing System

A. I only save those for which I have an immediate need.

B. I have more fun collecting business cards than using them. I have yet to develop a filing system, so I may find cards in the darndest places.

C. I date all my cards in the upper right-hand corner and file them alphabetically by company name.

D. I collect a limited amount, and I know when and where I got each of them.

Cars

A. Cadillacs or BMWs are for me.

B. Corvettes or sports cars, in general, are my choice!

C. Station wagons are so practical for business and family.

D. Reading *Consumer Reports* is a must for me before I buy a car.

Correspondence

A. I like it brief and informal . . . if I write at all.

B. I use lots of exclamation points and underlines to show my enthusiasm.

C. Sincerity and warmth are my goals.

D. I like formality. I often add attachments for more clarity.

Desktops

A. I like to delegate to others so I can keep routine items off my desk and work on the really big things.

B. I haven't seen the top of my desk since I bought it. In fact, I frequently use the floor for filing.

C. I file things as soon as I am done with them. I also keep my "pending" files updated.

D. My desktop may *look* messy; however, I know where *everything* is.

Facial Expressions

A. I maintain direct eye contact. I show impatience when people don't get to the point quickly.

B. I have lively, animated facial expressions. I show my feelings, and since I am optimistic, I like to share my enthusiasm with everyone I meet.

C. I have a friendly, warm smile. It's hard to get me perturbed.

D. I don't like people to know what I am thinking; I am comfortable being called stoic.

Goals

A. I have one goal — to get immediate results in everything I do and to eliminate anything that stands in my way.

B. My goals? They're in my head. I haven't had a chance to write them down yet.

C. I set them in December for the following year. Then, I type and file them by month in a twelve-part folder.

D. I believe long-term planning is important for success.

Handshakes

A. I shake hands firmly and with a purpose.

B. I am often so busy speaking with my hands I forget to even shake.

C. I am known for my gentle handshake. It can be firm, but mostly I want people to feel my sincerity.

D. My handshakes are formal. I do it more because of society dictates than because I want to. I don't particularly like being touched.

Information Gathering

A. I hire somebody to do my research. I get irritated when they don't deliver on time.

B. I need to concentrate on this area more. I often fire before I aim.

C. I budget time in the library in the weekly schedule I set on Sundays.

D. It is imperative that I have all the data before I make a decision. I take whatever time I need to get it.

Listening

A. I listen best when what the speaker says fits my agenda. I like people to get to the bottom line quickly.

B. It's hard for me to listen. I have so much to say.

C. I try to understand what others are saying and pay attention even if I am not that interested. I don't want to hurt their feelings.

D. I assess what is being said and listen for consistency. I carefully control my responses.

Making an Entrance

A. People "feel" when I enter a room. My confident posture contributes to a powerful aura.

B. I usually add excitement when I enter a room. I enjoy being in the spotlight.

C. I often slip into a room unnoticed and remain in the background.

D. I pride myself in observing more than being observed.

Office Enhancements

A. I proudly show off my awards and trophies.

B. I like to show off photographs of me and business associates and inspirational posters. I never have enough space!

C. Family photographs make me feel warm and fuzzy.

D. I like to display my diplomas, certificates, and credentials in an unassuming way.

Phone Calls

A. This is John. I'll pick you up at noon. We're going to Joe's Eatery.

B. Hi! Isn't the weather lovely? I had the greatest weekend.

C. Hi, this is Bonnie. Is this a good time for you?

D. Hello, this is Mrs. Jones. I'm following up as promised in my April 10 letter.

Reading a Newspaper

A. I read the business advice column first so I know *what* the latest networking/sales techniques are.

B. I read the personal profiles first so I know *who* is important to know.

C. I read the entire newspaper, starting on page one. I like orderliness, and I read the paper *how* it was assembled.

D. I write the editor whenever I find a grammatical or factual error. I want to know *why* it was allowed to happen.

Sales Calls

A. I am brief, clear, and to the point. I keep small talk to a minimum.

B. I view it as a social interaction. If the client wants me there, I'll spend as much time as necessary.

C. I establish rapport with a customer. I patiently listen and give personal assurances.

D. I use a logical, methodical approach, with plenty of backup data.

Answer Key

	A Dauntless	B Indefatigable	C Supportive	D Careful
Appearance				
Business Card Filing System				
Cars				
Correspondence				
Desktops				
Facial Expressions				
Goals				
Handshakes				
Information Gathering				
Listening				
Making an Entrance				
Office Enhancements				
Phone Calls				
Reading a Newspaper				
Sales Calls				
Totals will equal 150.				

- If your highest number is in Column A, you are a *Dauntless Networker*.

- If your highest number is in Column B, you are an *Indefatigable Networker*.

- If your highest number is in Column C, you are a *Supportive Networker*.

- If your highest number is in Column D, you are a *Careful Networker*.

Some of you will find you clearly prefer one style above the rest. Others will find two styles that are nearly equal. In that case, you feel comfortable exhibiting either style and let the situation dictate. Still others will find a tendency to prefer three styles equally, and a much smaller percentage will find a nearly equal distribution among all four styles.

The above excerpt from Breakthrough Networking *is used with permission.*

It's Not *Your* Confidence That Counts

Martin Lawson

When it comes to getting referrals from your network, confidence is a vital component — not *your* confidence, but the confidence your fellow network members have in you. None of them want to risk their personal reputations by referring business, information, or contacts to a stranger. And even though you may have known many of your fellow networkers for quite some time, until they've gained a certain level of confidence that referring contacts to you will not harm their reputation with their clients, associates, friends, or family, you're still a stranger.

What exactly is this level of confidence? The referral confidence curve shown here illustrates the dynamics of the process. Your success in getting referrals depends partly on your competence, of course, but more on how far up the confidence curve the referrer's confidence in you has progressed.

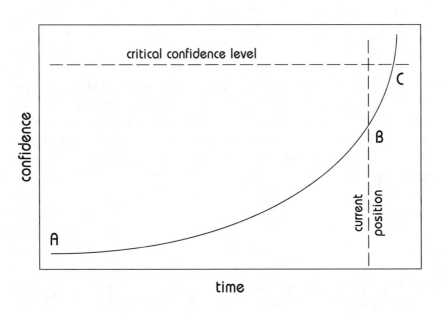

The shape of the curve shows why planning referral-based marketing means cultivating long-term relationships. Confidence grows slowly at first, then more quickly as the relationship matures. The level of confidence required reflects the level of risk perceived by the referrer.

GETTING THERE

How long will it take you to reach the critical level of confidence with your networking friends? Aside from the quality of your products or services, this depends on four main factors:

1. Your profession. The more significant the business being referred, the greater the risk to the referrer's reputation. It you're a florist, it may only take a week or two for people who try your services to recommend you on the basis of their experience with you. The risk associated with referring a florist is usually small — unless you're bidding on a large corporate account that also may be your referrer's top client. If you're a lawyer, accountant, or investment advisor, it may take you six months or a year to reach the critical confidence level. However, since the stakes are higher, your referrer stands to gain more if the results are successful. She will enhance her reputation as someone who knows the right people to get things done.

2. How well you educate others about your business. Don't assume that your fellow networkers understand your company or industry well enough to refer you confidently. Most have enough of a job keeping up with their own business and personal concerns. You have to educate them, and keep on educating them as long as you're in business. The best way is to speak to large, receptive groups; a networking group is ideal, because everybody is expected to address the group at regular intervals. Make your presentation interesting and stimulating. Tell them how your product or service improves business or life. Tell them who, what, when, where, and how. Each time you speak, present a new aspect of your business. Let your knowledge and eloquence persuade them that you are very good at what you do. They will grow confident that you cannot seriously injure their reputations with their contacts, and your name will come to mind whenever a referral opportunity arises.

3. The help you give others in moving up their own referral confidence curves. If you can endorse the quality of products or services offered by a networking partner — that is, increase others' confidence in him — your partner will be disposed to return the favor. Testimonials from one or two of your partners may, in turn, trigger a much larger and more valuable referral from another partner who was waiting for more evidence before taking a risk on you.

4. The time you invest in learning about others' businesses. If you want someone to learn about the value of your products or services, you have to spend time learning about the value of theirs. The best way to do this is one-on-one: "John, I'd like to be able to refer more business to you, but I need a deeper understanding of what your company does and how you operate. Could we get together one day next week to discuss this?" Although you don't say so, John understands that he will learn something more about your business at the same time. Serious master networkers meet regularly to raise each other's understanding of their businesses.

Staying for the Long Haul

It's not always easy to know how far you've progressed up your confidence curve. Many networkers spend a lot of time and effort trying to build others' confidence in them, then, on the brink of success, grow discouraged and stop attending meetings. (In terms of the graph, they work hard long enough to get from point A to point B, then quit, never realizing how close they are to point C.) How would you feel if someone found you a terrific referral about two weeks after you dropped out of sight?

Here's what you can do to gain perspective on your efforts and the results they are producing. Ask yourself the following four questions, and keep asking them over and over until you have attained success and the answers become obvious.

1. Are you being realistic about the time it will take, in your profession, to gain the critical level of confidence?

2. Are you regularly making stimulating, educational presentations to your fellow networkers about the value you provide to your clients?

3. Are you doing business with others in your group so you can give them dynamic testimonials and steer business to them in hopes they will return the favor?

4. Are you meeting regularly with your networking colleagues to learn about their businesses so you can confidently refer your contacts to them?

If you're following these simple tactics, then you are well along the road to getting all the referrals from others' networks that you deserve.

The Self-Assessment

Donna Fisher and Sandy Vilas

Our goal is to inspire you to be a power networker and enjoy the benefits and satisfaction of networking in your daily life. Whether you consider yourself a novice, intermediate, or expert networker, there is room for enhancement. The networking profile that follows will help you identify to what extent you are currently practicing the principles, tools, techniques, and attitude of a powerful networker. It will also reinforce the ideas you already practice, present new tools for greater effectiveness, and identify the steps you can take to achieve consistent networking success.

To determine your networking profile, score yourself on a scale of 1 to 5 (1 = never, 2 = occasionally, 3 = regularly, 4 = frequently, 5 = always) in terms of how each statement applies to the way you currently live your life. Be honest with yourself. This is your opportunity to assess your present level of expertise before you start on a path to a new and exciting world of networking.

When you complete the series of statements, total your score and check to see where you rated yourself on the scale from Lone Ranger to power networker. You may notice that you have been a Lone Ranger most of your life or that you have already developed expertise and mastery in the area of networking. . . .

Know Your Own Power as a Networker

1. I know the values and principles that are important in my life.

2. I can list five major accomplishments that I am proud of in my life.

3. I am clear about my expertise and the resource I can be for others.

4. I have given up the Lone Ranger mentality.

5. I know my own power as a networker.

6. I have a written list of long- and short-term goals that I review and revise regularly.

7. I have a network diagram that represents the magnitude and diversity of my network.

Be Gracious and Courteous as You Network

8. My presentation professionally represents who I am and what I do.

9. I introduce myself in a way that is clear, concise, and personable, and that generates interest.

10. I am at ease in groups and use conversation generators effectively.

11. I reintroduce myself to people rather than waiting for them to remember me.

12. I focus on people as they are introduced to me so that I remember their name and who they are.

13. I am comfortable playing host at networking events.

14. I am comfortable promoting and creating visibility for myself and my business.

15. I am gracious and courteous with everyone I meet.

Handle Business Cards with Respect

16. My business cards are attractive and representative of who I am and what I do.

17. I have sufficient business cards handy for each situation.

18. I give out my business cards appropriately.

19. I make notations on business cards that I receive as memory joggers and follow-up reminders.

Nurture Your Network with Acknowledgments

20. I receive and give acknowledgments daily.

21. I acknowledge the people who inspire me whether or not I personally know them.

22. I nurture my network with calls, notes, and gifts in a timely and appropriate manner.

23. I have personalized notecards.

24. I graciously receive and accept acknowledgment and support.

Manage Yourself as a Resource

25. I have established an effective system for organizing and retrieving my network.

26. My business card file is organized and up to date.

27. I use a time management system effectively.

28. My daily action list is completed each day with items transferred or checked off.

29. I do what is in front of me rather than creating more items on my action list.

30. I return phone calls within twenty-four hours.

31. I organize my thoughts before making a phone call to referrals, leads, or people in my network.

32. I say no to events, activities, and meetings that drain my time, energy, or focus.

33. I prepare for networking events in order to maximize the opportunity.

Be Effective with Your Requests

34. I ask for and use the support of others.

35. I make requests of my network in a clear, concise, and nondemanding manner.

36. I consistently find opportunities to ask, "Who do you know who . . . ?"

37. I follow up promptly on leads.

38. I gain value from every contact.

Create Visibility through Participation

39. I am a member of a professional organization.

40. I serve on a committee or board of an organization.

41. I regularly give referrals to and make requests of my network.

42. I am aware of and use the "three-foot rule."

43. I consistently reevaluate and add to my network.

Develop a Personal Networking Approach

44. I trust and follow my intuition.

45. I am committed to the success of the people in my network.

46. I am known for the high level of service I provide.

47. I am an active and perceptive listener.

48. I operate with integrity and professionalism in all my interactions and endeavors.

49. I approach each contact and opportunity with an open mind.

Network to Enhance Your World

50. I am known as a powerful networker with an established and resourceful network.

51. I use networking to benefit myself and others personally as well as professionally.

52. I keep my network in the forefront of my thinking.

53. I am a role model for power networking.

54. I see the world as one big network.

55. Networking is a way of life for me.

Scores

275–237	Powerful
236–200	Effective
199–164	Resourceful
163–128	Branching Out
127–92	Timid
91–55	Lone Ranger

The above excerpt from Power Networking *is used with permission.*

23

The Road to Mastery

NOW IT'S TIME TO WRAP UP THIS PACKAGE OF NETWORKING WISDOM WITH A FEW short summaries. Lance Mead shares what he has learned about networking in the ten years since he attended a pivotal breakfast meeting; Dr. Philip E. Humbert lists his top ten networking dos and don'ts; Reed and Kathy Morgan offer a bit of homespun wisdom about doing what the smart ones do; John Meyer and John Milton Fogg compare networking to their favorite outdoor sports; and Emory Cowan reminds us to serve no wine before its time.

Nine Keys to Mastery

Lance Mead

A number of years ago, my client and friend Ray invited me to attend a business networking breakfast. I nearly declined. After all, I was a successful businessman. I knew all I needed to know about networking. I was a longtime member of the chamber of commerce, Rotary International, Kiwanis, and the Elks. I was networked to the hilt.

But I accepted Ray's invitation — and it opened my eyes. What I had been doing was no more then fantasy networking, a haphazard, half-hearted attempt at marketing myself by hanging out with people who had other priorities. The breakfast meeting showed me the real thing: referral networking, the purposeful and systematic generation of business referrals.

Since that breakfast meeting ten years ago, I've made it my avocation to study networking and to learn its most effective strategies and techniques from the masters. Here are nine of the most important points I've learned.

1. Embrace the "Givers gain" philosophy. Whether meeting an old friend or a new contact, the master networker's first thought is, What can I do to help? It's more than a strategy, it's a way of life. I don't think about getting something from the person I'm talking with; I know, from long experience, that whatever good I can do will eventually come back to me in another form. I realize now, too, that it's not what you know that makes the difference, it's who you know; people like to help those they know best. When I help my friends, business keeps coming back to me, time and time again.

2. Work in a disciplined structure. To make your network a valuable asset, you have to be well organized. You need a systematic way of developing contacts, keeping track of appointments, and following up on obligations. People need to know what to expect from you.

> Going to a networking meeting without a purposeful plan is a terrible waste of time.

3. Attend networking events. Networking meetings are for feeding, nurturing, and renewing your network connections, as well as for making new contacts. You can't do this if you don't show up. Commit to regular attendance, even when you're feeling tired or would rather be sailing. I thought I was doing Ray a favor by attending that first business networking meeting, but it was the other way around. Today I'm glad I went — and more important, listened.

4. Plan your networking. Going to a networking meeting without a purposeful plan is a terrible waste of time. Be prepared. Have a well-thought-out plan for working the room, networking with significant participants, or having meaningful conversations with key people. You can spot the folks who come without a plan: they stare into space waiting for the event to end.

5. Accept the teachings of a mentor. Emulating someone you admire is a great strategy for success. But the rewards of mentoring flow both ways: successful people often want others to benefit from their experience and wisdom. They want to be emulated, quoted, and recognized for their achievements. And there are few higher-quality contacts than a mentor, who is usually an accomplished, respected expert. If you adopt the attitudes and behaviors of one of the best, one day you may become a mentor yourself.

6. Become a great storyteller. People like to hear a good yarn, whether it's a true story about your rise to prominence or a shaggy-dog story about nothing in particular. Most people aren't good at telling their own story; they assume everybody knows it. But your story needs to be out there, so your contacts can tell it to others when they refer business to you. If you want it to be a good story, you'd best supply the details yourself rather than rely on someone else's imagination or fiction-writing talents.

7. Have a database of resources to help other people. Knowledge is power. Cultivate a reputation as a person who knows the people who can get things done. If you are seen as a person with power, a gatekeeper to what others need, a clearinghouse of sources, you can ensure that people will stay in touch with you and send you plenty of business.

8. Keep an open mind. The most important thing you can know is that you don't know it all. If your mind is open to new ideas, you can learn something every day, everywhere you go. Because I thought I knew all I needed to know about networking, I almost didn't go to that first meeting. The things I didn't know, and that I began to learn that day, have made all the difference in my success.

9. Make relationships a part of your life. I don't know who you know, and you don't know who I know, and we'll never know if we don't develop an effective relationship by networking and communicating. People will not share contacts with you just because you are smart and nice. They will share information and contacts because they share a relationship with you.

It's hard for me to imagine where I would be now had I chosen not to attend that first meeting, where I met Dr. Ivan Misner, founder of BNI. You never know who will have an impact on your business or your life.

Top Ten Dos and Don'ts for Referrals

Philip E. Humbert

Every professional practice depends on a steady flow of appropriate referrals. Building an effective network of colleagues who regularly refer clients can be difficult, but nothing is more critical to a profitable, efficient, and satisfying private practice. Accountants, attorneys, chiropractors, and physicians (and other professionals) depend on referrals. The following tips will help:

1. **DO:** Be visible and well-liked! Know lots of people and be sure they know who you are and what you do. This is obvious, but bears repeating: Get out of the office and mingle!

2. **DON'T:** Inappropriately use acquaintances or membership lists to build your practice. People hate being put on the spot!

3. **DO:** Join and contribute to worthwhile groups and causes. You have to put in before you can take out. Be known as a generous, friendly person with lots to give. Participate in your community!

4. **DON'T:** Grab the spotlight or chair every committee. Don't turn down positions of leadership or responsibility, but don't be pushy. Let people discover you!

5. **DO:** Show up! Whatever your current circle of friends and relationships, this week go someplace else! Keep adding new circles of influence and expand the range of your interests and involvements.

6. **DON'T:** Expect colleagues with similar credentials and expertise to be referral sources. They have their own businesses to build and are unlikely to share clients with you. Be realistic about this. Build your network of friends and associates, but don't put them on the spot by asking them to refer their own clients to you.

7. **DO:** Reach beyond your profession for business connections. Look to business owners, salespeople, educators, and managers. Anyone who connects with lots of people and who does not compete with you is a potential partner.

8. DON'T: Rush into business relationships. Have lunch, get acquainted, but never push a business card or brochure on anyone. Conveniently "forget" them at the office, and send a follow-up letter a couple days later.

9. DO: Make sure your business connections run both ways. Referring clients must make business sense to both sides. Make sure your work produces increased income, more convenience, better outcomes, or other specific benefits to your referral sources. This is only fair.

10. DON'T: Panic or try to rush. Most successful practices only need a handful of great referral sources. Select and cultivate them wisely and patiently. Build slowly and well. It pays huge dividends!

"If It Ain't Broke, Don't Fix It!"

Reed and Kathy Morgan

During the corporate takeovers, mergers, and buyouts of the late 1980s, Oklahoma-based Gaylord Entertainment Company purchased Nashville's *Grand Ole Opry.* The *Grand Ole Opry,* performed live to audiences and broadcast each weekend, was the longest-running program in the history of radio. It was a tradition. It was a success. It was an institution.

Rumors of impending "changes and fixes" by the new owners had been reported for weeks. Backstage at the corporate transition press conference, *Grand Ole Opry* comedienne Minnie Pearl offered the following advice to CEO Edward L. Gaylord regarding his new company: "If it ain't broke, don't fix it!" During his introduction, Mr. Gaylord announced that Minnie Pearl's advice would be accepted. He said: "The Opry certainly wasn't broke — so nobody will be fixing or changing it."

Competent, successful, professional businesspeople around the world repeat the same disastrous mistake: reinventing the wheel. They are hard-driven, results-oriented, winner-take-all types who are very eager for success — fast. New job or business, high goals, critical earnings requirements, short time frames. Do this, try that, reload, shoot from the hip, reassign duties and authority. . . . They keep trying new, different, and unproven methods to achieve their results, often with failure and frustration as the result.

The sure way to success is less glamorous, slower, more tedious, but much more likely to be successful. The sure way to success is to copy success. Don't reinvent the wheel; instead, use the principles and methods perfected by others to serve as your basis for competing.

We all know the drill; we've used it since childhood. "Learn from the mistakes and successes of others," we were told. Our earliest personal role models were our grandparents, parents, teachers, ministers, neighbors, friends, and other adults. As grownups, our business success models should be successful, recognized leaders who achieve high goals. There is a successful model for every product and industry. Find yours.

The first step toward success in networking or marketing your business is to identify one or more success models. Find the best examples of all-around success and replicate the best of the best. Study them, interview them, read their articles and books, attend their seminars and training sessions. Use them as mentors if possible. Learn all you can about what they do and don't do. Their program ain't broke — so don't fix it. Replicate it.

1. Identify the individuals or programs that are your success models. Learn all you can about the organization, activity, content, presentation, and philosophy they use to achieve success.

2. Model the key elements of your effort after the best elements of your success models. You can combine the best elements of several models.

3. Implement your new model sequentially. Introduce each step of your success model in a logical sequence, and always respond to market feedback.

4. Master the skills with repetitive practice. Modify what you've learned from others to better fit your personality and skills.

5. Replicate the best of the success models you've chosen. Practice regularly, repetitively, and consistently, and seek constant improvement.

You will owe your success in part to those who have helped you both actively and by being good examples. You must repay their good deeds by helping others achieve success.

Better Than Par

John Meyer

Taking friends, clients, and prospects to the golf course for an afternoon of fun, food, and exercise has always been a popular way to enhance and solidify a potentially profitable relationship. But there's a difference between being an amateur and being a pro — both on the golf course and in networking.

Among golfers, the difference is not as profound as you might think. The top pros go around the course in about sixty-nine strokes; top amateurs, seventy-one. But the margin is crucial. The top ten pros average about $1.5 million a year in prizes; amateurs make $0.00. Those two strokes make a lot of difference — about $750,000 per stroke!

In networking, being a pro rather than an amateur is similarly rewarding. In fact, there are a lot of parallels between professional golfers and professional networkers. Here are a few of the principles involved in shaving a few points off your score and winning the big bucks.

EQUIPMENT

To play golf professionally, you need the best clubs, balls, tees, shoes. The top networker needs high-quality business cards, a professionally produced name tag, a business card caddy, a top-flight contact management system. The top pro golfer's equipment is provided by manufacturers; some pro networking organizations provide networking equipment as part of the membership fees.

PRACTICE

The only way to become a master is to practice. I recently heard Lee Trevino advise a golf neophyte: "If you go out and play a five-hour round of golf on a weekend, then you should go out and practice for five hours on the range before you go to the course again."

What does "practice" mean, in networking terms? It means getting good at getting contacts: the better you get, the closer to the green you find yourself. Spend as much time as you can going out and meeting people. Sometimes this seems to be a lot of effort with no immediate payoff. But it will eventually pay off in close networking relationships and profitable referrals. It's like practicing your tee and fairway shots.

What about your short game? PGA Tour golfers know they make more money sinking a three-foot putt than hitting a 300-yard drive. In networking, the pitch or chip shots that get you on the green are the short commercials and longer presentations that you use to keep your group thinking about your products or services. The putt for the money? That's when you create a valuable networking partner or close a business deal.

The more you practice these shots, the better you will become at executing them successfully. A pro golfer spends about twenty hours a week playing golf for a living. The rest of the week is spent practicing on the driving range and the putting green. In the days before a major tournament, the ratio of practice to play may approach four to one.

The professional networker should take to heart this four-to-one ratio. Practice your commercials and presentations. Work on your skills at communicating, managing contacts, and following up.

THE NUMBER ONE RULE

Top pro golfers have one characteristic above all others: they are passionate about pitting their hard-won skills against the rules and coming out on top. Master networkers have this same passion. They love helping others — a love that comes from an understanding that the way to receive business is to give business. The master networker plays by the number-one networking rule: "Givers gain."

Like Riding a Bicycle

John Milton Fogg

"**W**hat specifically do you advise me to do right now to build my networking skills?" Here's what you do: Go get a bicycle — yes, I'm serious, get a bicycle. Great. Now, I want you to pretend that you are from Mars. (For the others of you — and you know who you are — pretend you're from Venus.) There are no bicycles on those planets. Imagine that you have never seen a bicycle before. Pretty weird contraption, ain't it? What do you suppose it's for? Go ahead, pick it up. Turn it over. If you set it down on the handlebars and seat and step across it, you could probably sit right in

> Most people don't have a clue about what networking really is, let alone how to "ride" it.

that V-shaped place. Yeah, that round thing with all the teeth is pretty uncomfortable. (No, don't move those pedals — that would really hurt!)

My friends, that bicycle is a complete mystery — to someone who's never seen one before. Sure, given enough time and a truly playful, curious attitude, a Martian might get around to sitting on it and might even make it go. Eventually.

That bicycle is just like networking. Most people don't have a clue about what networking really is, let alone how to "ride" it. And until they do. . . .

Okay, my Martian (or Venusian) friend — I'm going to teach you how to ride a bicycle. Ready? Good. Here's a book about bicycles — read it. Here's a video about bicycles — watch it. Here's an audio — listen to it. Then, come to a training retreat. The best bicycle rider in the world will be there, and he'll show you how to ride; he'll give you some great tips and techniques on riding, on maintaining your bicycle, on the differences between mountain bikes and road racers, and. . . .

Great. Now you know all about bicycles. You've read books and seen videos about the design of the bicycle, its evolution, the physics of riding, the different parts of the bike and what they do and how they work together. You've seen other people ride up and down mountains and watched Lance Armstrong cross the finish line at the Tour d' Altoona. You now know, beyond the shadow of a doubt, that riding a bicycle is possible. ("If they can do it, I can do it.") And you even got to ride on the crossbar with the "best bicycle rider in the world" in the parking lot.

Tell the truth: you still don't get what it's like to be a bicycle rider, do you? All that knowledge simply doesn't do it. Even that experience doesn't cut it. Sure, you've got some ideas about bikes and riding — but a rider you are not.

Now let's stop being metaphorical for a minute and think about a real bicycle — your first bike. How did you learn to ride it? Probably started with a tricycle. Learned how to steer with those handle bars; how to pedal and make it go. And stop, too — learned that one fast! Probably banged into things, fell off, went out of control down a hill — but since you're reading this, we know you survived. And then, that first two-wheeler. Actually, four — two were "training" wheels. Principle's pretty much the same, but oh, this puppy is bigger and faster — much faster. Then, one day, those two little red wheels came off. All right! Were you scared? Somewhere between excited and frightened? Was it exhilarating? Of course.

By the way, did you do this bike thing alone? No — your older brother or sister or mom or dad was right there beside you. Showed you how to lean the sucker over a bit so you could hoist your leg across to the other side, how to position that right pedal at about one o'clock, the whole routine. And they held onto your bike so you wouldn't fall. And they ran alongside you and kept holding on to the seat. And all the while they were doing this, what were they saying to you? "Fall, you little creep! Crash and die!" No, of course not: they were your biggest cheerleaders. "You can do it! That's right! That's great! You're doin' it — you're terrific!"

Then, that magic moment when the person running alongside let go — and you rode your bike! I'll bet each one of you can remember that feeling — that moment when you got it. Balance, strength, direction, timing, equipment, arms, legs, eyes, brain, judgment — it all came together. You got it! You were being a bicycle rider!

Okay, now you can think "networking" again. You see, you get networking just like you got it when you first rode a bike. Has that happened for you? Yes, I know that you know what networking is, how it works — but are you *being* a networker? Were you taught to be a networker the way you were taught to ride a bike? (Most people aren't.) Are you teaching your people to ride the networking bicycle? (Most people don't — you can't teach what you don't know.)

Get the distinction. "Grok" it. Learn how to be a networker. Then teach others how to do and be what you know how to do and be.

How do you do that? The same way you learned to ride a bicycle — exactly the same way.

Making Wine

Emory Cowan

Building a word-of-mouth marketing plan requires developing a trusted network of partners — which means cultivating relationships. But relationships require time, energy, persistence, and, most of all, patience.

I believe that patience gives us the most difficulty. We live in a quick-fix, immediate-gratification society where patience is neither valued nor encouraged. We want our sales now, our business fully grown now, our satisfaction in wealth now.

But when I grow impatient with the tedious process of developing relationships, one of life's many humbling lessons comes back to remind and instruct me: Drink no wine before its time.

Many years ago, I bought some peaches at the farmers' market in Atlanta. They were the famous Georgia peaches, grown in orchards in the Fort Valley region and renowned for their sweet, juicy taste and wonderful aroma. I took them home, visions of peach pies and cobblers dancing in my head. We ate some right away; most sat out on the kitchen counter.

One morning I was awakened by the aroma of peaches filling the house. I knew that something would have to be done with them soon or they would spoil. Wine, I thought. Why not make some peach wine?

I knew my parents, who lived fifteen miles away, had an old ceramic crock and an old family recipe for fermenting wine from fruit. I found the crock, cleaned it, and, on the way home, bought cheese-cloth for the top, along with yeast and sugar for the ingredients.

By the time I got home, my excitement over this project was so great that I could almost taste new wine as I cut up the peaches, added the sugar and yeast, and closed the top with the cheesecloth.

But the process of making wine is slow, and I was impatient. With the crock safely stashed in the cool basement, I drove home from work each day with growing excitement. I would go immediately to the crock and smell the brew. As the days went by I became more intent on having the wine ready for consumption. But it was not happening fast enough for me.

So, one afternoon, frustrated that it was taking so long, I carried the crock to the kitchen, determined to speed up the process of fermentation. I removed the contents, used a blender to further emulsify the peaches, and added more sugar and yeast. Smug and satisfied, I returned the crock to the basement, and three days later I had — vinegar.

My vinegar-making triumph has become a life-shaping parable for me. When I am tempted to rush the process of forming relationships, whether in business, in a networking group, or in my personal life, I am reminded that some things just take time to happen. I am aware that letting my impatience force the process can turn the potential of new wine into vinegar.

Patience in developing relationships is a virtue. It leads to solid networked contacts who can help you with your business, your interests, and your life.

Bibliography

Baber, Anne, and Lynne Waymon. *Great Connections: Small Talk and Networking for Businesspeople (Second Ed.).* Manassas Park, Va.: Impact Publications, 1992.

Baber, Anne, and Lynne Waymon. *Smart Networking: How to Turn Contacts into Cash, Clients, & Career Success.* Dubuque, Iowa: Kendall/Hunt Publishing, 1997.

Bell, Catherine. *Your Image Potential.* Kingston, Ontario: Catherine Bell, 1997.

Bjorseth, Lillian. *Breakthrough Networking: Building Relationships That Last.* Lisle, Ill.: Duoforce, 1996.

Blanchard, Ken, and Robert Lorber. *Putting the One-Minute Manager to Work.* New York: William Morrow and Co., 1984.

Bly, Bob. *The Copywriter's Handbook.* New York: Owl, 1992.

Boe, Anne. *Networking Success.* Encinitas, Calif.: Seaside Press, 1994.

Boe, Anne, and Bettie B. Youngs. *Is Your "Net" Working?* New York: Wiley & Sons, 1989.

Burg, Bob. *Endless Referrals: Network Your Everyday Contacts into Sales.* New York: McGraw-Hill, 1994.

Byrum-Robinson, B., and D. Womeldroff. "Networking Skills Inventory." In *The 1990 Annual: Developing Human Resources,* edited by J. William Pfeiffer. San Diego: University Associates, 1990.

Canfield, Jack, and Mark Victor Hansen. *Dare to Win.* Deerfield Beach, Fla.: Health Communications, 1988.

Cashman, Kevin J. *Networking: Building Relationships, Building Success.* St. Paul, Minn.: Devine Multi-Media Publishing, 1994.

Cates, Bill. *Unlimited Referrals: Secrets That Turn Business Relationships into Gold.* Wheaton, Md.: Thunder Hill Press, 1996.

Chopra, Deepak. *The Seven Spiritual Laws of Success.* Novato, Calif.: New World Library, 1995.

Craig, Robert L., ed. *Training and Development Handbook.* New York: McGraw-Hill, 1987.

Daniels, Aubrey. *How to Bring Out the Best in People.* New York: McGraw-Hill, 1993.

Davidson, Jeff. *Marketing on a Shoestring.* New York: Wiley & Sons, 1988.

Davis, Robert, and Laura Miller. *Total Quality Introductions* (audiocassette). Upland, Calif.: Robert Davis Associates, 1991.

De Raffele, Frank J. Jr., and Edward D. Hendricks. *Successful Business Networking.* Worcester, Mass.: Chandler House Press, 1998.

Edwards, Paul, and Sarah Edwards. *The Best Home Businesses for the 21st Century: The Inside Information You Need to Know to Select a Home-Based Business That's Right for You.* Los Angeles: Jeremy P. Tarcher, 1999.

Edwards, Paul, and Sarah Edwards. *Working from Home: Everything You Need to Know about Living and Working under the Same Roof.* Los Angeles: Jeremy P. Tarcher, 1999.

Edwards, Paul, Sarah Edwards, and Rick Benzel. *Teaming Up: The Small Business Guide to Collaborating with Others to Boost Your Earnings and Expand Your Horizons.* New York: Tarcher/Putnam, 1997.

Edwards, Paul, Sarah Edwards, and Laura Douglas. *Getting Business to Come to You: A Complete Do-It-Yourself Guide to Attracting All the Business You Can Enjoy.* Los Angeles: Jeremy P. Tarcher, 1998.

Fisher, Donna. *People Power: 12 Power Principles to Enrich Your Business, Career & Personal Networks.* Austin: Bard Press, 1995.

Fisher, Donna, and Sandy Vilas. *Power Networking: 59 Secrets for Personal & Professional Success (Second Ed.).* Austin: Bard Press, 2000.

Fogg, John Milton. *The Greatest Networker in the World.* Roseville, Calif.: Prima Publishing, 1997.

Fraser, George. *Success Runs in Our Race: The Complete Guide to Effective Networking in the African-American Community.* New York: Avon Books, 1994.

Goodman, Morris E. *The Miracle Man: An Inspiring Story of Motivation and Courage.* Virginia Beach, Va.: Miracle Man Productions, 1991.

Holtz, Herman. *Great Promo Pieces: Create Your Own Brochures, Broadsides, Ads, Flyers and Newsletters That Get Results.* New York: Wiley & Sons, 1991.

Henderson, Robyn. *How to Master Networking.* Sydney: Prentice Hall Australia, 1997.

Henderson, Robyn. *Networking for $uccess.* Collaroy Plateau, Australia: Murray Child & Company, 1998.

Jolley, Willie. *It Only Takes a Minute to Change Your Life.* New York: St. Martin's Press, 1997.

Kaufmann, Mel. *The Link: The Missing Link in Your Financial Empire*. San Pedro, Calif.: TRM, 1997.

Kay, Herb. *How to Get Filthy, Stinking Rich and Still Have Time for Great Sex: An Entrepreneur's Guide to Wealth and Happiness*. Austin: Bard Press, 2000.

Krannich, Robert L., and Caryl Rae Krannich. *Network Your Way to Job and Career Success*. Alexandria, Va.: Impact Publications, 1989.

Levinson, Jay Conrad. *Guerrilla Marketing: Secrets for Making Big Profits from Your Small Business*. New York: Houghton Mifflin, 1993.

Linn, Susann. *Directory of Orange County Networking Organizations, 1999 edition*. Corona Del Mar, Calif.: Susann Linn, 1998.

Mackay, Harvey. *Dig Your Well Before You're Thirsty*. New York: Doubleday, 1997.

Mackay, Harvey. *Swim With the Sharks Without Being Eaten Alive*. New York: Random House/Ballantine, 1996.

McBride, Joe. *Tooting Your Own Horn: A Professional's Guide to Marketing and Promoting Yourself Without Becoming Totally Obnoxious* (audiocassette). Spokane, Wash.: Joe McBride/Jump Start Press, 1998.

Misner, Ivan R. *Networking for Success*. Claremont, Calif.: Business Paradigm Productions, 1987.

Misner, Ivan R. *Seven Second Marketing: How to Use Memory Hooks to Make You Instantly Stand Out in a Crowd*. Austin: Bard Press, 1996.

Misner, Ivan R. *The World's Best Known Marketing Secret: Building Your Business with Word-of-Mouth Marketing (Revised Ed.)*. Austin: Bard Press, 2000.

Misner, Ivan R., and Robert Davis. *Business by Referral: A Sure-Fire Way to Generate New Business*. Austin: Bard Press, 1998.

Naisbitt, John. *Megatrends: Ten New Directions Transforming Our Lives*. New York: Warner Books, 1982.

Naisbitt, John, and Patricia Aburdenem. *Re-Inventing the Corporation*. New York: Warner Books, 1985.

Office of the President. *The State of Small Business: A Report of the President*. Washington, D.C.: U.S. Government Printing Office, 1987.

Osborn, Alex. *Applied Imagination*. New York: Charles Scribner, 1953.

Peters, Tom. *Thriving on Chaos: Handbook for a Management Revolution*. New York: Alfred A. Knopf, 1987.

Poe, Richard. *Wave 4: Network Marketing in the 21st Century*. Roseville, Calif.: Prima Publishing, 1999.

Ries, Al, and Jack Trout. *Positioning: The Battle for Your Mind.* New York: McGraw-Hill, 1981.

RoAne, Susan. *How to Work a Room: Learn the Strategies of Savvy Socializing — for Business and Personal Success.* New York: Warner Books, 1991.

RoAne, Susan. *The Secrets of Savvy Networking.* New York: Warner Books, 1993.

Rogers, Everett M., and D. Lawrence Kincaid. *Communication Networks: Toward a New Paradigm for Research.* New York: Free Press, 1981.

Scheele, Adele. *Skills for Success.* New York: William Morrow and Co., 1979.

Sheer, Mark. *Referrals: Earn More Money in Less Time and Have More Fun.* Mission Viejo, Calif.: Mark Sheer Seminars, 1993.

Sheldon, Betsy, and Joyce Hadley. *The Smart Woman's Guide to Networking.* Franklin Lakes, N.J.: Career Press, 1995.

Small Business Administration. *1988 Annual Report.* Washington, D.C.: U.S. Government Printing Office, 1988.

Stanley, Thomas. *Marketing to the Affluent.* Homewood, Ill.: BusinessOne-Irwin, 1988.

Sukenick, Ron. *Networking Your Way to Success: A Proven Method for Building, Developing and Implementing a Network of Your Own Key Contacts.* Dubuque, Iowa: Kendall/Hunt Publishing, 1995.

Toffler, Alvin. *Power Shift: Knowledge, Wealth, and Violence at the Edge of the 21st Century.* New York: Bantam Books, 1990.

Toffler, Alvin. *The Third Wave.* New York: William Morrow and Co., 1980.

Tye, Joe. *Never Fear, Never Quit: A Story of Courage and Perseverance.* Solon, Iowa: Paradox 21 Press, 1995.

U.S. Chamber of Commerce. *1992 Survey of Local Chambers of Commerce.* Washington, D.C.: Office of Chamber of Commerce Relations, 1992.

U.S. Department of Commerce. *Enterprise Statistics.* Washington, D.C.: U.S. Government Printing Office, 1977.

Wilson, Jerry R. *Word-of-Mouth Marketing.* New York: John Wiley & Sons, 1991.

Woods, Donald R., and Shirley D. Ormerod. *Networking: How to Enrich Your Life and Get Things Done.* San Diego, Calif.: Pfeiffer & Co., 1993.

Contributors

The following contact information is available on BNI's Masters of Networking website, www.MastersofNetworking.com, where it will be regularly updated.

Jeremy M. Allen founded Youth Excellence in Birmingham, Alabama, while attending Samford University. The company provides dynamic training, motivational and inspirational seminars and workshops for fifteen- to nineteen-year-olds across America. Jeremy serves on various boards of directors and committees, including the Homewood Chamber of Commerce, the Shelby County Chapter of the Red Cross, Leadership Shelby County, Young Business Leaders, and Junior Achievement. Recently, Jeremy was chosen as Birmingham's youngest-ever up and coming "Top 40 Under 40." As executive director of BNI for Birmingham and Huntsville, Alabama, he has twice earned an annual Top Ten Regions award. He is currently working on a motivational book and CD set entitled *Success and Significance*. Contact: jeremy@bni.com.

Anne Baber writes articles on business topics, is an adjunct professor with Webster University, presents workshops, seminars, and keynotes on business networking and workplace communication, and is president of Baber & Associates. Before starting her own business, she was director of corporate communications for United Telecom. She is coauthor, with Lynne Waymon, of *Smart Networking* and *Great Connections*. Contact: Baber & Associates, 13433 W. 80th Terrace, Lenexa, KS 66215, 913-894-4212, fax 913-492-6575, 800-352-2939, ababer@contactscount.com.

Candace Bailly, who worked as a naval intelligence analyst in the Pentagon, opened BNI's San Diego region and became its director. Now a BNI executive director for Oregon and Southwest Washington, she is currently coauthoring (with Dr. Ivan Misner) a book on creating brilliant business cards. Candace is a member of BNI's Founders' Circle (2000–2001). She has a B.S. degree in business administration. Contact: PO Box 57, Sherwood, OR 97140, 503-925-8251, fax 503-925-9890, crbailly@bni.com, www.bni-oregon.com.

Anna D. Banks has more than twenty-two years of experience in accounting and finance with the federal government, has managed a financial planning and tax preparation firm, and served as corporate secretary and director of the National Association of Tax Practitioners. She has a B.S. degree from Douglass College,

Rutgers University. Anna received the 1999 Professional Achievement Award from the Lenni-Lenape Girl Scout Council's Women of Distinction Committee. She is an area director of BNI for the New Jersey area. Contact: PO Box 246, S. Orange, NJ 07079-0246, 973-673-3539, njbni@bellatlantic.net.

Bill Becks spent twenty-four years with the Addiction Research Foundation in the province of Ontario, Canada, latterly as director of community programs. He is a director of the Children's Aid Society. Currently executive director of BNI in Central North Ontario, he has a B.A. in sociology and a master's degree in social work. Contact: 705-487-1917, becks@csolve.net.

Catherine Bell, a board member of the Association of Image Consultants International (AICI), began her career in fashion design and teaching. Her company, Prime Impressions, specializes in image issues that affect the success of individuals and corporate management. A freelance writer, Catherine has self-published *Managing Your Image Potential,* a handbook on professional appearance and protocol. She is an assistant director of BNI. Contact: Prime Impressions, 574 Princess St., Ste. 100, Kingston, Ontario, Canada K7L 1C9, 613-549-9996, fax 613-549-4117, image@kos.net, www.webwoods.com/prime.

Lillian D. Bjorseth is founder and president of Duoforce Enterprises Inc., a company that teaches networking skills and interpersonal relationship building. She has coached top executives at AT&T in communication and public relations skills. She is the author of the *Breakthrough Networking: Building Relationships That Last* book and audiotape series and the *Nothing Happens Until We Communicate* audiotape and workbook series. Lillian is a member of the National Speakers Association and vice president of marketing communication for the Illinois chapter. Contact: 2221 Ridgewood Rd., PO Box 1154, Lisle, IL 60532, 630-983-5308, fax 630-983-5312, lillian@duoforce.com, www.duoforce.com.

Victor Blumenthal has thirty-five years of experience managing multimillion-dollar profit centers for Honeywell, Automatic Data Processing, and Avery Dennison, and six years as president of a manufacturing company. He is an executive director of BNI for Cape Cod and Southeast Massachusetts. Contact: 508-563-6834, fax 508-563-2049, vicblu@bni.com.

David Bullock visited South Africa immediately after receiving his degree in industrial economics from Nottingham University, England. After working with the Southern Rhodesian government in various positions, he returned to England before a posting in Indonesia with Unilever, where he became the general manager in 1975. Since then, David has operated as a specialist recruiter in the Far East and is currently an executive director for BNI. Contact: Wootton Wawen, England, 44-1789-488-085, david@bni-swmids.org.uk.

Bob Burg, president of Burg Communications, Inc., is a professional speaker and consultant on the topics of communication skills and business networking. A former television news anchor, salesperson, and sales manager, he is a much-sought-after keynote speaker for major corporations, associations, and sales organizations throughout North America. He is the author of *Endless Referrals*. Contact: Burg Communications, Inc., PO Box 7002, Jupiter, FL 33468-7002, 561-575-2114 or 800-726-3667, fax 561-575-2304, www.Burg.com.

Craig Campana is an author, motivational speaker, and networking trainer whose seventeen-year career in television, publishing, advertising, and business consulting includes working with director Steven Speilberg on the visual history *Survivors of the Shoah*. He founded the first chapter of Business Network Int'l. in Wisconsin and since has grown the region to over sixty chapters. A member of BNI's Founders' Circle for four years, he is a certified networking trainer and a nominee for BNI National Director of the Year 2000. He is a contributing author to *Confessions of Shameless Self-Promoters* (spring 2001) and is coauthoring his own book about career path networking. Contact: 262-781-7194, fax 262-781-7219, referrals@bniwis.com, www.bniwis.com.

Phillip Campbell, entrepreneur and network professional, began his career in the U.S. Marine Corps, Special Operations. He has successfully developed many businesses, including his current ones, Network Publishing & Network Marketing Products, and PremiumSteaks.com. As a network consultant, he has worked with new organizations such as Go-Givers Network and has lectured on networking for civic, business, and education groups, including California Polytechnic. Contact: 516 N. Diamond Bar Blvd. #400, Diamond Bar, CA 91765-1007, 888-NTWK-PUB (888-689-5782), 909-397-0707, fax 909-397-0767, ntwkpub@earthlink.net, www.premiumsteaks.com.

Jack Canfield is one of America's leading experts in the development of human potential and personal effectiveness. Besides being coauthor of the best-selling *Chicken Soup* book series, he is the author and narrator of several best-selling audio- and videocassette programs, including *Chicken Soup for the Soul — Live, Self-Esteem and Peak Performance*, and *How to Build High Self-Esteem*. He is regularly seen on television shows such as *Good Morning America, 20/20, CBS Eye to Eye*, and *NBC Nightly News*. Jack addresses over 100 groups each year. His clients include professional associations, school districts, government agencies, churches, sales organizations, and corporations. Contact: www.jackcanfield.com.

Bill Cates speaks to salespeople in dozens of industries on how to increase sales and build a business through referrals. He has worked in customer service management at American Airlines and has created and sold a book publishing company. In addition to authoring the book *Unlimited Referrals*, he has written several audiocassette albums on sales and sales management, including *Break the Voice Mail Barrier, No More Cold Calls, Where Did the Time Go?* and *Creating Influence.* Contact: 2915 Fenimore Road, Silver Spring, MD 20902-2600, 800-488-5464, 301-949-6789, fax 301-949-8564.

Deepak Chopra is the best-selling author of *The Seven Spiritual Laws of Success; Ageless Body, Timeless Mind; Quantum Healing; and Creating Affluence,* as well as audio and video programs that promote health and well-being. His books have been translated into more than twenty-five languages, and he lectures widely throughout North America, South America, India, Europe, Japan, and Australia. He is the executive director of the Institute of Mind-Body Medicine and Human Potential at Sharp HealthCare in San Diego. Contact: 858-551-7788, www.chopra.com.

Emory G. Cowan Jr., Ph.D., is president and CEO of the Colorado School of Professional Psychology. He is a retired U.S. Army chaplain, a retired United Methodist Church clergyperson, and was an assistant professor of psychology at Chapman University, where he directed the Colorado Springs Academic Center's graduate programs in psychology. Contact: www.bnicolorado.com.

Marjorie S. Cowan, M.A., was a Dale Carnegie instructor for the Sales Advantage and the Dale Carnegie courses for fifteen years, and is now a real estate broker. A graduate of Redlands University, Margie holds an M.A. in psychology from Chapman University. She also chairs the board of the nonprofit Switzer Counseling Center in Colorado Springs. A BNI member for over eleven years, Marjorie has directed chapter growth in the Front Range of Colorado since 1997. She is the executive director of BNI in Colorado. Contact: 5317 Cracker Barrel Circle, Colorado Springs, CO 80917-1803, 888-264-2656 (toll free), 719-596-8010, fax 719-570-0497, cowan@bni.com, www.bnicolorado.com.

Ed Craine has been an entrepreneur since he operated his own house painting business in high school. Ed received a B.A. in history in 1973 and an M.B.A. in finance and marketing from Cornell University. He is president of Smith-Craine Finance, a San Francisco mortgage company, and has been a BNI executive director since 1996 when he acquired the San Francisco/San Mateo franchise. Contact: 2645 Ocean Ave. #202, San Francisco, CA 94132, 415-406-2330, fax 415-406-2340, ecraine@smithcraine.com, www.smithcraine.com.

Robert Davis is a professional speaker, trainer, coach, and president of Robert Davis Associates. He is the author of *Implement Now, Perfect Later* and coauthor (with Ivan R. Misner) of *Business by Referral.* He is the president of the Greater Los Angeles Chapter of the National Speakers Association. Robert is also founder of the Recovering Perfectionist Club. Contact: 909-681-0686, RDavisNSA@aol.com.

Frank J. De Raffele Jr. is president of ProActive Consulting, Inc., author of the book *Successful Business Networking*, an executive director for BNI, a business columnist, and the executive producer and co-host of the radio program *Business Talk Network*. He is also an internationally acclaimed motivational speaker and trainer. He has received international recognition in the *Toronto Star* and the *Globe and Mail* of Canada and has been featured in *Success, Employment Review,* and *Professional Selling* magazines and on many national radio and television programs. Contact: 1260 North Avenue, Beacon, NY 12508, 845-838-2805, fax 845-440-0508, fderaffele@aol.com.

Norm Dominguez, currently BNI's national director in San Dimas, California, joined BNI in 1987 after an extensive career in sales and marketing. He became an executive director in May 1989 with chapters in Arizona and New Mexico. He has served on the BNI Franchise Advisory Board and as a district director, and he developed the educational coordinator position and chapter medallion program. Contact: BNI, 199 S. Monte Vista Ave., Ste. 6, San Dimas, CA 91773-3080, 909-305-1818, fax 909-305-1811, norm@bni.com.

Sandy Donovan began her career in sales and later moved into radio promotions and public relations. She became a BNI director in South Florida in January 1997, where she now conducts workshops and seminars for companies and business organizations on increasing sales through referrals. Contact: sandybni@bellsouth.net.

Paul and Sarah Edwards, known to many as "The Self-Employment Experts," are the authors of the best-selling *Working from Home* book series and coauthors (with Rick Benzel) of *Teaming Up*. They give advice to audiences of their radio and television shows, on line, and through their magazine columns in *Home Office Computing* and *Small Business Computing* magazines. Contact: c/o "Q&A," *Home Office Computing* magazine, 730 Broadway, New York, NY 10003, www.homeworks.com.

Bruce Elliott spent over twenty years in the Canadian traffic and transportation industry as a professional civil engineer. He operated several small businesses before opening BNI regions in Ontario and Alberta. He has lectured at colleges and universities across Canada. Bruce and his wife, Eleanor, helped create BNI Canada. They operate a 100-acre farm near Stratford, Ontario. Contact: 519-475-4643, 888-375-1904, bni@execulink.com, www.bnicanada.ca.

Todd A. Evans is an executive director of BNI for Manitoba, Canada, and a past executive director (now assistant director) for Eastern Ontario and Western Quebec. He is vice president of business development for Crossdraw Technologies Inc., marketing web applications to assist in collaboration, consultation, customer service, and customer retention. Contact: Crossdraw Inc., 800-280 Albert St., Ottawa, Ontario, Canada K1P 5G8, 613-292-2647, fax 613-239-0328, toddevans@bnieast.com, www.bnieast.com, www.crossdraw.com.

Donna Fisher, CSP, conducts keynote presentations and seminars on the importance of people skills, networking, and the personal touch in today's high-tech culture. Her clients include Hewlett Packard, Chase Bank, and Arthur Andersen. She has held sales, marketing, and management positions with Exxon, McDonnell Douglas Automation Company, and the University of Houston. She is a member of the Business Owners Advisory Board of the American Business Women's Association and has written two best-selling business books, *Power Networking* (with Sandy Vilas) and *People Power*. Contact: 6524 San Felipe, Ste. 138, Houston, TX 77057, 800-934-9675, donna@donnafisher.com, www.donnafisher.com.

Tom Fleming is the director of training for the Certified Networker Program in Massachusetts, a college-level course teaching business professionals how to become more productive and effective networkers. He has been working with BNI for the last five years while launching various business ventures. Tom's experience also includes ten years with various Fortune 500 companies, a business degree from Boston University, and an MBA from Babson College. Tom aspires to continue to educate and motivate others through his speaking engagements. Contact: 617-376-0537, TomF@bni.com.

John Milton Fogg is the founder of *Upline* and *Network Marketing Lifestyles* magazines and the author or editor of more than twenty-four books and audio programs, including *The Greatest Networker in the World*. Contact: 4881 Parson's Green, Charlottesville, VA 22903, 804-823-2343, jmf@greatestnetworker.com, www.greatestnetworker.com.

James A. Fontanella is founder and president of Renaissance Executive Forums, an international organization that offers a variety of services designed specifically for the top executive, such as its advisory board forums, in which business chief executives and owners provide peer review. Contact: Renaissance Executive Forums, Inc., 7855 Ivanhoe Avenue, Ste. 300, La Jolla, CA 92037, 858-551-6600, fax 858-551-8777, jim@executiveforums.com, www.executiveforums.com.

George C. Fraser, who received his executive training at Dartmouth College, is the founder and chairman of the board of SuccessSource, Inc., a source of products and programs to promote networking within the African-American community. He is the author of the book *Success Runs in Our Race* and publisher of *SuccessGuide: The Networking Guide to Black Resources*. He has been a manager at Procter & Gamble, United Way, and Ford. Contact: SuccessSource, Inc., 1949 E. 105th St. #100, Cleveland, OH 44106, 216-791-9330.

Robert French, who lives in Canterbury, England, was a successful farmer for twenty years, during which time he represented the interests of farmers by becoming active in agricultural politics. He now runs a large marketing organization for businesspeople wishing to grow their businesses through highly focused networking in Europe and Asia. Contact: 44-1227-700-352, robert_french@invictanet.co.uk.

Dan Georgevich is an executive director for BNI in Michigan. In this role, Dan supports over sixty BNI chapters, helping business professionals increase their sales. His accomplishments include conducting Certified Networker Program training and doing on-line interactive sessions on the Internet for international audiences. Dan has been recognized with national awards for his contributions to helping others get more business through word-of-mouth marketing. Contact: 810-323-3800, fax 810-323-3838, dang@bni-mi.com, www.bni-mi.com.

Nancy Giacomuzzi has been a real estate agent for more than seventeen years and has served in a variety of professional organizations. She was instrumental in establishing BNI in Minnesota. As an executive director for thirty chapters, she speaks to groups throughout the state. Contact: 800-416-0759, 612-986-6266, fax 952-920-6496, nancygi@worldnet.att.net, www.bni-mn.com.

Morris E. Goodman is the author of the book *The Miracle Man* and, with Zig Ziglar, the creator of the motivational movie of the same name. He was a highly successful life insurance salesman in his thirties at the time of the events chronicled in his book. He has authored many cassette tape albums on goal-setting, self-esteem, and self-worth. He is a speaker and trainer to Fortune 500 companies and associations all over the world. Contact: 4176 Cheswick Lane, Virginia Beach, VA 23455, 757-490-9262, goodman@skybiz.com.

Carol S. Grebe served for sixteen years as administrative director for five children's mental health outpatient facilities in Southern California. She is now a BNI executive director for the San Francisco North Bay and Sacramento regions, with more than 750 members in thirty-seven chapters. She is also coordinator for BNI's Networking Online and a member of the BNI Founders' Circle. Contact: BNI, 925 Lakeville St. #331, Petaluma, CA 94952-3329, 707-773-1370, fax 707-773-1114, bnisfbay@aol.com, www.bni-sfbay.com.

Cynthia Greenawalt-Carvajal, BNI's executive director in the Fort Lauderdale/Miami area, is a management consultant, business coach, and entrepreneur. With her degree from the Wharton School of Business, the University of Pennsylvania, and ten years of study in shifting leadership paradigms, she provides entrepreneurs, business owners, and sales teams with access to breakthrough results in their productivity and effectiveness. A former All-American swimmer, she contributes on a global level as an investor in The Hunger Project. She is currently recording her first collection of songs on CD, promoting music that stirs the human spirit. Contact: 516 SW 18th Street, Suite 2, Ft. Lauderdale, FL 33315, 954-455-9400, fax 954-779-3068, cynthia@bni.com, www.bni.com.

Joyce Hadley (Copeland) is coauthor (with Betsy Sheldon) of *The Smart Woman's Guide to Networking*. She and Sheldon were co-editors of a consumer travel magazine in the 1980s and their collaboration turned into a long-lasting friendship and professional relationship. She is now a full-time writer on careers. Her latest book, published January 2000, is *Where the Jobs Are: The Hottest Careers for the 21st Century*.

Mark Victor Hansen is coauthor of the best-selling series *Chicken Soup for the Soul* and author of *Dare to Win* and other bestsellers. A popular professional speaker on sales excellence and personal empowerment, he addresses thousands of people each year through corporate programs, national trade and professional associations, and educational and philanthropic institutions around the world. Contact: Mark Victor Hansen and Associates, PO Box 7665, Newport Beach, CA 92658-7665, 800-433-2314 (outside Calif.), 714-759-9304 (inside Calif., outside U.S.).

Robyn Henderson is an international business educator based in Australia who has authored five books on networking, business building, and self-promotion. She has had ten years' career experience in sales and thirteen years in the hospitality industry. Robyn's speaking career has taken her to more than ten countries, with over 150 presentations each year, all without advertising. She received the 2000 Nevin Award from the National Speakers Association of Australia, one of only three women in the world to win this award. Contact: Networking to Win, PO Box 195, Coogee NSW 2034, Australia, 61-2-9369-1025, fax 61-2-9369-1053, inetwork@ozemail.com.au, www.networkingtowin.com.au.

Edward D. Hendricks is director of the Center for Corporate Education and Professional Development and the Institute for Non-Profit Leadership at Sacred Heart University, Fairfield, Connecticut. He was president of Edward D. Hendricks & Associates and CEO of the International Association of Management Consulting Firms, and he has been featured on CBS's *American Business Journal* and on CNN International as an expert on leadership, consulting, and training. He lectures and consults internationally on networking, marketing, mergers, and leadership. He is the author of *The Insider's Guide to Consulting Success*. Contact: fax 203-374-2694, hendrice@sacredheart.edu.

Connie Hinton was the first secretary to be promoted into a management position in the Federal Reserve Bank Kansas City. Having served as BNI's executive director in Idaho and Washington for the last four years, she is widely regarded as a specialist in business networking. She was instrumental in creating an Internet chat program for her company in Seattle. Contact: BNI NW, 800-286-0508, fax 425-391-0817, connie@bninw.com, www.bninw.com.

Nancy Holland achieved world championship as a member of the Canadian National Ski Team, competed in two Winter Olympics, and was inducted into the Quebec Ski Hall of Fame. After retiring from competition, Nancy directed several ski schools in Quebec. She now owns her own marketing business, gives motivational presentations in Canada, France, and the United States, and is the founding co–national director of BNI Canada. Contact: 154 Tyrrel Ave., Toronto, Ontario, Canada M6G 2G7, 416-652-9098, 800-365-2276, nancy@bnicanada.ca.

Wes Holsapple II is president of BDS, Business Development Solutions, which specializes in preparing organizations for success by developing the management, supervision, sales, and marketing abilities of their people. Previously, Wes was area manager and trainer for Dale Carnegie Training. He is executive director of BNI for Mississippi. Contact: 800-870-2969, wes@bnims.com.

Philip E. Humbert, Ph.D., is a professional speaker, master networker, and personal success coach. As a psychologist, entrepreneur, and business leader, he understands the challenges of balancing financial and professional success with a rich and satisfying personal life. He is the author of *Making Money, Creating Wealth: Your Guide to Financial Independence,* and publishes the world's most popular coaching newsletter. Contact: Resources for Success!, PO Box 50910, Eugene, OR 97405, 541-342-1030, fax 541-345-2099, Coach@philiphumbert.com, www.philiphumbert.com.

Mel Kaufmann began his career in relationship-building in 1982 as a marketing representative for the Wilshire Chamber of Commerce. He gave talks to members about how to translate membership into career and financial success. He is author of the book *The Link.* Contact: TRM, 308 S. Miraleste Dr. #59, San Pedro, CA 90732, 310-831-2799, fax 310-519-0571.

Herb Kay joined the navy at seventeen, became a Russian linguist, learned to fly, started a retail business, failed, started over, and built a successful investment business. He now appears on national television as a TV financial expert, starts new ventures, makes lots of money as an entrepreneur, and manages millions of dollars for people all over the country. He wrote *How to Get Filthy, Stinking Rich and Still Have Time for Great Sex,* a guide to the art of making money and enjoying the process. Contact: HKRichMaster@aol.com, www.herbkay.com.

Gillian Lawson and her husband, Martin, have worked in fundraising for several years and have raised more than $1.5 million for charity. Gillian has sung with the London Symphony Chorus in many countries, including the United States and Russia, and also finds time to serve as a justice of the peace in a busy Magistrates' Court on the outskirts of London. She is a national director for BNI and with her husband was responsible for importing the BNI concept into the United Kingdom and Ireland. Contact: MGLawson@aol.com.

Martin Lawson was educated in South Africa, then spent fifteen years managing businesses for large corporations. In the fifteen years since, he has depended on effective networking to run his own consulting business, advising some of the leading private and public sector businesses in the United Kingdom, Europe, and the United States. In 1997, he and his wife, Gillian, introduced BNI into the United Kingdom and Ireland, and they are currently extending their operations into the German-speaking countries. Contact: MGLawson@aol.com.

Steve Lawson grew up in South Africa and obtained his degree in economics in England. He has lived on five different continents. In 1975 he started his own communications company in Canada, which he still runs today. Steve is an executive director for BNI Canada, which he and his wife were instrumental in developing. Steve is actively involved in the expansion of BNI in the United Kingdom and Europe. Contact: 416-410-5461, fax 905-513-7872, lawsonsmail@home.com.

Mike Levin is the founding national director for BNI in South Africa. He has over twenty years' experience in the retail and catering industry, working with companies such as Woolworths and Ackermans. He has lived in Capetown for more than thirty years, and he played field hockey with the championship team for over twenty of them. His goals include helping people reach their own goals. Contact: mike@bni.com.za.

Jay Conrad Levinson is the president of his own marketing and consulting firm. He lectures nationwide on guerrilla business techniques for major companies, professional organizations, and universities. He wrote the bestseller *The Guerrilla Approach to Marketing* and, following a remarkable series of books on this philosophy of business, updated it in *Guerrilla Marketing*. Contact: Guerrilla Marketing International, 260 Cascade Dr., PO Box 1336, Mill Valley, CA 94942, 800-748-6444 (415-381-8361 in Calif.).

Susann Linn, author and publisher of *Susann Linn's Directory of Orange County Networking Organizations*, attends fifty to sixty networking meetings per month. She is a noted columnist, trainer, and keynote speaker on the art of networking and holds regular public networking seminars for salespeople, entrepreneurs, and job seekers. Contact: Networking Directory, 3334 E. Coast Hwy., Ste. 291, Corona Del Mar, CA 92625, 949-786-1320, ntwrkqn@pacbell.net.

Linda Macedonio and her husband, Mike, are the executive directors for BNI in Rhode Island and Bristol County, Massachusetts. They often speak before professional and women's organizations, teaching members strategies for improving their networking techniques. Linda recently sold her bookkeeping business, Professional Bookkeeping Service. Contact: Mary Lou Renner, BNI, 32 Lois Lane, N. Attleboro, MA 02760, 508-695-7271, fax 508-695-7056, mikem@bni.com, www.bniri.com.

Harvey Mackay is one of America's most sought-after business motivational speakers, a nationally syndicated business-advice columnist, and an active corporate CEO. He is the author of the *New York Times* bestsellers *Dig Your Well Before You're Thirsty, Swim With the Sharks Without Being Eaten Alive,* and *Beware the Naked Man Who Offers You His Shirt*. Contact: Mackay Envelope Company, 2100 Elm St. S.E., Minneapolis, MN 55414, harvey@mackay.com, www.mackay.com.

Mary Anne Marriott's ten-year career in the financial counseling industry included helping develop and implement a counseling program for the insolvency profession, as well as writing a chapter on financial counseling for a book designed to assist problem gamblers. She left this field to become an entrepreneur and establish BNI chapters in the Atlantic Provinces of Canada. She and her sister are partners in a telecommunications business. Contact: 902-857-1990, fax 902-857-1076, mamarriott@bni.com.

Kathleen Mathy, a CPA and principal in her own firm in Sugar Land, Texas, received her master's degree in clinical pathology from the University of Iowa. She has been the Houston BNI executive director since 1994 and was named Woman of the Year by the American Business Women's Association of Ft. Bend County, Texas. She writes a monthly tax column. Contact: 281-491-5821, director@bnihouston.com, www.bnihouston.com.

Joe McBride is a professional speaker and marketing consultant based in Little Rock, Arkansas. He works often with entrepreneurial professionals, helping them understand the relationship between their activities outside their office and the acquisition of new clients. Joe is the author of the audiocassette program *Tooting Your Own Horn: A Professional's Guide to Marketing and Promoting Yourself Without Becoming Totally Obnoxious*. Contact: McBride Presentations, 4 Single Oaks Drive, North Little Rock, AR 72120, 501-833-5617, fax 501-833-3584, joespeaks@swbell.net, www.intl-speakers-network.com/jmcbride.

Lance Mead has owned and operated travel agencies, restaurants, hotels, leasing companies, and other businesses over a thirty-year period on the U.S. East Coast. He has also been vice chairman of the Democratic Party in the Bronx, a board member of Kiwi Airlines, consultant to the governor of Puerto Rico, and a featured speaker for various companies and media. He attended the U.S. Military Academy at West Point. He is co–national director of BNI South Africa and executive director for thirteen regions of BNI in the U.S. Contact: 600 Tuckahoe Road, Yonkers, NY 10710, 877-407-4621, fax 914-793-3440, jlance@bni.com, www.bni-newyork.com, www.bni-newjersey.com.

John R. Meyer retired from a career in banking and is now a district director for BNI's Midwest region and a member of the Founders' Circle. He was one of the first BNI directors qualified to teach the Certified Networker Program. In 1999 he received the Davis College Outstanding Alumni Achievement Award. He stays connected with his community through various organizations. Contact: 419-471-0788, fax 419-474-9142, bni.ohio@worldnet.att.net, www.bni-ohio.com.

Elisabeth L. Misner is a member of the board of the Leroy Haynes Center for Children and Family Services in La Verne, California. A BNI member since 1986, she is now its special projects director. She has coordinated BNI's internal mentoring project and has served as editor of the newsletter *SuccessNet*, which has a circulation of 40,000. She assists in training BNI directors and in editing Dr. Misner's books. Contact: BNI, 199 S. Monte Vista Ave., Ste. 6, San Dimas, CA 91773-3080, 800-688-9394, 909-305-1818, fax 909-305-1811, beth@bni.com, www.MastersofNetworking.com.

Reed Morgan and **Kathy Morgan** are BNI directors in Kentucky and Middle Tennessee. Reed has nearly thirty years' experience as an independent representative for a specialty book and magazine printing company. Kathy is an educator who, with her husband, teaches communication skills, management techniques, and networking to business professionals. Both are Certified Networker Program trainers with bachelor's and master's degrees. Together Reed and Kathy, who live in Nashville, have chartered nearly fifty BNI chapters hosting about 1,000 members. They have received national BNI awards for growth, customer service, and productivity. Contact: PO Box 158529, Nashville, TN 37215-8529, 888-BNI-KYTN (888-264-5986), fax 503-210-1892, reedprint@home.com, mrmorgan@bni.com, www.bnikentucky.com.

Cindy Mount is director of Traicor International, a productivity and performance training company based in Peterborough, Ontario. She studied education and business administration at the University of Alberta and worked for nineteen years in the public sector before launching her own businesses in 1996. Traicor's clients include Merrill Lynch, ScotiaMcLeod, Investors Group, and Johnson & Johnson. Ms. Mount is currently an area membership director with the National Association of Professional Organizers, a director with Junior Achievement, and a past president with BNI and the Entrepreneurs Association.

Contact: Traicor International, 266 Charlotte St., Suite 304, Peterborough, Ontario, Canada K9J 2V4, 877-TRAICOR (877-872-4267), 705-740-2547, fax 705-740-0659, cm@traicor.com, www.traicor.com.

John Naisbitt, speaker and adviser on social, economic, political, and technological trends to many of the world's leading corporations, is chairman of the Naisbitt Group, a Washington, D.C.–based research and consulting firm, and publisher of the quarterly *Trend Report*. He is the author of several international bestsellers, including *Megatrends, Global Paradox,* and *High Tech, High Touch*. He has been an executive at IBM and Eastman Kodak. Contact: www.naisbitt.com.

Karyanne Newton has been the owner of KLS Images in Progress for ten years. She has many years of experience in entrepreneurial coaching, public speaking, and strategic business consulting. As a BNI director in Ontario since 1996, she specializes in workshops and seminars on network communications. She was BNI Canada's first recipient of the Notable Merit Award for Outstanding Performance. Contact: Karyanne Newton: 5983 Greensboro Dr., Mississauga, Ontario, Canada L5M 5S5, 905-812-8653, kls_karyanne@yahoo.com.

Alice Ostrower began her career as an educator and motivational speaker in the United States, Canada, and Australia by promoting her Connecticut decorating business. She joined BNI and changed her focus to networking. As an executive director for BNI, she oversees franchises in Connecticut, Western Massachusetts, parts of Florida, and Albany, New York. Known for her humorous and informative workshops, lectures, and seminars, she is in great demand as a keynote speaker. Contact: PO Box 99, Avon, CT 06001, 860-658-7545, alicenet@bni.com.

Ian Pendlebury worked for sixteen years in the downstream oil industry in Australia. In July 1997 he established BNI in Australia, and some eighteen months later helped introduce it into New Zealand. He is now the national director of BNI Australia. Contact: ian@bni.com.au.

Debby Peters worked fourteen years to achieve success as a salesperson and then sales manager before moving to Toledo, Ohio, and founding Sales . . . And More!, a company that provides sales training, coaching, and teleclasses. A member of BNI, Debby advises customers and clients on networking, a technique she used to grow her company. Contact: PO Box 1121, Perrysburg, OH 43552, 419-833-5182, debby@salesandmore.com, www.salesandmore.com.

Tom Peters is the coauthor of *In Search of Excellence* (with Robert H. Waterman Jr.) and *A Passion for Excellence* (with Nancy Austin), and the author of *Thriving on Chaos, Liberation Management, The Tom Peters Seminar, The Pursuit of Wow!, The Circle of Innovation,* and the *Reinventing Work* series. He is the founder of the Tom

Peters Company, with offices in Palo Alto, Boston, Chicago, Cincinnati, and London. Contact: tom@tompeters.com.

Richard Poe studied creative writing and Russian at Syracuse University and later worked as a reporter for the *New York Post*. He is editor of David Horowitz's *Front Page Magazine* (frontpagemag.com) and writes a regular column for Christopher Ruddy's NewsMax.com. His first book, *How to Profit from the Coming Russian Boom* (McGraw-Hill, 1993), was followed by the bestseller *Wave 3: The New Era in Network Marketing* (Prima, 1994) and several best-selling sequels, including *Wave 4: Network Marketing in the 21st Century*. Contact: richardpoe.com.

Arlette S. Poland, an attorney for over twenty years, has been a networker since her high school days. Thanks to BNI she has honed that skill to make her practice a success, creating an effective niche for herself as The Lemon Law Lawyer of the Desert, and to build a great network of friends and business connections. Contact: 760-862-1212, asp005@juno.com.

Arthur Radtke is managing partner of Business Referral Institute, which offers training to sales and professional organizations on increasing revenues through referrals and strategic alliances. Art serves on BNI's Franchise Advisory Board. He and his wife, Lisa, are BNI directors in Virginia, North Carolina, and Tampa Bay, Florida. Together they have chartered over 100 BNI chapters hosting nearly 2,000 members and have received national awards for growth, customer service, training, and creativity. Since 1981, Art has worked with large corporations such as First Data Corp. and operated his own marine company in Richmond, Virginia. Contact: 13705 Pebble Creek Lane, Midlothian, VA 23112-4725, 888-479-2534, fax 804-763-4068, Aradtke@bni.com, virginia@bni.com.

Susan RoAne, keynote speaker and seminar leader to Fortune 500 companies and universities, is founder of The RoAne Group. She has developed and taught courses at UCLA, the University of Hawaii, and the University of California at Berkeley. She is author of *How to Work a Room* and *The Secrets of Savvy Networking*. Contact: The RoAne Group, 320 Via Casitas, Ste. 310, Greenbrae, CA 94904, 415-461-3915, fax 415-461-6172, Susan@SusanRoAne.com, www.susanroane.com.

Stacia Robinson, president of Stacia Robinson & Co. of Montgomery, Alabama, is an innovative speaker on diversity in advertising, youth entrepreneurship, and word-of-mouth marketing. She serves on the boards of Leadership Montgomery, Partners in Education, Montgomery Education Foundation, and the United Way. An executive director of BNI, Stacia chairs the Cross-Cultural Council. Contact: PO Box 210894, Montgomery, AL 36121-0894, 334-279-1824, fax 334-277-8193, sfrobinson@bni.com, www.bni.com.

Darrell Ross is the BNI director for British Columbia, Canada. He has a strong background in sales, marketing, and managing people. He has actively built BNI throughout BC and currently looks after thirty-five chapters with over 500 member/clients. Darrell has an honors degree in public administration and a wealth of experience from extensive travel through Europe, Asia, the Middle East, and North America. **Donna Ross** has a background in fashion modeling and, more recently, therapeutic massage and yoga. Contact: 1873 Nelson St., Ste. 701, Vancouver, British Columbia, Canada V6G 1M9, 877-419-4264, 604-689-0553, fax 604-689-0560, ddross@imag.net.

Patti Salvucci's hard work and passion for cultivating relationships has allowed her to succeed in the food and hospitality sector, in sales training, and in establishing a referral-marketing business. In the past five years she has built one of the world's largest and most successful BNI regions and is now active on BNI's board of advisors. Patti and a colleague recently launched the Certified Networker Program in Massachusetts, a college course on how to network effectively. She is a popular keynote speaker in North America and abroad. Contact: 508-788-9029, fax 508-788-8002, patti@bni.com.

Deanna Tucci Schmitt parlayed successful experiences as a salesperson and then sales and communications trainer into a career as a BNI executive director when she brought BNI to the Greater Pittsburgh region in 1998. In her previous sales career, networking played a significant role when she called on accountants, attorneys and bankers in order to develop the relationships that encouraged them to refer their clients to her. Contact: 507 Fruitwood Dr., Bethel Park, PA 15102-1337, 412-831-5254, fax 412-831-7384, dtschmitt@bni.com, www.bni.com.

Jerry Schwartz, a professional networking consultant, is an executive director for BNI Maryland, overseeing sixty-five chapters in Maryland and the District of Columbia, and a district director for BNI Corporate for the Northeast U.S. Jerry has been a motivational business speaker for corporations and organizations throughout North America and has made guest appearances on local radio and television shows. He is a member of BNI's Founders' Circle. Contact: PO Box 286, Riderwood, MD 21139, 410-484-6109, fax 410-484-0047, jerry@bnimaryland.com, www.bnimaryland.com.

Mark Sheer is a business consultant, experienced in finance and tax planning, who focuses on recruiting, training, motivating, and maintaining a top-notch sales force. He coaches financial professionals on referral marketing and other human resource specialties. He is the author and publisher of *Referrals*. Contact: Mark Sheer Seminars, 28829 Paseo Campana, Mission Viejo, CA 92692, 949-588-5931, fax 949-588-5932.

Betsy Sheldon is coauthor (with Joyce Hadley) of *The Smart Woman's Guide to Networking*. She and Hadley were co-editors of a consumer travel magazine in the 1980s and their collaboration turned into a long-lasting friendship and professional relationship. She is now editor-in-chief of *Journey Online Magazine*. Contact: 317-259-0245, www.ambassadair.com.

Pam Sheldon, business owner, speaker, writer, politician, and rural dogmaster, is the owner of the largest BNI franchise in Canada and three BNI franchises in New York State, as well as co–national director for BNI Australia. Her presentations on structured referral marketing have won admiration from audiences worldwide. Contact: RR #3, 6323 Side Road 15, Milton, Ontario, Canada L9T 2X7, 905-878-5570, 888-416-3833, bnigh@interhop.net, www.bniniagara.com.

Sim Chow Boon parlayed his experience as an electronics technician in the Singapore Navy into a career as an analytical strategist. After he met Mervin Yeo in the sales force of an international insurance company in Singapore, the two of them collaborated to form a successful employment business in 1996. In 1999 they founded BNI Singapore. Contact: gces@pacific.net.sg.

Scott T. Simon received an MBA from Central Missouri State University, worked for General Foods Corporation as a regional sales representative, then entered the real estate business in 1975, specializing in land transactions for large corporations and later adding full property management and development divisions. He is an executive director for BNI's St. Louis region, which has thirty-eight chapters. Contact: 11939 Manchester Road #150, St. Louis, MO 63131, 314-822-1030, fax 314-822-3001, scottsimon@bnistl.com, www.bnistl.com.

Mike Smith uses his twenty-five years of experience in finance, management, and business ownership as a foundation for his keynote speaking and business training activities. He was recently asked to co-host a nationally syndicated radio show, *Vacation Time*, in Orlando. As a BNI franchise owner in St. Louis, Mike and his partner achieved the "Top Ten Regions" list. Contact: 407-855-6369, fax 407-855-6984.

Ronald M. Stark, Attorney at Law, is the BNI regional director for Riverside County, California, and an attorney of twenty-five years, with a practice limited to living trusts and probate. Contact: 9841 Oakmount Blvd., Desert Hot Springs, CA 92240, 760-251-6570, fax 760-329-5262, baronstark@aol.com.

Ron Sukenick is a conceptual thinker and speaker who teaches audiences to build their own networks of key contacts. He developed the IBN Business Network and Business 500, achievement-oriented programs for top management and entrepreneurs. He is vice president of the nationally known Factory Direct Table Pad Co. of Indianapolis and author of *Networking Your Way to Success,* which describes a proven method for building, developing, and implementing networks of key contacts. Contact: The Sukenick Group, 5443 N. Arlington Ave., Indianapolis, IN 46226, 317-543-9166, fax 317-543-9177, rsukenick@tablepads.com.

Leslie Taylor has been in sales and training for over twenty years. Her tapes, which help businesspeople learn to present their business in a minute or less, are a favorite tool of entrepreneurs and salespeople in many countries. Based in Las Vegas, Leslie is a district director with BNI. In addition to her work with BNI, Leslie is vice president of marketing for KeepCareSimple.com, an organization committed to getting information, referrals, and tools to caregivers. Contact: 3462 Sioux Way, Las Vegas, NV 89109, 702-731-6065, LLTaylor@bni.com.

Carol Thompson, president of Thompson Group, an Austin-based marketing and PR firm, has served on the San Antonio branch of the Federal Reserve Board and as chair of the Greater Austin Chamber of Commerce. Founder of Thompson Executive Search, she is a national speaker, covering topics such as business networking and business etiquette for a wide variety of groups, including marketing associations, chamber of commerce conferences, Women in Technology groups, and entrepreneurship and leadership programs. Contact: The Thompson Group, PO Box 26716, Austin, TX 78755, 512-418-8869, fax 512-418-1209, carol@thompson-group.com, www.thompson-group.com.

Bob Travis is a registered pharmacist. He has served his profession over the past thirty years as vice president and president of the State Pharmacy Association, as well as chairman of its House of Delegates. Bob's interest in marketing and management inspired him to develop a networking career through BNI. In 1995 he became the first executive director of BNI in South Carolina. Contact: 232 Weeping Cherry Lane, Columbia, SC 29212, 803-732-9123, fax 803-781-8162, bob@bobtravis.com, www.bobtravis.com.

Joe Tye, president of Paradox 21 Inc., is the author of seven books on personal and business success, including *Never Fear, Never Quit; Your Dreams Are Too Small; The Healing Tree;* and the forthcoming *Leadership of the Ring: J.R.R. Tolkien's Strategies for Building a Winning Team.* He is a frequent speaker on "The Twelve Core Action Values for Personal Leadership Effectiveness," a comprehensive leadership development program developed by his company. Tye earned a master's degree in healthcare administration from the University of Iowa and an MBA from the Stanford Graduate School of Business. Contact: Paradox 21 Inc., PO Box 490, Solon, IA 52333-0490, 319-644-3889, fax 319-644-3963, joe@nfnq.com, nfnq.com.

Sandy Vilas, before becoming CEO of CoachInc.com, the world's largest training and coaching services organization for personal and business coaches, was a successful training and sales consultant with a wide range of clients across the country. CoachInc.com has been mentioned in *Newsweek*, the *Times* of London, *Entrepreneur*, and *Inc.*, and on the *NBC Nightly News* and CNN's *Impact*. He is coauthor (with Donna Fisher) of *Power Networking*. Contact: Coach U, PO Box 881595, Steamboat Springs, CO 80488-1595, 970-870-3302 or 941-387-8440, 800-482-6224 (coachu), fax 800-329-5655, www.coachu.com, President@coachu.com.

Hazel Walker runs her own employee benefit agency, serves on the board of managers for the State PTA of Indiana, and has served many years as president and otherwise on the Warren Township PTA Council in Indianapolis. She is also on the Indianapolis Chamber of Commerce Action Committee. She is an executive director for BNI in Central Indiana. Contact: PO Box 19827, Indianapolis, IN 46219, 317-891-0355, fax 317-894-8733, hazel@bni.com.

Lynne Waymon, president of Great Connections, consults with associations and corporations on making the most of networking opportunities. She provides keynotes, training seminars, and coaching for people who depend on networking for career and business success. She also gives keynotes and seminars on career development, negotiation skills, and the power of influence. She is coauthor, with Anne Baber, of *Smart Networking* and *Great Connections*. Contact: Great Connections, 622 Ritchie Ave., Silver Spring, MD 20910, 800-352-2939, 301-589-8633, fax 301-589-8639, Lwaymon@aol.com, www.ContactsCount.com.

Jerry R. Wilson is president of Jerry Wilson and Associates, a consulting firm specializing in speaking and training for companies from Fortune 500–size down to small businesses. He has written articles for *Success* magazine, *Master Salesmanship*, and *Personal Selling Power*, and has authored the book *Word of Mouth Marketing*. Contact: Jerry Wilson and Associates, 5335 N. Tacoma Ave., Ste. 1, PO Box 55182, Indianapolis, IN 46205, 800-428-5666, 317-257-6876.

Mervin Yeo's experience in sales and marketing made him an effective communicator and led to his association with Sim Chow Boon in an international insurance company in Singapore. They collaborated to start an employment business in 1996, where their past experience gave them an edge that turned the partnership into a successful business venture. In 1999 they founded BNI Singapore. Contact: bnispore@bni.com.

Acknowledgments

We wish to acknowledge and thank all the BNI directors who encouraged this project with their enthusiastic good wishes, especially the many master networkers who contributed to this book. We are particularly grateful to all the published authors who kindly contributed their articles to this project, a generosity that we believe has helped produce a book second to none on the subject of business networking. It takes a leap of faith to offer one's good name to a new project, which is exactly what the published authors did by agreeing to share their insight and wisdom. Thank you all for your contributions to this important message.

Ivan Misner and Don Morgan

I would like to offer a heartfelt thank you to all my staff, particularly Norm Dominguez and Amy Brown, for helping to run my company so well that I have the time to work on a project such as this. Also, a big thanks to the most creative person I know: my wife and partner in life, who makes my house a home and life a lot more fun. Her support and help made this book possible for me.

I would also like to thank my friend and coauthor Don Morgan, whose contributions to this book were outstanding. When I conceived this idea many years ago, he was the first and only person I considered for the project. It is to my benefit that he graciously accepted.

Finally, a special thank you to Ray Bard, Jeff Morris, and the staff at Bard Press for their commitment to excellence, their insightful understanding of the material, their expertise, care, and attention. Without their help, this book could not have been completed.

Ivan Misner

My personal appreciation is extended to Christel and Margaret at BNI Canada, who did much of my other work, and especially to Nancy Holland, who always inspires me and who piloted the BNI Canada ship, and even passed up a few ski days, giving me more time for this project.

I particularly wish to thank Dr. Ivan Misner, who invited me to coauthor *Masters of Networking* as we walked through downtown Toronto several years ago, and whose generous invitation allowed me to achieve one of my life's objectives.

Don Morgan

Index

A

B

O

P

About BNI

BNI (Business Network Int'l.) was founded by Dr. Ivan Misner in 1985 as a way for businesspeople to generate referrals in a structured, professional environment. The organization, now the world's largest referral network, has tens of thousands of members on almost every continent of the world. Since its inception, members of BNI have passed millions of referrals, generating billions of dollars for the participants.

The primary purpose of the organization is to pass qualified business referrals to the members. The philosophy of BNI may be summed up in two simple words: "Givers gain." If you give business to people, you will get business from them. BNI allows only one person per profession to join a chapter. The program is designed for businesspeople to develop long-term relationships, thereby creating a basis for trust and, inevitably, referrals. The mission of the organization is to teach business professionals that the word-of-mouth process is more about farming than hunting: it's about the cultivation of professional relationships in a structured business environment for the mutual benefit of all.

You can contact BNI on the Internet at bni@bni.com or visit its websites at www.bni.com. and www.MastersofNetworking.com.

Ivan R. Misner, Ph.D., is the founder and CEO of BNI (Business Network Int'l.), the largest business networking organization in the world. Founded in 1985, BNI now has thousands of chapters throughout North America, Europe, Australia, Asia, and Africa. Each year, BNI generates millions of referrals resulting in hundreds of millions of dollars worth of business for its members.

Dr. Misner's Ph.D. is from the University of Southern California. He has written four books, including the best-selling *The World's Best Known Marketing Secret*. Dr. Misner is also on the business administration faculty at the University of La Verne.

Called the "Networking Guru" by *Entrepreneur* magazine, Dr. Misner is a keynote speaker for major corporations and associations throughout the world. He has been featured in the *Wall Street Journal, Los Angeles Times, New York Times, CEO Magazine*, and numerous TV and radio shows, including CNBC television. He and his wife, Elisabeth, live in La Verne, California, with their three children, Ashley, Cassie, and Trey. Contact: misner@bni.com.

Don Morgan, M.A., is the founding national director of BNI Canada and executive director of BNI Chicago. In his thirty-year career as an organizational consultant, psychotherapist, educator, and entrepreneur, he has focused on using communication tools to help people and organizations achieve their goals. With his master's degree in community mental health, Morgan has provided direction for many new businesses in the health care,

retail, and service industries. He has received honorary recognition from the Ontario Ministry of Health for his involvement as board member, consultant, and director in developing community mental health services. He has taught at the University of Western Ontario and other colleges. A talented speaker, Morgan turns his unique analytic perspective and humor into thought-provoking motivational presentations.

For the past fifteen years, Morgan and his partner, Olympic skier Nancy Holland, have worked to develop word-of-mouth marketing strategies for their business clients. Having lived and worked in three countries, Don and Nancy now live in Toronto, where they are both passionate about skiing and sailing. Contact: morgan@bnicanada.ca.